Paul Emmerson

Busines English Handbook

Advanced

The whole of business in one book

MACMILLAN

Macmillan Education
4 Crinan Street
London N1 9XW
A division of Springer Nature Limited
Companies and representatives throughout the world

ISBN 978-1-4050-8603-5

Text © Paul Emmerson 2007
Design and illustration © Springer Nature Limited 2007

First published 2007

All rights reserved; no part of this publication may be reproduced, stored in a retrieval system, transmitted in any form, or by any means, electronic, mechanical, photocopying, recording, or otherwise, without the prior written permission of the publishers.

Designed by Carolyn Gibson
Illustrated by Glyn Goodwin and Peter Harper
Cover design by Designers Collective

Author's acknowledgements
First and foremost, a very big thank you to Karen Spiller for combining roles of freelance project manager, content editor and copy editor, and providing input and creativity at every turn.

Thanks are also due to Anna Cowper, Karen White and Balvir Koura at Macmillan, to Clare Shaw, to Carolyn Gibson for her work on the graphic design, and to Marna Warner for transcribing all the original interviews on which the audio scripts are based. And of course the book would not be the same without the wonderful drawings of Glyn Goodwin. Find him on the web at www.glyngoodwin.co.uk

The author would like to thank colleagues at the International House Executive Centre (London) for channelling interviewees his way. An especial thanks to Fiona Johnston in this regard. The usual gratitude is due to my Director of Studies, Maurice Cassidy, for facilitating my writing and teaching and the balance between the two.

Thanks also to all my students who acted as guinea-pigs for early versions of these units. A special mention is due to the students from Campus 02 in Graz, Austria.

Finally, I would like to thank Roger Harrison for the time and trouble he took to prepare the interview, and for his very valuable comments on the contents of the related unit.

The publishers would like to thank all the people who gave up their time to be interviewed for the listening material: Alain Caffi, Andras Feher, Anke Hofer, Dave Heywood, Elena Podlipalina, Fernando Gil, Francisco Ruiz, Francois Bitouzet, Jon Greenhill, Kate Irving, Laura Parrini, Livio Russo, Lorenzo Beccattini, Maria Fernanda Cunha, Marian Wigg, Michele Olivieri, Robert Rozanski and Roger Harrison. Thanks also to Bronwyn Steck, Dr Thomas Lavelle, Annette Nolan, Elena Ivanova Angelova, Dr Ilona Mathe, Danuta Korta, Lauri Tolkki, Sabine Schumann, Keith Hanna and Ingrid Abele for their valuable input.

Whilst every effort has been made to locate the owners of copyright material in this book, there may have been some cases when the publishers have been unable to contact the owners. We should be grateful to hear from anyone who recognises copyright material and who is unacknowledged. We shall be pleased to make the necessary amendments in future editions of the book.

Printed and bound in Spain

2022 2021 2020 2019 2018
19 18 17 16 15 14 13

Contents

To the student

Who is this book for?

This book is for learners of English at **upper-intermediate** or **advanced** level (CEF levels B2 and C1) who want to consolidate and extend their knowledge of business English. It can be used either by university students studying on a business-related course, or by people already working and following a career in business.

The book is **self-study**. That means that you can use it on your own, without a teacher. You can also use it in class, and at the end of each unit there are short speaking or writing activities for classroom use.

Why was this book written?

Conventional coursebooks cover some areas of business, not all. They have texts and articles that may be out of date, or that include a lot of language that is not relevant. The Business English Handbook is different:

- It aims to cover all the main topic areas and all the main communication skills in one book.
- It aims to be highly focused, with language being chosen for maximum usefulness and just the right degree of challenge for high-level learners.
- Where there is a difference between British and American English, the word or term most frequently used in international business contexts has been used. The alternative word or term is given in brackets.
- It provides interesting and motivating listening activities, linked to the units.

If you work through this book from beginning to end, you will have covered the whole of business. You will have studied all the most important vocabulary and all the most important speaking and writing techniques needed for work or study.

How is the book organized?

One unit consists of four pages:

- Two pages of input: a text on the left and a mind map on the right. There is a close relationship between the two.
- Two pages of practice exercises. These are mostly based on the language in the input pages, but occasionally there is some new language that is closely related.

In the book there are twenty-four units. These are divided into two sections of twelve units each:

- The first half of the book covers the major business topics. Look at the contents page. You will see that the book begins with two units that give an overview of the business world. Following this, there are two units on management. Then there are units covering all the main functional areas of business: production and operations, sales and marketing, finance, human resources and information technology.

- The second half of the book covers business communication skills. This part of the book begins with a unit on the language of trends. It then has units on presentations, discussions and social English. Following this there are two units that deal with the question of style in speaking and writing – first clarity and directness, then politeness and indirectness. Then there are three units all with the title 'Developing an argument' – the language in these units is relevant for discussions, presentations and report writing. The theme of writing is explored in more detail in the next unit, called 'Writing paragraphs'. This will be useful for both university students (academic writing) and business people (report writing). Finally a unit on 'CV and job interview' will help those people looking for a job – now or in the future.

Audio CD and listening exercises

There is an audio CD attached to this book. It contains ten listening activities. Listen at home, in your car, or in class. Try the exercises (pages 104–108). Finally listen again and read the script.

Website references

You will notice website references at the bottom of the page in units 1–12. These have been included so that you can follow up the topic on your own, according to your interests. The sites contain a lot of material that will give you good reading practice and also help you with papers and projects if you are a student. We have included the home page only, with a few brief hints to help you navigate to the relevant pages. You may have to click around the site a little before you find what you want.

How should I use this book?

You can study any unit in any order (with the exception of units 20–22).

The author recommends that you look at the input, try the exercises, and then finally **look back at the input again**. This will help you to memorize it and will give you the greatest chance of using the language actively sooner rather than later.

To the teacher

What is *Business English Handbook*?

Think of it as a super-charged workbook. During a course it will supplement any classroom material that you already use. At the end of a course it will provide follow-up and review. It allows your students to consolidate what they have already learned, as well as filling in the gaps for things that you didn't have time for.

Can I use *Business English Handbook* as my main coursebook?

You can use it as your main coursebook in some situations, namely those where you want intensive lexical input and practice followed by extended speaking and writing activities. Many students will appreciate the focus and relevance of the language, and find this motivating. Others will want a more conventional main coursebook.

How can I make the input communicative?

There are several ways to turn the double page spread of input into communicative activities:

A Students brainstorm mind maps and then compare with the book

1 Put the central title of the mind map on the board, and then draw the inner lines with their headings. Ask students to work in pairs to copy what is on the board, and then to extend each branch with their own ideas. Elicit an idea or two for each branch to get started.
2 When the students finish, regroup them into new pairs. They explain their maps to their new partners.
3 Take whole-class feedback, building up an extended mind map on the board, using the best ideas.
4 Finally, the students look at the version in the book. Let them study it for a few minutes, and then compare with the version on the board.
5 For students in work, a good follow-up for homework would be to make a personalized mind map (with the same central title) based on their own jobs. In the next class they explain their mind maps – either in pairs or as a presentation to the whole class. University students who are not in work can do a similar activity based on what they have studied on the rest of their course.

B Students predict topic ideas and then compare with the text on the left-hand page

Write up on the board the sub-headings or some key topic words from the text on the left-hand page. Then ask the students to work in pairs to predict what ideas the text will mention. Take whole class feedback, writing ideas on the board. Finally the students read the text in the book to compare and contrast.

C Teacher-facilitated discussion as preparation for looking at the text or mind map

Begin by simply writing the unit heading on the board. Then you, the teacher, lead a whole-class discussion as a warmer. Students keep their books closed but you have it open in front of you as a reference. You carefully strike a balance between a) guiding the discussion so that some of the ideas in the book will be familiar to the students when they open it and b) allowing the discussion to follow the interests of the students, even if the ideas are not mentioned in the book. After the discussion the students open their books and read the text and look at the mind map. This will be an easier and more interesting task following your warmer.

D Students prepare half of the input for homework, then peer teach in class

Divide the class into A/B pairs at the end of a lesson, with A being given the left-hand page text and B the mind map. Their homework task is to read their own page carefully, checking any unknown words in a dictionary, and thinking about the general ideas in the unit (relating it to their own jobs or academic studies, doing some Internet research, etc). Back in class, put students into the A/B pairs. They begin by silently reading the half of the input that they did not prepare. Then they take turns to explain what they prepared for homework. Any final discussion can be kept within the same pair or opened out to the whole class.

How can I work with the exercises and speaking / writing tasks?

Having studied the input pages, ask the students to do the exercises. Usually students do not have to look back in order to complete them.

At the end of each unit there are speaking or writing activities. Let the discussions run. Take notes on errors, lacks, pronunciation – whatever will help the students to express themselves more clearly. Then allow plenty of time at the end of the lesson to deal with these points in a feedback slot. Use feedback to extend language (collocations, related words, opposites) as well as just correct it.

Help the process of language acquisition by encouraging students to re-read the input silently in class: just before speaking / writing, after a week, after a month.

What are the listening activities?

On the audio CD there are ten listening activities featuring business people being interviewed about their work. They are designed to be used independently. They finish with further opportunities for speaking practice, based on whatever the students found interesting in the script.

1 Industries and companies

Going to work for a large company is like getting on a train. Are you going sixty miles an hour or is the train going sixty miles an hour and you're just sitting still?
J Paul Getty (1892–1976), American industrialist

Industry groups

A national economy can be described in terms of its main sectors and industries. (See the mind map opposite.) This mind map is a simplified version of the 'Global Industry Classification Standard', developed by Morgan Stanley and Standard and Poor's and used in publications like *Business Week*.

Another way to classify an economy is:

- Primary industries, which include agriculture, forestry and mining.
- Secondary industries, which include construction and manufacturing. Manufacturing itself is often divided into capital goods (eg equipment and machinery used to produce other goods), durable goods (eg cars, washing machines) and non-durable goods (eg food, clothing).
- Service industries, which include banking, entertainment, tourism.

An economy can also be divided into:

- The private sector, which includes large corporations, SMEs (= small and medium-sized enterprises) and individuals working on a self-employed basis.
- The public sector, where there are schools and hospitals as well as SOEs (= state-owned enterprises) such as railways and the post office.

Types of business

Within each industry there can be a variety of types of business organization, each with their own legal structure. A business can be:

- A sole trader (US: sole proprietorship). Here the business is owned by one person, who is 'self-employed'. That individual has unlimited liability – they are personally responsible for any debts. A self-employed professional will refer to themselves as a 'freelancer'.
- A partnership. Here two or more people run the business together. Lawyers, architects and auditing firms are typical partnerships.
- A limited liability company. Here there is a legal distinction between the company and the owners, so the company is responsible for any debts, not the owners. The owners therefore have 'limited liability'. This type of company is often quite small, and includes many family-run businesses. The company is referred to as a 'private' company because shares cannot be sold to members of the public. In official documents, the company name is followed by Ltd (UK) meaning 'limited', or Llc (US) meaning 'limited liability company'.

- A public limited company (US: a corporation). Here the company is owned by shareholders (US: stockholders), who might be:
  - large financial institutions (eg pension funds or investment banks).
  - other companies.
  - members of the public (and for this reason the company is called a 'public' company).

The shareholders receive a share of the profits every year (paid as dividends), and will also get a capital gain or loss when they sell their shares (because the price can go up or down on the stock market). These are large companies, and are run by managers under the supervision of a Board. In official documents, the company name is followed by PLC (UK) or Inc or Corp (US).

- A franchise. This type of company includes McDonald's and the Body Shop. Here the business owner allows other people (franchisees) to set up in business using the company's brand name, products and reputation. The franchisee has varying degrees of control over how products are marketed and sold.

Business expansion

There are various ways that a company can grow:

1 Internal growth: stay private. The company increases its sales, number of employees, etc, but stays as a private company, perhaps run by the original founders of the business (often family members).
2 Internal growth: IPO. The company moves from being a small, family-owned firm to being a large corporation with a stock-market listing. The process of issuing shares for the first time is called an IPO (initial public offering).
3 Internal growth: 'trade sale' to a much larger company in the same sector. In this case the original small company is absorbed and its name often disappears. Many start-ups in the IT and biotechnology areas sell themselves in this way. (Microsoft, Intel and Google all grew by buying start-ups.)
4 Merger. Two established companies join to form one (eg Mercedes and Chrysler).
5 Acquisition (= takeover). One established company buys another. The first step in an acquisition is often to take a controlling stake in the other company – buying a large number of shares but without complete ownership. The acquired company often keeps its original trading name, becoming a subsidiary of the larger 'parent company'.

Further information www.gics.standardandpoors.com ● www.businessnameusa.com ● www.sba.gov/managing

Energy equipment and services

Oil and gas

Chemicals
Construction materials
Containers and packaging
Metals and mining
Paper and forest products

Cleaning, auditing, human resources and employment, office supplies, security, waste management, etc

Automobiles and components

Household durables (consumer electronics, homebuilding, household appliances, etc)

Leisure equipment and products

Textiles, apparel and luxury goods

Consumer services (hotels and restaurants, leisure facilities, education services)

Media (advertising, broadcasting, movies and entertainment, publishing)

Retailing (distributors, Internet and catalogue retail, general merchandise stores, speciality retail)

Energy

Commercial services and supplies

Consumer discretionary

Materials

Capital goods

Aerospace and defence
Building products
Construction and engineering
Electrical equipment
Industrial conglomerates
Machinery
Trading companies and distributors

INDUSTRY GROUPS

Consumer staples

Food, beverage and tobacco production

Food and drug retailing

Household and personal products

Industrials

Health care

Health care equipment and services

Pharmaceuticals, biotechnology and life sciences

Transportation

Air freight and logistics
Airlines
Marine
Road and rail
Transportation infrastructure

Financials

Diversified financials

Diversified financial services
Consumer finance

Capital markets (asset management, investment banking and brokerage)

Banks

Information technology

Semiconductors and semiconductor equipment

Utilities

Real estate

Insurance

Software and services

Internet software and services

IT Services (consulting, data processing, etc)

Software (applications, systems, home entertainment)

Telecommunication services

Electric utilities
Gas utilities
Water utilities
Multi-utilities

Technology hardware and equipment

Communications equipment
Computers and peripherals
Electronic equipment and instruments

Diversified telecommunication services (fixed-line, fibre-optic and wireless)

Wireless telecommunication services

1 Industries and companies: Exercises

1.1 Fill in the missing letters.

1 Goods that are carried by ship, train or aircraft are called 'fr_ _ _ _t'.

2 A product used in the home is a 'ho_ _ _ _ _ld product'.

3 Pieces of electrical equipment used in people's homes are 'app_ _ _ _ _ _s'.

4 The words 'clothing' and 'drinks' are conversational. In a business context you often see the words 'app_ _ _l' and 'bev_ _ _ _s'.

5 Rooms, equipment or services that are provided for a particular purpose are 'fac_ _ _ _ _ _s'.

6 Another term for 'property' is 'r_ _ _ e_ _ _ _ _'.

7 The business of buying and selling shares is called 'br_ _ _ _age'.

8 Public services used by everyone are 'u_ _ _ _ _ _ _s'.

1.2 The words *appliance*, *device*, ~~equipment~~ and *machinery* are similar. Complete the collocations by choosing the best one.

1 kitchen / office / standard _equipment_

2 heavy / agricultural / construction _____

3 a handheld / labour-saving / safety _____

4 a household / domestic / electrical _____

1.3 Underline the correct words.

1 Goods that are needed and used all the time are in the *consumer discretionary / consumer staples* sector.

2 Goods that are not basic to people's lives are in the *consumer discretionary / consumer staples* sector.

1.4 First match the company names in the box to the descriptions below. Then write the industry group from the mind map (see first example).

> Cisco   Citigroup   ~~ExxonMobil~~   GE (General Electric)
> Intel   Pfizer   Proctor & Gamble   Wal-Mart
> PwC (PriceWaterhouseCoopers)   UPS (United Parcels Service)

1 The world's largest oil producer and distributor.
   ExxonMobil / _Oil and gas_

2 Provides auditing, tax and consulting services to other businesses. _____ / _____

3 An international company, its services include current accounts (AmE checking accounts), insurance, stock brokerage, investment banking and consumer finance. _____ / _____

4 Designs and manufactures microprocessors and specialized integrated circuits. _____ / _____

5 The world's #1 maker of household and personal products; more than twenty of its brands are billion-dollar sellers (including Ariel, Fairy, Gillette, Pampers and Pantene). _____ / _____

6 One of America's largest and most diverse corporations, its products cover power generation, jet engines, financial services, medical imaging, etc. The name of its industry group reflects the wide range of activities. _____ / _____

7 A global health care company, famous for making Viagra; its competitors include GlaxoSmithKline and Novartis. _____ / _____

8 The largest private employer in the US; $9 out of every $100 that Americans spend on shopping is spent in their stores. _____ / _____

9 A worldwide delivery company; it also offers customs handling, international trade management and supply chain design. _____ / _____

10 Manufactures hardware such as switches and routers that allow the Internet to function and computers to talk to each other. _____ / _____

1.5 Complete the definitions using the words in the box.

> household appliances   business solutions
> consumer durables   fabrication   finished goods
> food and beverages   non-durable goods   raw materials.

1 Manufacturing is the transformation of _____ into _____ . Some industries, like semiconductors and steel, use the term _____ in place of 'manufacturing'.

2 _____ are manufactured goods that are not destroyed by use, such as automobiles, _____ or furniture.

3 _____ generally last for only a short time. Common examples are _____ , apparel, office stationery and gasoline.

4 Sometimes a manufacturing company positions itself as a service company. Microsoft, IBM and SAP are good examples. They offer not just products, but _____ .

1.6 Complete each explanation with a pair of words from the box. The words may not be in the correct order.

> acquisition / merger   debt / liability   enterprise / venture
> firm / partnership   freelancer / self-employed
> senior management team / Board

1 The _____ is elected by the shareholders and is responsible to them. It can hire and fire the CEO, but the _____ (including the CEO) run the company on a day-to-day basis.

2 A _____ is a new business activity, and it collocates with the word 'capital' to mean money available to expand a successful start-up. An _____ is either a company, or any large important project. Used without the article it collocates with 'free' and 'private' to give a synonym for 'capitalism'.

3 A _____ is simply money that somebody owes. A _____ refers to an amount of money that a company owes, but it can also mean the legal responsibility for paying for something.

4 Many people work for themselves, with the legal status of sole trader. If they are a plumber or a shop-keeper, they are likely to refer to themselves as _____ . If they are a professional who works for several companies (eg a journalist or independent consultant), they are likely to refer to themselves as a _____ .

5 The word _____ can just be a synonym for 'company'. But it is more often used for a small company providing a professional service, such as a _____ of accountants, lawyers or architects.

6 A _____ is when two companies join to form one. The suggestion is that the process is welcomed by both sides. An _____ is when one company buys another. The process could be unwelcome by the smaller company, who might feel that they are being taken over.

1.7 The text below explains the process of becoming a public company. Fill in each gap with a word from the box.

appoint	constraints	guarantee	held
issue	reinvested	run	underwriting

When a privately-owned company reaches a certain size, it may decide to 'go public' and
[1] _____ shares on the stock market. This process is called an Initial Public Offering (IPO), or a flotation, or a 'listing' on the exchange.

The process is complicated, and months of planning are involved. The business is probably being
[2] _____ by just a few key people who were the founding members. Before the IPO, they have to assemble an independent board, and one of the first tasks of the board is to [3] _____ auditors who will check the accounts for accuracy.

The firm also needs specialist advice about the best time to sell, the initial offer price of the shares, and who to sell them to. This is all handled by an investment bank, also appointed by the board. The investment bank takes some risk as they [4] _____ that all the shares will be purchased – referred to in legal terms as [5] _____ the issue.

The flotation will bring a huge amount of new capital into the business. Most of this is [6] _____ and used for expansion, but some will go to the people with privately- [7] _____ shares who started the original company. Nearly always these people then continue as part of the management team, although they may find it difficult to adjust to the red tape, shareholder pressure, and other [8] _____ of a listed company.

1.8 Complete the reasons for a merger or acquisition by matching the beginnings of sentences 1–8 with the best ending a)–h).

1 To expand the business quickly, particularly ☐
2 To expand more cheaply than by internal growth, although if ☐
3 To meet the needs of customers who are demanding additional products and services ☐
4 To gain economies of scale, ie have lower costs and ☐
5 To gain control of ☐
6 To gain market power: the larger, merged company will make the whole market less competitive ☐
7 To gain entry into a foreign market, or avoid ☐
8 To become and be ☐

a) a key supplier of raw materials or components.
b) and therefore prices and margins will increase.
c) seen as a global company.
d) if there is cash available on the balance sheet.
e) increased efficiency through larger size.
f) legal restrictions imposed on foreign-owned companies in that market.
g) that the company can't supply.
h) the market thinks a company is a takeover target, its share price will go up and it will become more expensive to buy.

Discussion topics

1 In five years' time, the industry group I'd most like to work in is … , because …

2 One day I want to be a freelancer working for myself – it'll be much more rewarding than being the CEO of a large corporation.
   ○ Agree   ○ Disagree

3 If I was an entrepreneur with a lot of money, I'd create a start-up company making / supplying / offering …

4 Most mergers fail to produce the expected benefits (fact). Why?

2 Globalization and economic policy

It's a recession when your neighbour loses his job; it's a depression when you lose your own.
Harry S. Truman (1884–1972), thirty-third president of the United States

Forces driving globalization

The main drivers of globalization are:

- Cost factors. Companies are looking for cheaper labour and manufacturing costs to enable them to stay competitive, so they outsource to other countries. The country receiving the inward investment benefits from the creation of jobs, skills development and technology transfer. Its low costs give it a major competitive advantage.
- Market factors. As domestic markets become saturated, so emerging markets offer new opportunities. The BRICs (Brazil, Russia, India, China) could dominate world trade in the 21st century, as the US did in the 20th and the UK in the 19th. In any case, companies need to establish a global presence because customers are also global. It is dangerous to stand aside as competitors merge and make alliances.
- Technology factors. The Internet makes comparison of supply chain costs easy for manufacturers, and comparison of final price easy for the end-user. Mobile communications allow employees to keep in touch all over the world. Software tools on company intranets allow managers to access information anywhere, anytime.
- Global business cycle. The 'business cycle' – shown below – used to happen separately in different national economies. With the integrated global economy, it is now international.
  - recovery (= upswing)
  - growth (= expansion / boom)
  - recession (= contraction / downturn)
  - depression (= slump)

In every turn of the cycle, the pace of globalization is likely to increase – particularly during the 'recovery' and 'growth' phases.

Remember that not all recessions lead to a depression – there might just be a mild slowdown in the economy (seen as a reduction in GDP – gross domestic product).

Company strategy in the face of globalization

If a company wants to trade outside its own national borders, it has three basic strategies, depending on the level of involvement in the foreign market. These three are not mutually exclusive, and one can often lead to another:

1 Import / Export. This is the lowest risk but also gives the lowest profit potential. Related options include franchising and foreign licensing.
2 Outsourcing. If companies want a deeper level of involvement, with a long-term contractual agreement, they can outsource (= subcontract) some or all of their manufacturing. Increasingly, service jobs are also being outsourced.
3 Foreign direct investment (FDI). This is the highest risk but gives the most control and shows the most commitment to the global market. Here companies buy property and businesses in the foreign nation. FDI includes acquisitions to create overseas divisions (= subsidiaries), joint ventures and strategic alliances. A joint venture is where two or more companies share the costs and profits in a particular market, but keep their separate identities.

Political strategy in the face of globalization

Politicians can make two basic responses:

1 Being in favour of market forces and deregulation. In this case, politicians will try to make their labour markets more flexible, for example by making it easier to hire and fire people. They will lower taxes to encourage private investment and private spending. They will cut red tape (= bureaucracy) to make it easier to start a new business. They will encourage free trade.
2 Being in favour of subsidies and protectionism. In this case, politicians will try to protect the job security and social benefits of people who already have a job. They will support high taxes in order to pay for social programmes and other government spending. They will try to protect national businesses and jobs with measures such as tariffs (= taxes) and quotas (= limits) on imports.

Measuring and analysing global trade

When analysing trade, important concepts are:

- Balance of trade. This is the difference between a nation's imports and exports. If a country exports more to its trading partners than it imports, then it has a 'trade surplus'. Otherwise it has a 'trade deficit'.
- Balance of payments. This is a much wider measure – it includes imports and exports of goods as above, but also includes services and investments.
- Exchange rates. Currencies (dollars, euros, yen, etc) fluctuate against each other according to supply and demand. If the value of a currency falls, exports increase (because they become cheaper for overseas customers) and foreign investment is stimulated (because domestic assets are cheaper for foreigners). On the other hand, imported goods become more expensive, and consumers feel this as a drop in their living standards.

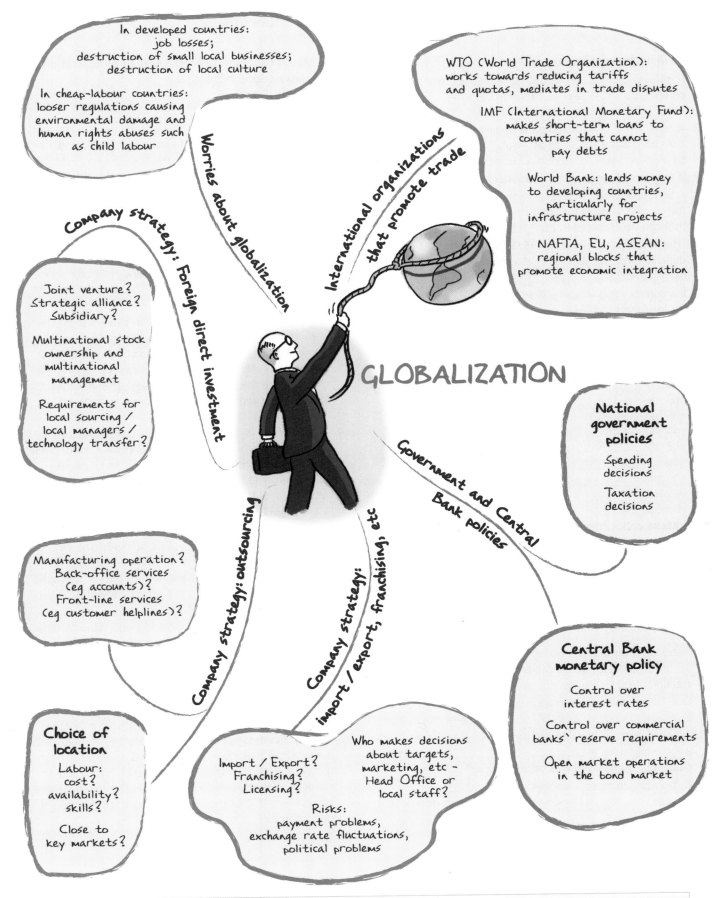

In developed countries:
job losses;
destruction of small local businesses;
destruction of local culture

In cheap-labour countries:
looser regulations causing
environmental damage and
human rights abuses such
as child labour

Worries about globalization

International organizations that promote trade

WTO (World Trade Organization):
works towards reducing tariffs
and quotas, mediates in trade disputes

IMF (International Monetary Fund):
makes short-term loans to
countries that cannot
pay debts

World Bank: lends money
to developing countries,
particularly for
infrastructure projects

NAFTA, EU, ASEAN:
regional blocks that
promote economic integration

Company strategy: Foreign direct investment

Joint venture?
Strategic alliance?
Subsidiary?

Multinational stock
ownership and
multinational
management

Requirements for
local sourcing /
local managers /
technology transfer?

GLOBALIZATION

Government and Central Bank policies

National
government
policies

Spending
decisions

Taxation
decisions

Manufacturing operation?
Back-office services
(eg accounts)?
Front-line services
(eg customer helplines)?

Company strategy: outsourcing

Company strategy: import / export, franchising, etc

Choice of location

Labour:
cost?
availability?
skills?

Close to
key markets?

Import / Export?
Franchising?
Licensing?

Who makes decisions
about targets,
marketing, etc -
Head Office or
local staff?

Risks:
payment problems,
exchange rate fluctuations,
political problems

Central Bank monetary policy

Control over
interest rates

Control over commercial
banks' reserve requirements

Open market operations
in the bond market

2 Globalization and economic policy: Exercises

2.1 Fill in the missing letters.

1 It is dangerous for a company to stand aside while competitors m_ _ _e (= join together), form j_ _ _t ven_ _ _es, or create overseas divisions.

2 A 'sub_ _ _ _ _ _y' (= company owned by another company) is not the same as a 'sub_ _ _y' (= money paid by a government to support a business).

3 A less formal synonym for 'bureaucracy' is 'r_ _ t_ _ _'.

4 A technical word for taxes on imported goods is 'ta_ _ _ _s'. A word for limits on the quantity of goods that can be imported is 'qu_ _ _s'.

5 'The euro against the dollar' (€/$) is currently 1.28. 'The dollar against the yen' ($/¥) is currently 115. These are examples of 'ex_ _ _ _ge r_ _ _s'.

6 If a currency falls in value, domestic a_ _ _ts are cheaper for foreigners to buy.

2.2 Find words with a similar meaning and then put them in order to show the business cycle.

boom   contraction   depression   downturn
expansion   ~~growth~~   ~~recession~~   ~~recovery~~
slowdown   slump   upswing

↓ 1 _____recovery_____ / _____

↓ 2 _____growth_____ / _____ / _____

↓ 3 _____recession_____ / _____ /

_____ / _____

↓ 4 _____ / _____

2.3 Make collocations using one item from each box. Then use the collocations to complete the sentences.

competitive   contractual   deeper
~~inward~~   mobile   trade   trading

advantage   agreement   communications   ~~investment~~
involvement   partners   surplus

1 National governments encourage _____inward_____ _____investment_____ because it brings benefits such as the creation of jobs, skills development and technology transfer.

2 Low labour and manufacturing costs are a major _____ _____ in the global market.

3 Import / export is low-risk, but has a low profit potential. If a company wants a _____ _____ in the global market they will look at outsourcing.

4 Outsourcing involves a long-term _____ _____ with a low-cost provider of goods or services.

5 _____ _____ make it easy for managers to stay in touch with colleagues and Head Office.

6 If a country exports more to its _____ _____ than it imports, it has a _____ _____ (= positive balance of trade).

2.4 Match the company responses to globalization to their descriptions 1–7 below.

foreign subsidiary   import / export   joint venture
franchising   outsourcing   strategic alliance   licensing

1 A company gives the right to manufacture its product to a foreign company for a fee (= royalty). This has been done successfully by Coca-Cola and Disneyworld, although in other cases the local producer may choose to use a different brand name. _____

2 Similar to 1, but the term is usually used for small businesses in the retail and service sector like McDonalds and The Body Shop. Head Office has tighter control of the local business operation than in 1, and the name and brand image are always retained.

_____

3 A company (usually small or medium-sized) trades directly with another separate company in the foreign market. Sometimes an intermediary (eg a local agent) matches buyers and sellers and provides services like dealing with customs and documentation. Retailers often use this strategy for supplies of clothing, furniture, toys, etc.

_____

4 A partnership in which two or more companies (often from different countries) join to undertake a major project or start a business activity. Volkswagen and General Motors entered the Chinese market through this route.

_____

5 A long-term partnership similar to 4, but it may be between two companies of very different sizes, such as a large manufacturer and one of its suppliers. The relationship is not as close as 4, so there is usually no sharing of costs, risks, management or profits. Motorola and Oracle have both used this approach (with suppliers and customers respectively). _____

6 An international company uses a low-cost manufacturer in another country, and then sells the products under its own brand name in other markets. Also called 'contract manufacturing'. This has been done by many firms in the IT area (for software development as well as hardware) and in the automobile industry. _____

7 A parent company directly owns a company in another country. Business operations are under the control of local management, although Head Office is responsible for global strategy. Examples include Nestlé, Toyota and Siemens. Some people think that the term 'multinational corporation' (MNC) should only be used for this type of organization. _____

2.5 There are a variety of policy responses to changes in the economic climate. Read the texts and then answer the questions below.

Fiscal policy refers to the government's efforts to keep the economy stable by increasing or decreasing taxes and government spending.

High tax rates slow the economy because they take money out of the private sector and put it into the hands of government. They also discourage small businesses by decreasing profit margins and making effort less rewarding. But high taxes also mean that more money is available to spend on education, health, defence, highways and social programmes. In practice, most governments spend more than they collect in taxes, creating a national debt. Reducing this deficit is politically unpopular as it involves cutting public services.

Monetary policy refers to the role that central banks have in controlling the money supply. If there is more money in circulation, demand in the economy increases, but so does inflation. Central banks ('the Fed' in the US; 'the ECB' in the EU) can act in three main ways:

1 Raising and lowering interest rates

The central bank controls the 'base rate' (AmE discount rate) – how much commercial banks have to pay to borrow money from them. This rate is passed on (with some additional percentage as profit) to any customer who needs a loan. At this point it is referred to as the interest rate. When the economy is booming, the central bank raises rates. This makes borrowing more expensive. So businesses borrow less, and the economy slows as companies spend less on labour, plant, equipment, etc. The opposite is true when the central bank lowers rates: businesses borrow more and the economy takes off.

2 Reserve requirements

The central bank tells commercial banks what percentage of their customer accounts must be physically kept in the bank as cash. When reserve requirements are raised, banks have less money available to make loans and the economy cools.

3 Open-market operations

The central bank buys and sells bonds. To cool the economy (decrease the money supply) they sell bonds to the public. The money received in payment is no longer in circulation for the purchase of goods and services. To stimulate the economy (increase the money supply) they buy back bonds from the public, and the money they pay enters circulation.

With these three tools central banks can operate either an 'expansionary' or a 'restrictive' monetary policy.

According to the texts, are these statements true (T) or false (F).

1 Fiscal policy consists of taxation and spending decisions, and is under the control of governments. Monetary policy consists of interest rate and other money supply decisions, and is under the control of central banks. T / F

2 Government spending resulting from high taxes gives a stimulus to small businesses. T / F

3 High taxes can give new opportunities for certain businesses (eg in the defense or medical supplies sectors). T / F

4 Raising interest rates is a way of stimulating the economy. T / F

Underline the correct words.

5 Having an 'expansionary monetary policy' is the same thing as *increasing / decreasing* the amount of money in circulation, which will *provide a stimulus to / cool* the economy, which over the long term runs the risk of creating *inflation / deflation*.

Now underline all the measures that can be taken – according to the text – if fighting inflation (ie slowing the economy) is the only consideration of policy.

6 *increasing / decreasing* taxation

7 *increasing / decreasing* interest rates

8 *increasing / decreasing* the reserve requirements of banks

9 *increasing / decreasing* the sale of bonds by the central bank

Discussion topics

1 Globalization is great! Everyone benefits. I don't see workers in poor countries complaining – they prefer to work for international companies.
○ Agree   ○ Disagree

2 Look out! Your job is at risk from outsourcing. Retrain now as a hairdresser, cleaner, chef or taxi driver to avoid future unemployment.
○ Agree   ○ Disagree

3 No-one can control the economy.
○ Agree   ○ Disagree

4 How strong is the economy in your country? Is it going to grow or decline over the next few years?

3 Corporate strategy and structure

If one does not know to which port one is sailing, no wind is favourable.
Seneca (ca 4 BC–AD 65), Roman philosopher, statesman and dramatist

Strategy and planning

Strategy and planning begins with analysis, and a well-known tool to do this is a SWOT analysis (looking at the internal Strengths and Weaknesses of the company, and the external Opportunities and Threats). Planning itself can be categorized into two main types depending on the time-scale and purpose of the planning.

- Strategic planning is concerned with the longer term and 'the big picture'. It is the process of defining the company's mission, determining the overall goals of the organization and allocating resources to reach those goals. It is done by top and middle managers.
- Operational planning is concerned with translating the general, long-term goals into more specific, concrete objectives. It involves monitoring the day-to-day work of departments. It is done by middle and supervisory managers.

Company structure

Having decided on its strategy, a business needs to organize itself into a structure that best suits its objectives. This can be done in several ways.

- Organization by function. The company is divided into departments such as production, finance, marketing, human resources.
- Organization by product. The company brings together staff who are involved in the same product line.
- Organization by customer type. The company is organized around different sectors of the market. Large customers are called 'key accounts'.
- Organization by geographical area. The company is organized according to regions.

A large multinational may use several of the above: for example a functional division initially (at an international level), then a national structure for each country, and within this some level of division according to customer types.

The business must also decide on the best way to organize its management hierarchy (= chain of command). The company is run by top (= senior) managers with job titles such as: Chief Executive Officer (CEO), Chief Operating Officer (COO), and a series of Vice-Presidents or Directors of different departments. Top management set a direction for the organization and aim to inspire employees with their vision for the company's future. This vision is often written down in a mission statement.

The next level is middle management, where managers are in charge of (AmE head up) a department, division, branch, etc. Middle managers develop detailed plans and procedures based on the firm's overall strategy.

Finally there is supervisory (AmE first-line) management, and typical job titles are: Supervisor, Team Leader, Section Chief. Supervisory managers are responsible for assigning non-managerial employees to specific jobs and evaluating their performance. They have to implement plans developed higher up the hierarchy.

In some companies – or for specific projects – there can be a matrix structure with cross-functional teams. Here employees from different parts of the organization work together and bureaucracy is reduced.

Above everything there is the Board, chaired by a Chairman or President, which gets involved in 'big picture' strategic planning and meets perhaps once a month. The CEO will be on the Board, but most Board members are not involved in running the company – they are elected by and responsible to the shareholders. Their main interest is shareholder value: getting a good return on investment in terms of both dividend payments and a rising share price.

Centralization vs Decentralization

A key issue for the company is to decide on the degree of centralization. Should authority be kept at Head Office (centralization)? If so, this would mean:

- A strong corporate image.
- Decisions made by experienced managers who see the whole picture, not just one part of the business.
- Standardized procedures which could lead to economies of scale (lower costs) and simpler distribution channels.

But decentralization also has advantages:

- Lower-level managers are more familiar with local conditions and can therefore give a stronger customer focus.
- The delegation of decision-making is likely to lead to a higher level of morale at the grassroots.

There are other closely-related questions. Should the structure be 'vertical', with many layers of management, or 'flat', with fewer layers? And how many subordinates should each manager supervise?

Monitoring and adapting plans (comparing actual data with forecasts, acting on feedback from customers and suppliers, acting on reports prepared by first-line managers)

Controlling budgets

Implementing plans, procedures and projects

Ensuring that objectives are SMART (specific, measurable, agreed, realistic and time specific)

Identifying customer needs, eg through market research

Identifying ways to lower costs and reduce waste

Determining staffing needs

SWOT Analysis: market position

Analysing the product portfolio, including stage in the life cycle of main products

Analysing figures for profit centres (that add value) and cost centres (that spend budgets)

Operational (day-to-day) issues for supervisory and middle managers

Analysis of current position

STRATEGY AND PLANNING

'Big picture' issues for Board and senior managers

General issues for senior and middle managers

Setting overall sales and revenue goals

Setting budgets and making long-term forecasts of costs

Improving distribution channels

Identifying new markets

Identifying opportunities for new products

Pricing policy: value-for-money products vs high quality / premium price products

Building brand loyalty

Investing in technology, plant and equipment

Integrating on-line and off-line procedures (eg for sales and for customer service)

Evaluating current markets: development, consolidation, or withdrawal?

Prioritizing sales growth and market share, or earnings growth and profitability?

Business development: looking at possible takeover targets, mergers, alliances; entering new markets (from zero? buying local company? joint venture?)

Product diversification, or focus on core business?

Marketing strategy: worldwide or multidomestic?

Identifying major cost savings: looking for internal efficiencies, setting up production in low-cost countries (outsourcing)

Increasing shareholder value: share price and dividends

Image, reputation and social responsibility

3 Corporate strategy and structure: Exercises

3.1 Fill in the missing letters.

1 Inside a company, large customers are often referred to as 'k_ _ a_ _ _ _ _ _s'.

2 COO stands for 'C_ _ _f O_ _ _ _ _ _g O_ _ _ _ _r'.

3 A matrix structure brings together people from different parts of the organization to work as c_ _ _ _-f_ _ _ _ _ _ _l t_ _ _s.

4 The delegation of decision-making is likely to lead to a higher level of morale at 'the gra_ _ _oots' (= the ordinary people in an organization rather than its leaders).

5 Each manager supervises a number of sub_ _ _ _ _ _ _s.

6 In relation to an existing market, the 'big picture' strategy can be one of dev_ _ _ _ _nt (growth), conso_ _ _ _ion (making the existing situation stronger), or wi_ _ _ _wal (leaving the market completely).

3.2 Complete each phrase 1–10 with an ending a)–j).

1 Operational planning translates general goals ☐
2 It is usual to divide an organization ☐
3 Some companies are organized according ☐
4 The Board gets involved ☐
5 Senior managers set ☐
6 Middle managers develop detailed plans based ☐
7 First-line managers implement plans ☐
8 First-line managers are also responsible ☐
9 A cross-functional team brings ☐
10 Subordinates work ☐

a) a direction for the company.
b) developed higher up the hierarchy.
c) for assigning employees to specific jobs.
d) in major strategy issues.
e) into functional departments.
f) into more concrete objectives.
g) on the overall strategy.
h) to geographical regions.
i) together staff from different parts of the company.
j) under the supervision of a first-line manager.

3.3 The mixed-up letters make words that describe departments or functional areas inside a company. Put the letters in the right order.

1 haumn rruoeecss
2 cmoesutr scrieevs
3 qtuialy crotnol
4 rsaceerh and dvnolpmeeet
5 pbiluc rnotilaes
6 pejcrot mmeegnnaat
7 aiiisdttrnmaon
8 bnlliig
9 pdroctoiun
10 lgael
11 siihnppg
12 facnine
13 metakrnig
14 atnccous
15 pasuirchng (= buying, BrE)
16 pcroenremut (= buying, AmE)

3.4 Pairs of words in bold have been switched – one from each column. Put them back in their correct places.

1 market **channel**
2 cost **value**
3 earnings **business**
4 management **loyalty**
5 customer **statement**
6 product **share**
7 core **growth**
8 distribution **research**
9 mission **needs**
10 market **portfolio**
11 shareholder **centre**
12 brand **hierarchy**

3.5 Which of the collocations in exercise 3.4 refer to:

1 using a questionnaire to carry out a survey
   _____ market research _____

2 the main activity of a company that generates most of its profits _____

3 financial benefits (= increase in share price and dividends) for the owners of the company _____

4 the whole range of products that a company sells
   _____

5 when customers are faithful to a particular product
   _____

6 a business unit that spends money but does not generate revenue _____

7 a continuing increase in profits _____

8 what is shown in an organigram (= organization chart)
   _____

9 senior management's vision for the company
   _____

10 how a product gets from the manufacturer to the end-user _____

3.6 Match the verbs in the box with their definitions below. Be careful – some are very similar.

adapt	assign	~~check~~	control	coordinate
determine	ensure	evaluate	implement	monitor

1 make sure that everything is correct or the way you expect it _____ check _____

2 organize people so that they work together effectively
   _____

3 give someone a job to do _____

4 carry out; make a plan start to work _____

5 have the power to make decisions; make something operate in the way that you want _____

6 make certain that something happens _____

7 change something to fit a new situation _____

8 watch or measure something carefully for a period of time to see how it changes _____

9 (formal) think about or test something before deciding its value, suitability or effectiveness _____

10 (formal) control what something will be; officially decide something; find out _____

3.7 Use the words in the box to complete the SWOT analysis below.

alliance	barriers	climate	debt	depth	one-stop
outdated	overhead	range	shortage	start-up	
state-of-the-art	tailor-made	transfer	workflow		

Strengths (strong points, internal)

- a large market share
- a well-structured distribution network
- motivated and well-trained staff
- ^{1}_____ (= cutting edge) products
- ^{2}_____ (= customized / personalized) products
- all services provided in one place: a '^{3}_____ shop'
- a well-known, high-value brand

Weaknesses (weak points, internal)

- a lack of new products
- a lack of managerial ^{4}_____ (= amount of knowledge and experience)
- ^{5}_____ (= old fashioned) production methods
- high levels of ^{6}_____ (= money owed to banks and other creditors)
- slow ^{7}_____ (= progress of work done) due to inflexible procedures
- an over-reliance on a limited ^{8}_____ of products
- high direct costs (= production costs) and high indirect costs (^{9}_____ eg utility bills)

Opportunities (future chances in the market)

- new foreign markets
- an improving economic ^{10}_____
- outsourcing
- a key supplier who might want to make a strategic ^{11}_____
- new product ideas: either from market research or from sales reps talking directly to customers

Threats (future dangers in the market)

- greater competition
- low-cost production in Southeast Asia
- technology ^{12}_____ to Southeast Asia (so that low-cost countries start using high-tech equipment)
- high ^{13}_____ costs of a new facility
- political risk: regulation, taxes, trade ^{14}_____ (eg quotas and tariffs)
- the market approaching saturation
- possible ^{15}_____ of components or raw materials
- reduced pricing power due to merger of two important customers

3.8 Look back at the completed SWOT analysis in exercise 3.7 and find a word that means:

1 a situation in which you do not have enough of something _____

2 depending too much on something _____

3 'sales staff' (the answer is a short form of a longer word) _____

4 a building used for a particular purpose (especially for manufacturing) _____

5 when everyone who wants the product already has it _____

3.9 Tick (✓) the one statement that is true.

1 *Targets* and *goals* tend to be more general. *Objectives* and *aims* tend to be more specific, with *aims* being the most concrete and measurable. ☐

2 *Aims* and *goals* tend to be more general. *Objectives* and *targets* tend to be more specific, with *targets* being the most concrete and measurable. ☐

3.10 Managers should make sure that business objectives are SMART. Can you remember what these letters stand for? Don't look back at the mind map until you have tried to think!

Sp _ _ _ _ c, Mea _ _ _ _ le, Ag _ _ _ d, Rea _ _ _ ic, and Ti _ _-specific

Discussion topics

1 Bosses just take the credit for the work of lower-level employees. Who needs them?
   ○ Agree   ○ Disagree

2 The continual emphasis on shareholder value in American-style companies produces high levels of stress amongst employees and an inability to think about the longer term.
   ○ Agree   ○ Disagree

3 Think of two companies operating in the same market (eg Coke and Pepsi, Yahoo and Google, Audi and BMW, Gucci and Armani). Compare their strategies.

4 Make a quick SWOT analysis for a company / country / city / educational institution that you know. Present it to some colleagues and ask for questions.

4 Managing people

If I had to sum up in a word what makes a good manager, I'd say decisiveness. You can use the fanciest computers to gather the numbers, but in the end you have to set a timetable and act.
Lee Iacocca (1924–), American industrialist

Motivation

The ability to motivate others and improve morale is a 'soft skill' – difficult to acquire and almost impossible to measure. Four key thinkers contributed to this field in the 1950s and 60s, and their work is still the basis for contemporary approaches:

1 Maslow developed his 'hierarchy of needs'.
   ↑ self-actualization needs
   ↑ ego (self-esteem) needs
   ↑ social needs
   ↑ security needs
   ↑ physiological needs

   We move to the next stage up only when the lower need is met. And as soon as any need is met, then it is no longer a motivator. The bottom two are usually not an issue in business (unless you are hungry or in danger). After that, our next need is to feel accepted and part of a group (social need). If that happens, then next we have ego needs: recognition and acknowledgement from others, as well as a sense of status or importance. Finally, if that need is met, we want self-fulfilment ('self-actualization' in Maslow's terms): to achieve, to develop to our fullest potential.

2 Herzberg expressed similar ideas. He agreed that the most important motivators at work were sense of achievement, earned recognition and interest in the job itself. But then there was another set of job factors ('hygiene' or 'maintenance' factors) that do not motivate employees, but can cause dissatisfaction if they are missing. These include salary, job security, working conditions and good relations with co-workers.

3 McGregor observed that managers generally fall into two categories: Theory X and Theory Y. Theory X managers believe that most people dislike work and must be controlled and directed to achieve the organization's goals. Theory Y managers believe that most people like work and actively seek responsibility. They believe in empowerment (= giving employees the authority to make decisions without traditional managerial approval) and enabling (= giving them the tools).

4 Drucker believed in 'management by objectives' (MBO). MBO calls on managers to work with employees to formulate clear, ambitious but achievable goals. There has to be monitoring and measurement to ensure objectives are being met, and workers who achieve their objectives can be rewarded with pay rises, bonuses, etc.

Communication

Communication is two-way: top-down and bottom-up. It can also be external: the PR (public relations) function handles this.

Inside an organization, informal communication happens all the time: everyone enjoys discussing 'office politics' at the water cooler and picking up information 'on the grapevine' (= passed from one person to another in conversation). Formal communication is through the medium of meetings, presentations, reports, etc, and these are covered in the second half of this book. But two other key communication skills are not possible to practise in a book:

● 'Active listening'. This means listening with full attention, not interrupting except to ask for clarification, and giving consideration to the other person's point of view.
● 'Assertiveness'. This means stating your needs and opinions confidently and clearly, without on the one hand being indirect or 'suffering in silence', or on the other being aggressive and rude.

Teamwork

A team (or 'taskforce' or 'working party') needs a variety of personality types to perform well:

● 'Head' people who are good at thinking and problem-solving.
● 'Hands' people who are good at doing and acting.
● 'Heart' people who are good at networking and resolving conflicts.

Once a team has been set up, it usually goes through the five stages of development identified by Bruce Tuckman:

1 Forming. People get to know each other.
2 Storming. This refers both to 'brainstorming' as ideas get suggested for the first time, and also to conflicts that arise as team members clarify their roles and expectations.
3 Norming. Members sort out a way of working together and begin to 'own' and share the team objectives.
4 Performing. Members focus on solving problems and doing tasks. Progress can be seen as they pass various milestones (= events that mark an important stage in a process).
5 Adjourning. The job is finished, and there is often a public recognition and celebration of achievements.

MANAGING PEOPLE

Making decisions with colleagues

1. Accept there is a problem, define the situation and identify objectives

2. Collect information and ideas (use of 'working parties')

3. Analyse information and develop alternatives

4. Make a decision on the best alternative

5. Communicate the decision and begin implementation

6. Evaluate the final results (use of reports)

Leading (CEO level)

Qualities of leaders

Leaders are different to managers

Leaders see the big picture: they have the vision and commitment to make radical changes

Leaders are creative and innovative, looking for new solutions to old problems

Leaders are alone at the top, managers have colleagues and teams

Leadership styles

Autocratic: instructions given to subordinates

Democratic: sharing responsibility and decision-making

Laissez-faire: minimal supervision

Supervising and directing

1. Establish clear standards

2. Monitor performance

3. Compare results against established standards and communicate results / deviations to employees involved

4. Take corrective action if necessary

5. Provide positive feedback and reward people for work well done

Managing teams

Work teams
Problem-solving teams
Cross-functional teams
Project teams

Team roles

'Head' people
'Hands' people
'Heart' people

Stages of team development: forming, storming, norming, performing, adjourning

Communicating

External (Public Relations) as well as internal

Informal as well as formal

Top-down as well as bottom-up

Assertiveness

Active listening

Motivating

Theories

Maslow
Herzberg
McGregor
Drucker

Salary and promotion (See unit 11)

Job design

Empowerment and enabling
Job enrichment

4.1 Fill in the missing letters:

1 The level of confidence and positive feelings that people have, especially people who work together, is their level of 'mo_ _ _e' (slightly different to 'motivation', which is linked to doing things).

2 When we have the recognition and respect of others, it adds greatly to our 'self-es_ _ _m' (= feeling that we are valued and important).

3 When we have been successful, it is good to have the 'ackn_ _ _ _ _ _ _ _nt' (= public recognition and thanks) of others.

4 Developing to our fullest potential was called 'self-actualization' by Maslow. A more common term is 'self-ful_ _ _ment'.

5 Being successful after a lot of effort gives us a 'sense of ach_ _ _ _ _nt'.

6 Giving people more control over their work is called 'emp_ _ _ _ _ _nt'.

7 Giving someone the tools and skills to do something is called 'en_ _ _ing' them.

8 Successful managers are neither passive nor aggressive. Instead, they are 'ass_ _ _ _ve'.

9 Business leaders need to have vision and 'comm_ _ _ _nt' (= enthusiasm, determination and a strong belief in what they are doing).

4.2 Decide whether the phrases below best describe managers (M) or leaders (L).

1 welcome change ☐　　5 good at motivating ☐

2 welcome stability ☐　　6 good at supervising ☐

3 look at the details ☐　　7 four make a team ☐

4 look at the big picture ☐　8 four is three too many ☐

4.3 Read the text then answer the questions below.

The work of Maslow and Herzberg has been developed into the theory of 'job enrichment'. This theory states that there are five characteristics affecting an individual's motivation and performance:

1 Skill variety. The extent to which a job demands different skills.

2 Task identity. The degree to which a job has a visible outcome.

3 Task significance. The degree to which a job has an impact on the work of others.

4 Autonomy. The degree of freedom and choice that people have in scheduling work and determining procedures.

5 Feedback. The amount of direct and clear information that is received about performance.

The first three factors above contribute to the meaningfulness of the job. The fourth gives a feeling of responsibility. The fifth contributes to a feeling of achievement and recognition.

Job enrichment tries to maximize the above five factors within the constraints of the organization. It also includes two specific strategies:

● job enlargement – combining a series of tasks into one challenging and interesting assignment

● job rotation – moving employees from one job to another.

Find a word in the text which means:

1 making something better and more enjoyable _____

2 result _____

3 power to make independent decisions _____

4 quality of being serious, useful and important _____

5 making something bigger _____

6 piece of work that you must do as part of your job or course of study _____

4.4 Read about a decision-making process at Xerox.

[1]In the 1990s Xerox was in trouble. [2]Anne Mulcahy, a company insider, realized how serious the situation was – customers were leaving, morale was low, and the company product line was too unfocused. [3]She became CEO in 2000 and immediately began a listening tour, seeking insights from employees, customers and industry experts on where the company had gone wrong. [4]What strategic options were open to Xerox? [5]It could focus on laser or ink-jet, high-end or low-end, single-function or multi-function. [6]And which areas of the business were going to be cut? [7]R&D was traditionally strong at Xerox but used up a lot of internal resources. [8]Mulcahy and her team worked out a plan. [9]First, they would focus on cash generation, second they would cut costs wherever possible (R&D was saved from this), and finally they would focus exclusively on areas where Xerox had a competitive advantage. [10]Mulcahy took time to explain this plan to front-line employees. [11]In addition, she made sure that everyone explained it to customers as well, and made many customer visits herself.

Now write the sentence numbers that match the stages below.

a) Accept there is a problem; define the situation. ☐2☐

b) Collect information and ideas. ☐

c) Analyse information and develop alternatives. ☐ to ☐

d) Make a decision on the best alternative. ☐ to ☐

e) Communicate the decision and begin implementation. ☐ to ☐

4.5 Study the collocations related to decision making. Check any unknown words in a dictionary.

achieve, define, establish, fail in, fall short of, fulfil, identify, meet, reach, set	an objective
address, cause, clear up, create, deal with, give rise to, handle, overcome, resolve, solve, tackle	a problem
accept, agree to / with, come up with, make, offer, put forward, reject, rule out, take up, turn down	a suggestion
arrive at, come to, defer, make, overrule, overturn, postpone, put off, reach, reverse, take	a decision
collective, critical, crucial, difficult, hard, important, joint, key, major, tough, unanimous	decision
anticipated, desirable, eventual, expected, favourable, final, likely, satisfactory, successful	outcome

Now divide the words in each box into three groups, based on their meaning.

achieve, meet, reach, fulfil	define, identify, establish, set	fail in, fall short of	an objective
			a problem
			a suggestion
			a decision
			decision
			outcome

4.6 Match the team roles in the box to the descriptions below. This exercise is based on the ideas of Belbin and Margerison-McCann.

Coordinator	Innovator	Evaluator	Finisher
Implementer	Promoter	Shaper	Specialist	Team worker

'Head' people

1 _____ – solves difficult problems with creative ideas; not afraid to challenge norms; may ignore details

2 _____ – thinks carefully and accurately about things; listens patiently; may lack energy to inspire others

3 _____ – has expert knowledge in key areas; may be uninterested in all other areas

'Hands' people

4 _____ – takes basic ideas and makes them work in practice; methodical and organized; can be slow

5 _____ – gets involved quickly with lots of energy; more interested in the final result than the process; may be impatient

6 _____ – likes completing things on time, on budget, and to specification; can worry too much

'Heart' people

7 _____ – central person who makes sure everyone works well together; helps everyone focus; can be seen as too controlling

8 _____ – caring, a good listener, and works hard to resolve problems; may have difficulty making decisions

9 _____ – enthusiastic, sees the big picture and good at explaining it to people outside the group; can be too optimistic and lose initial energy

4.7 Change each adjective describing people into its opposite.

1	accurate	_ _accurate / _ _precise
2	careful	care_ _ _ _
3	conservative	inn_ _ _ _ve / ra_ _ _al
4	decisive	_ _decisive / hes_ _ _ _ _
5	efficient	_ _efficient / wa_ _eful
6	enthusiastic	_ _enthusiastic / b_ _ed
7	flexible	_ _flexible / r_ _id
8	hands-on	l_ _ _ez-f_ _ _e
9	lazy	h_ _ _-w_ _ _ing
10	patient	_ _patient
11	polite	_ _polite / r_ _ _
12	reliable	_ _ reliable

4.8 Complete each sentence using either sensible or sensitive. These adjectives are often confused.

1 He reacts to things in an emotional way and is easily offended, he's very _____.

2 He's reasonable, practical and mature, he's very _____.

Discussion topics

1 All this Maslow and Herzberg stuff is garbage. There's only one thing that motivates people: money.
   ○ Agree   ○ Disagree

2 All this stuff about teamwork is garbage. If you want to do a job properly, do it yourself.
   ○ Agree   ○ Disagree

3 The best communicator inside an organization that I have ever known is _____ (name). He / She is such a good communicator because …

4 Looking at the nine team roles in exercise 4.6, I think I am a _____ (role) because …
   Someone who I really enjoy working with is called _____ (name). He / She is a _____ (role) because …

5 Operations management

The first rule of any technology used in a business is that automation applied to an efficient operation will magnify the efficiency. The second is that automation applied to an inefficient operation will magnify the inefficiency.
Bill Gates (1955–), co-founder of Microsoft Corporation

What is 'operations'?

Operations has been defined as 'the use of resources that are devoted to the production and delivery of products and services'. In fact it is the 'core business' of the company, with other functions like marketing, finance and human resources simply acting in support. It includes product development, managing the supply chain, production planning and control, billing and shipping, and all those day-to-day activities covered by the term 'administration'.

The operations function has five basic performance objectives. They mean different things for the organization and the customer:

	For the organization	*For the customer*
Quality	error-free process	products that are on-spec
Cost	high level of productivity	competitive price
Dependability	operational stability	reliable delivery (quantity and time)
Flexibility	ability to respond to change	volume and delivery adjustments; wide and frequently updated product range
Speed	fast throughput	short 'lead-time'

'on-spec' = having the required specifications
'lead-time' = time from placing the order to receiving delivery

Developing new products

Initial ideas for a new product may come from marketing or operations. These ideas are turned into a 'concept brief' – this is a clear statement describing the form, function, purpose and benefits of the product. Immediate operational issues arise:

- Feasibility. Can we actually do (or make) this? Do we have the skills/capacity/resources?
- Vulnerability. Being pessimistic, what could go wrong? What is the downside risk?
- What materials, parts and components will be needed?
- Is it possible to reduce production costs by reducing design complexity? In particular, are there opportunities for:
  a) standardization (restricted variety)?
  b) commonality (= using the same components)?
  c) modularization (= using sub-components that can be put together in different combinations)?
- How can we reduce the time-to-market (= time taken from concept brief to the launch) or the roll-out (= phased introduction) of the new product?

Managing the supply chain

A manufacturer might have a component maker as a first-tier supplier, but also the component maker's supplier (eg a raw materials company) as a second-tier supplier. Together, they form the 'upstream' or 'supply side' end of the network. Equally, they might have a distributor as a first-tier customer, but also the distributor's customer (eg a retailer) as a second-tier customer. Together, they form the 'downstream' or 'demand side' end of the network.

Supply chain management includes:

- Procurement (= sourcing + purchasing) from first-tier suppliers (AmE vendors).
- Materials management inside the plant. This includes inventory (= stock) management and production planning and control.
- Logistics (= distribution) to first-tier customers.

There are several important strategic issues:

- Should the company directly own any parts of the supply chain? If it does, then this is vertical integration.
- Should the company opt for single or multi-sourcing? Having just one supplier will mean good communication with a dependable partner, and also economies of scale (= cost savings from buying in large quantities). But disadvantages include risks associated with a failure of supply, and giving the supplier the chance to put upward pressure on prices.
- How much of the process can migrate to the web, eg finding the best price, delivery time and specifications through e-procurement?

These days many organizations, eg film companies have a 'virtual operation'. The organization buys in the range of functions it needs for a particular project, but at the end of the project this network disappears. This gives flexibility and speed, but the company is left with very few core competencies (= key areas of technical expertise) where it retains a competitive advantage.

Further information www.design-council.org.uk ● www.sussex.ac.uk/Users/dt31/TOMI/topics ● http://knowledge.wharton.upenn.edu

Materials processing technology

Use of computers to build a virtual prototype and test it

Use of computers to control the machine tools that shape pieces

Industrial robots to assemble parts

RFID tags (radio frequency identification) on individual items

Use of technology

Choice of location

Domestic production or outsourcing?

Labour costs, availability and skills?

Grants and subsidies?

Infrastructure: road and rail links?

Proximity to suppliers?

Convenience for customers?

Environmental considerations?

Additional issues for service sector: number of branches; relationship between online presence and physical business premises

Customer processing technology

Web-based ordering and after-sales

Hotel reservation systems, airline check-in systems, etc

EPOS (electronic point-of-sale) technology that handles payment and updates stock records in retail outlets

Stages in design

1. Initial idea and concept brief
2. Screening: is it a good idea? would it sell? is it suitable for our company?
3. Preliminary design
4. Feasibility studies, evaluation and improvement
5. Prototyping and final design
6. Roll-out

OPERATIONS MANAGEMENT

See unit 6

Production

Managing the supply chain

Developing new products

Other operational issues

1. Reduce production costs and time-to-market by reducing design complexity

2. Determine any changes that will be needed to the factory layout, machinery, planning and control procedures (capacity, inventory, quality)

3. Draw up a 'bill of materials' (list giving materials and parts needed)

Whole supply network includes first- and second-tier suppliers and customers

Original Equipment Manufacturer (OEM) supplies parts and components that are used by other companies

Procurement (= sourcing + purchasing) from first-tier suppliers

Logistics (distribution) to first-tier customers

Materials management inside the plant

Use of e-procurement

Packaging issues:

does the product need special packaging?

cost implications?

who makes the packaging?

5 Operations management: Exercises

5.1 Fill in the missing letters.

1 The time spent between the customer placing an order and receiving delivery is the 'l_ _ _-time'.

2 An initial idea for a new product has to be turned into a 'con _ _ _t b_ _ _f' that describes its form, function, purpose and benefits.

3 The chance of something happening or being successful is its 'fea_ _ _ility'.

4 The chance of damage or harm to something is its 'vul_ _ _ _ility'.

5 An organization's immediate suppliers are its 'first-t_ _r' suppliers. Together with these suppliers' own suppliers, they form the 'ups_ _ _ _m' end of the supply network.

6 'Pr_ _ _ _ _ment' = 'so_ _ _ing' (finding suppliers) + 'purchasing' (buying).

7 A close synonym of 'supplier', more common in American usage, is 'v_ _ _or'.

8 The key areas of technical expertise that a company has are its 'c_ _e comp_ _ _ _cies'.

5.2 Complete the phrases by matching an item from the first column with an item from the second.

1 technical	throughput
2 a high level	-free process
3 fast	expertise
4 a frequently	integration
5 downside	of scale
6 vertical	of productivity
7 economies	risk
8 an error	updated product range

5.3 Match the two parts of each phrase.

1 draw up	on prices
2 reduce	to the web
3 migrate an operation	a feasibility study
4 put upward pressure	advantage
5 have a competitive	into a concept brief
6 roll out	design complexity
7 carry out	a bill of materials
8 turn an initial idea	a new product

5.4 Match topics 1–12 with the conversation extracts a)–l) below.

1 EPOS technology ☐	7 prototyping ☐
2 commonality ☐	8 RFID tags ☐
3 feasibility ☐	9 roll-out ☐
4 economies of scale ☐	10 screening ☐
5 logistics ☐	11 standardization ☐
6 modularization ☐	12 vulnerability ☐

a) 'Which shipping company will we use? And when can we get the containers to the port?'

b) 'We should be ready to launch in the spring: first in France and then in Germany, Switzerland and Austria.'

c) 'We use chip-and-PIN cash registers in our stores, and inventory information is automatically updated.'

d) 'Yes, in theory it could be a successful product, but in practice we don't have the capacity or the resources.'

e) 'How much money could we lose if things don't go according to plan?'

f) 'We manufacture a wide range of cars, but a lot of the engine parts are the same – it makes maintenance much easier.'

g) 'We've got to build a working model and test it properly before we can go into production.'

h) 'The brainstorming session was useful, but a lot of these ideas just won't work in practice.'

i) 'If we place a large order we'll get a much better price.'

j) 'They make sub-assemblies for PCs in high volume, and then put them together according to the customer's own spec.'

k) 'There's a smart memory chip embedded into every item. We know exactly where it is in the store, as well as where and when it was made.'

l) 'It's a successful formula. Wherever you go in the world, we sell the same burgers prepared in the same way.'

5.5 Complete the text using these verbs: builds, compile, drilling, hooked up, specifies, tested, welding.

Computers are now used throughout manufacturing to design and develop individual parts. The designer [1]_____ various criteria such as size, shape, materials, etc and the software [2]_____ a virtual prototype. This is then [3]_____ using given parameters. Before moving to production the software can also [4]_____ (= make) a list of materials and quantities needed. Once the design specifications are complete, the computer is [5]_____ (= connected) directly to the machine tools that make the part from an initial piece of metal, plastic or wood. Machine tool actions include cutting, shaping, turning, [6]_____ (= making holes in) and [7]_____ (= joining together).

5.6 Match these words to their definitions below: criteria, parameters, specifications.

1 limits that affect how something can be done _____

2 detailed plans about how something is to be made, or exact measurements _____

3 standards that are used for making a decision about something _____

5.7 The following words collocate with 'criteria': ~~define, meet,~~ **specify, establish, fulfil, satisfy, set. Divide the words into two groups, based on the meaning.**

a) ___define___ = _____ = _____ = _____

b) ___meet___ = _____ = _____

Only one of these two groups collocates with 'parameters'. Which one?

5.8 Read the text about e-procurement then answer the questions below.

E-procurement means sourcing and purchasing online. Different suppliers' offerings are often brought together into a single catalog (BrE catalogue), the customer decides who to buy from, and then the whole transaction process is automated. The software is sophisticated: it allows both sides to negotiate solutions for certain foreseeable scenarios (eg penalties for late delivery).

But the process is not straightforward. First, for a modern manufacturing operation it is rarely a question of a series of one-time purchases from a small number of suppliers all offering a similar product. The supply-chain relationships are much more complex than that.

Second, it's not just about price. The procurement process also needs to evaluate product availability, supplier responsiveness, service levels, delivery history, and customer-satisfaction ratings. These do not show up on the system so easily and reliably.

Finally, e-procurement has to work for the supplier too. They receive a detailed RFQ (Request for Quotation), but how do they respond in a flexible way? For example:

- Can they adjust details of the RFQ and make counter-offers?
- Can they make a rush-order surcharge?
- Can they offer different products that the customer may not be aware of?
- And to build a long-term relationship, can they know the forecast requirements of this potential customer?

The main criticism of e-procurement is related to this last point: that it focuses too much on short-term individual purchases and driving down costs. It works against the development of a long-term relationship with a supplier. Treating your supplier as a partner might bring far greater returns in the long run.

Find a word from the text that matches the definitions. The answers are in the order they appear in the text.

1 complicated and advanced in design
2 predictable / anticipated
3 punishments for breaking a rule or contract
4 easy to understand or use
5 be easy to see or notice (phrasal verb)
6 the price someone will charge you for a piece of work
7 additional amount of money you must pay
8 predicted / anticipated
9 making an amount fall to a lower level (phrasal verb)
10 period of time ('term' can also be used in this expression)

5.9 Project management is a distinct area within operations management. Complete the sentences below with the words in the box:

> constraints Gantt chart milestones scope
> setbacks small print stakeholders track

1 Difficulties that stop the progress of a project are called

_____ .

2 All the people with an interest in the success of a project are collectively called the _____ .

3 A visual illustration of the different phases and activities in a project (composed of many horizontal bars) is called a

_____ .

4 Before you sign a contract, it's very important to read the

_____ .

5 The events that mark the key stages in a project are called

_____ .

6 The factors that limit your actions (such as time and cost) are called _____ .

7 The _____ of a project is the range of things that it deals with.

8 If a project is 'on- _____ ', it is going according to plan; if you 'keep _____ of something', you pay attention to it so that you know what is happening.

Discussion topics

1 In a customer-focused business, product development should be the responsibility of marketing, not operations.
  ○ Agree   ○ Disagree

2 A long-term relationship with just one supplier is better than having many suppliers.
  ○ Agree   ○ Disagree

3 The most interesting use of technology in business operations that I have heard of (or know) is …

4 Companies are becoming like 'virtual operations' – they seem to be there, but in fact only a few key people on permanent contracts keep everything running. More and more jobs are done by outside people on a short-term basis for individual projects.
  ○ Agree   ○ Disagree

6 Production

A business that makes nothing but money is a poor business.
Henry Ford (1863–1947), founder of The Ford Motor Company

Managing the production process

Manufacturing takes place in a plant (= factory / facility). The process can be 'capital-intensive' (= requiring a lot of finance) or 'labour-intensive' (= requiring manpower). If the operation is efficient at transforming inputs (= materials, labour and information) into finished goods, then there is a high level of productivity.

Key stages in the manufacturing process are:

- Planning. This involves trying to bring together customer demand with operational issues of volume, timing, and the purchase of materials. A 'bill of materials' is produced, this is compared with the existing inventory, and any necessary purchases are made.
- Sequencing. A supervisor decides which workstation (= machine and / or employee) will carry out which tasks in which order.
- Scheduling. The supervisor decides when particular tasks should start and finish.
- Dispatching. The supervisor authorizes tasks to begin (giving detailed instructions).
- Loading. Materials or parts are introduced to an operation so that it can begin. (A robot loads an assembly line with a new component, an operator loads a machine with raw materials.)
- Monitoring. This involves checking progress, eliminating bottlenecks, and identifying and solving problems.

Key issues are:

- Control of capacity – there might be a need to ramp up (= increase) production.
- Control of inventory.

Lean operations and JIT

Outside of a business context, 'lean' means 'thin in a healthy way' / 'no fat'. In a business context, it refers to an approach which tries to meet demand instantaneously with perfect quality and no waste. The most important idea of lean operations is that of minimizing inventory kept on the premises – both stock and work-in-progress (WIP). So parts, components, raw materials and other supplies are delivered to the factory just as they are needed. And once delivered, the throughput (= rate at which work goes through the system) is fast.

Note that with lean operations the capacity utilization (= ratio of actual output to potential output) is often low. This is a difference with traditional approaches. Note also that the need to carry inventory doesn't disappear – it just shifts to suppliers.

The techniques used for lean operations are often called 'just-in-time' (JIT) techniques. These include:

- Making every effort to eliminate waste.
- Developing working practices which support 'continuous improvement' (often called by its Japanese name 'kaizen').
- Involving all staff in quality initiatives.
- Improving the flow of work-in-progress around the plant by rearranging layout and using machines that are small, simple, robust and flexible.
- Reducing set-up and change-over times.
- Incorporating manufacturing considerations into the design process (reducing production costs by reducing design complexity).

Why use JIT techniques? Because materials, work-in-progress and finished goods that are not being used represent a waste of time, space and money.

Quality management

What is quality? Is it a manufacturing process free of errors and waste? Or is it having the best specifications, regardless of price? Is it perhaps a product that is 'fit for purpose', having only features that the user actually needs? Is value-for-money an important factor?

Most people would agree that quality includes: functionality, appearance, reliability, durability, ease of recovery from problems, and contact with company staff. But is there anything else, and how is quality to be measured?

Many years ago, 'quality control' meant taking samples of a product and doing tests to see if it met technical standards. Then 'quality assurance' widened its scope to include some non-operational functions such as customer service. Nowadays, 'total quality management' (TQM) covers the whole organization, from more traditional areas like process control and product testing to determining customer needs and dealing with complaints. It includes all the ideas of lean operations and JIT. And a whole industry has developed to provide international standards for measuring quality; amongst the best known are the ISO 9000 family and 'Six Sigma'. (This term is a statistical measure meaning fewer than 3.4 defects per million items produced.)

Modern approaches to manufacturing

Lean manufacturing and JIT

'Kanban' - using a 'pull' system where production responds quickly to real, observed demand. This contrasts with a 'push' system where production is based on forecasts of demand (which may not be accurate)

Flexible manufacturing: designing machines to do multiple tasks; reprogramming machine tools while they are running

Mass customization: tailoring products to meet the needs of a large number of individual customers

Types of production process

Continuous process: work in progress without stopping

Mass process: high volume, low variety

Batch process: groups of products of the same type move through the process

Job production: low volume, opportunities for customization

Project (as in 'project management'): highly customized products, long timescale

PRODUCTION

Control of capacity

Forecasting demand fluctuations: seasonality, etc

Maximizing capacity utilization (= making the best use of the capacity you have)

Monitoring equipment: set-up and change-over time / causes of breakdowns / speed losses / quality losses

Adjusting capacity:
Overtime / using part-time staff; subcontracting parts of the operation; changing demand through price; developing products with a different seasonal demand

Quality

Quality can be seen from a manufacturing or a customer point of view

Perfect quality comes at a price: is it justified?

Quality standards: internal technical standards, ISO 9000 family, Six Sigma

Checks on quality: what to check for? which stages in the production process? frequency? every product or just a sample?

Use of benchmarking (= comparison with best practice in the industry) as a tool for improvement

Control of inventory

Perpetual inventory system: software knows what was sold (and when and where); when inventory falls to a predefined 're-order level' there is a trigger to order more stock

Advantages of storing materials

Buy the best when it is available

Respond quickly and flexibly to changes in demand

Insure against unexpected problems

Buy in bulk to reduce costs

Disadvantages of storing materials

Ties up working capital

Has to be stored, insured and handled

Can deteriorate or be damaged

6 Production: Exercises

6.1 Fill in the missing letters.

1 A specific problem that causes delays to a whole process, is called a 'bo_ _ _ _eck'.

2 The amount of work that can be dealt with in a particular time period is the 'thr_ _ _ _put'.

3 Actual output divided by potential output is 'cap_ _ _ _y u_ _ _ _ _ _ion' (eg room occupancy rates in a hotel).

4 A product that serves its intended function, without any extra features, is described as 'f_ _-for-pu_ _ _ _e'.

5 If a product has good quality in relationship to its price, then it is 'good v_ _ _ _-for-m_ _ _ _'.

6 The characteristic of 'always working well' is 'r_ _ _ability'.

7 The characteristic of 'lasting a long time' is 'd_ _ _ _ility'.

8 A fault in the way something is made is a 'd_ _ _ _t'.

6.2 Match the different stages in the production process with their descriptions 1–6 below.

planning ☐   scheduling ☐   loading ☐
sequencing ☐   dispatching ☐   monitoring ☐

1 introducing materials to an operation so it can begin

2 authorizing a task to begin

3 bringing together customer demand with operational issues of volume, timing, materials, etc

4 checking progress and solving problems

5 deciding when tasks should start and finish

6 deciding which workstation will carry out which task in which order

6.3 Read about the relationship between WIP (work-in-progress) and different types of production process. As you read, imagine an example for each one.

1 In a *continuous process* there is a network of complex, capital-intensive machinery through which WIP flows without interruption. One example would be …

2 In a *mass process*, there is an assembly line where WIP moves along the line past workstations carrying out fixed operations. One example would be …

3 In a *batch process*, machinery and equipment are located in 'cells' around the plant, and WIP moves in groups to different cells; in each cell a variety of specialized operations can be carried out. One example would be …

4 In *job production*, there is a fixed position layout where the WIP does not move; instead operations are scheduled in sequence on it. One example would be …

5 In a *large-scale project*, the WIP is often off-site, or at the customer's own premises. One example would be …

Now complete each paragraph with the most appropriate example: *construction of a building, an automobile plant, aircraft manufacture, clothing manufacture, steel making.*

6.4 The word 'time' appears in a lot of expressions used in production and operations. Write each word next to its definition: *changeover time, cycle time, downtime, lead time.*

1 when equipment (or the whole line) stops working and production is lost _____

2 time between one job / batch finishing and the next one beginning (includes time taken to prepare machinery for the new process) _____

3 time required from receiving a customer order to final delivery; it includes order processing, pre-pack time, in-transit time, receiving and inspection _____

4 time taken for a given job / batch to pass through all the operations needed _____

Continue as before with these words: *lag time, overtime, set-up time, time-to-market.*

5 extra hours that someone works, beyond their contractual obligation (and often paid at a higher rate)

_____

6 time taken to prepare machinery and equipment for a new job / batch _____

7 time required from the initial concept for a new product to when it first goes on sale _____

8 any period of delay between one event and another (eg between giving an instruction and the operation beginning) _____

6.5 Complete this text about 'kaizen' using the words in the box.

| competitors | culture | cycle | improvement |
| marketplace | metrics | process | resistance |

Kaizen is a term used in lean manufacturing to mean continuous [1]_____. It describes a corporate [2]_____ where everyone works proactively (= taking action before a problem develops) to improve the manufacturing [3]_____ . This is essential in today's changing [4]_____ – someone is going to come up with a better, faster or cheaper way, and it will either be you or your [5]_____ .

How can you know if continuous improvement is happening? You establish a system of monitoring key [6]_____ (= variables that can be measured). For example, average [7]_____ times, or the time it takes to successfully complete a changeover. And employees must be involved, otherwise there will be a lot of [8]_____ .

6.6 Study the collocations below. Check any unknown words in a dictionary.

first-rate, high, low, inferior, outstanding, top, uneven, poor, variable	quality
assess, demand, evaluate, keep up, insist on, maintain, measure, preserve, test	quality
begin, boost, cut back (on), go into, increase, ramp up, reduce, scale down, speed up, start up	production
be in charge of, keep track of, monitor, rationalize, simplify, streamline, supervise	the process
excess, full, limited, maximum, reduced, peak, spare, total	capacity
carry, dispose of, get rid of, have, hold, keep, reduce, reorder, replace	inventory (= stock)

Now divide the words in each box into three groups, based on their meaning.

first-rate, high, top, outstanding	low, poor, inferior	uneven, variable	quality
			quality
			production
			the process
			capacity
			inventory

6.7 Read the text about quality standards.

The International Organization for Standardization is a worldwide federation of national standards bodies. They promote the 'ISO 9000' series of standards, and these cover a wide range of activities: determining customer needs, dealing with complaints, product testing, storage, etc.

Companies are audited to make sure that they deserve the ISO award, and this provides both a discipline for manufacturers and an assurance for customers. Another set of standards, the ISO 14000 series, covers environmental standards.

The ISO approach has been adopted worldwide, but it has its critics. People say that it encourages a recipe-based approach, sometimes called 'management by manual', rather than a more customized approach. Also, the whole process of keeping records and carrying out internal audits is expensive and time-consuming.

An alternative approach that is becoming very popular among large companies is 'Six Sigma'. This is a term from mathematics, but in a manufacturing context it means having a target of only 3.4 defects per million items. Like ISO, it now has a whole series of tools and techniques and is very expensive to implement. It recommends that organizations have a specially trained taskforce of internal consultants, dedicated full-time to improving processes. These people are ranked as Black Belt, Green Belt, etc.

A third approach to measuring performance against a standard is 'benchmarking'. This is not like ISO and Six Sigma because the standard is not pre-defined; instead the standard is simply the best practice of your competitors (or your own past results). The organization then tries to match (or even exceed) this best practice.

Cover the text. Make phrases by matching the columns.

1	cover a wide	worldwide
2	determine customer	range of activities
3	deal	to implement
4	be adopted	needs
5	keep	practice of your competitors
6	carry out internal	against a standard
7	be expensive	with complaints
8	be dedicated	records
9	measure performance	to improving processes
10	match the best	audits

Discussion topics

1 You are a teenager and you offer to wash your parents' car. This activity is similar to the manufacturing process described on page 26 (planning / sequencing / scheduling / dispatching / loading / monitoring) because … However it is different because …

2 The most high-quality, low-cost, customer-focused and environmentally-friendly production process I know is …

3 You run a small convenience store in a residential area. Discuss problems and solutions in relation to control of capacity and control of inventory. (See mind map.)

4 Lean operations, JIT, quality management, etc are now so widespread that very few products have faults.
   ○ Agree   ○ Disagree

> Business has only two functions – marketing and innovation.
> Peter Drucker (1909–2005), Austrian author of management-related literature

Marketing strategy

A marketing strategy includes the following:

- Analysis of the wider business environment. More specifically: the political / legal, economic, social / cultural, and technological factors operating in the external world. (The acronym 'PEST' is sometimes used here.)
- Identification and analysis of target markets for new products.
- Sales goals in terms of volume and revenue.
- The marketing budget.
- Elements of the marketing mix, and their timing.

The term 'marketing mix' is another name for the well-known four 'P's: product, price, place (ie distribution channel) and promotion. In this book, product and price are covered in the mind map opposite, and distribution and promotion in the next unit. Some writers would add a fifth 'P': packaging. The importance of packaging is often underestimated: it attracts the buyer's attention, it explains the benefits of the product inside, it describes the contents, and of course it also protects the product during handling and contributes to convenience and ease-of-use. And these days environmentally-friendly packaging can give a product a competitive advantage. There is even a sixth 'P': people. This refers to the knowledge, skills and personality of the pre-sales and after-sales staff who come into contact with the customer.

Marketers often use the term 'total product offer' to reinforce the diversity of elements that make up a 'product'. These include value-for-money (= relationship between quality and price), brand name and image, packaging, convenience of sales channel, store surroundings, service, speed of delivery, the guarantee, etc.

Market research

How do marketers identify the need for new products? How do they decide how to improve existing products? One very important way is by collecting data using market research. Other ways are listed under 'origin of new product ideas' in the mind map opposite.

The easiest data to collect is information that is already available (= secondary data). This may be internal company data such as the company's sales figures broken down according to different categories (customers, product lines, territories, etc). Alternatively, it may be external data found in published sources such as reports from government agencies, trade associations and professional research firms.

Another important source of secondary data is simply to look at consumer buying patterns in more developed markets where the product is already available.

Data collected for the first time (= primary data) is more difficult and expensive to obtain, but will give answers to the exact questions that marketers are interested in. It includes both quantitative information (eg carrying out a survey on a representative sample of people using a questionnaire) and qualitative information (through focus groups, face-to-face interviews, etc). Another important source of primary data is looking at the activity of competitors (= benchmarking), and this may include looking at their product range or their marketing strategy. A new area of research is ethnography: studying people's behaviour in natural environments.

Of all the techniques above, focus groups in particular can give very valuable information. A small group of consumers sit in a room and discuss a variety of pre-defined topics. They might be asked how they feel about a particular brand, which of various possible new advertising campaigns they prefer, what ideas they have for improving an existing product, etc. The interview is usually recorded for later analysis.

Market segmentation

Who is the target market for a product? An immediate distinction is whether it is an industrial product (B2B: business-to-business), or a consumer product (B2C: business-to-consumer) aimed at end-users. A third category might be products for use in hospitals, schools, public transport, etc (B2G: business-to-government). Various categories of industrial products are shown in the mind map.

In relation to consumer products, the 'mass market' is becoming an old-fashioned concept. Products are increasingly targeted at specific market segments. There are four basic methods for segmenting a market:

- Product-related: comfort, safety, luxury, good value-for-money, convenience, durability, etc.
- Demographic: age, gender, education, family life cycle, income, occupation, etc.
- Psychographic: attitudes, lifestyle, opinions, values, self-image, etc.
- Geographical: region, post code, etc.

Look back at 'product-related' segmentation above and notice from the examples how marketers are interested in benefits (from the customer's point of view) rather than features (from a purely product design point of view).

PRODUCT AND PRICE

Determining prices

Cost-based pricing: add a specific percentage (= markup) to the base cost to give the selling price

Breakeven analysis: determining the minimum sales volume that covers all the costs

Origin of new product ideas

Market research

Pre-sales and after-sales staff listening to customers

Customers making direct suggestions

Competitor activity (including attempts to 'reverse engineer' products – finding out how they were made and then copying the process)

The R&D department

External changes in the market

Key concepts

Product line: group of related products that are physically similar or intended for the same market

Product mix (product range): assortment of product lines and individual offerings

Product life cycle: introduction; growth; maturity; decline

Branding

Brand: a name, symbol or design (or some combination) that identifies a product

Trademark: a name or symbol that cannot be used by another producer

Brand loyalty passes through three stages:

1. Brand awareness (= brand recognition)
2. Brand preference
3. Brand insistence

Pricing strategies

Profitability: the normal business aim of achieving a return on investment by maximizing revenue and minimizing costs

Market share: increasing your percentage of the market by selling at a low price, even if it means that profits are also low

Matching the market leaders: setting price according to what is standard in the market, and then competing by emphasizing other benefits such as design, service, convenience

Prestige pricing: setting a high price to maintain an image of quality and exclusivity

Identifying the correct price point: in a price-sensitive market, increasing the price beyond a certain point will damage sales

Social objectives: governments can subsidize prices so that low-income groups can afford a basic product (typical examples are utilities and farm products)

Industrial (B2B) products

Installations: major capital items, heavy equipment, etc

Accessory equipment: hand tools, photocopiers, etc

Component parts: eg batteries purchased by an automaker

Raw materials: farm and natural products, eg wheat, steel, leather

Supplies: expense items that do not become part of the final product, eg copy paper

7 Marketing strategy and product development: Exercises

7.1 Fill in the missing letters.

1 Data collected by market research can be 'qu_ _ _itative' (= factual and numerical), or 'qu_ _itative' (= opinions and attitudes that are difficult to measure).

2 Another word for the final consumer of a product is the 'e_ _-u_ _r'.

3 The relationship between quality and price is referred to as 'v_ _ _ _-for-m_ _ _ _'. This phrase often has the word *good* in front, to mean 'cheap' ('cheap' can have a negative connotation).

4 Marketers tend to emphasize 'be_ _ _its' (= advantages for the customer) rather than 'fea_ _ _es' (from a product design point of view).

5 A name or symbol that has legal protection is called a 'registered tr_ _ _ _ _ _k'.

6 Two key concepts in pricing are 'm_ _ _-up' (= the % added to the cost to give the selling price) and 'br_ _ _even volume' (= the sales volume at which the product starts to make a profit).

7.2 Complete the text with the words in the box.

brand awareness	brand names	brand loyalty
market leader	market share	product lines
product mix	profitability	

Proctor & Gamble is a very well-known company in the household and personal goods sector. It has 22 different [1]_____ including baby care, cosmetics, household cleaners, laundry, oral care, etc. The combination of all these makes up P&G's [2]_____ (= product range). P&G has many well-known [3]_____ such as Ariel, Pampers, Pantene, but notice that the brand is not the same as the company name (although in other companies it is). P&G spends a very large marketing budget maintaining the [4]_____ of its customers – it wants them to be satisfied and committed to further purchases. But even larger sums are needed when it launches a new product – [5]_____ (= brand recognition) has to be built up from zero.

What about P&G's pricing policy? Well, they are a [6]_____ so they don't have to set artificially low prices to gain sales volume and [7]_____. Instead, they can focus on [8]_____ – maximizing revenue and minimizing costs.

7.3 Complete the text with the words in the box.

advertising budgets	consumer tastes	differentiate products
early adopters	making a loss	reaches saturation
similar offerings	withdrawn from the market	

The classic product life cycle is Introduction, Growth, Maturity and Decline. In the Introduction stage the product is promoted to create awareness. It has low sales and will still be [1]_____ . If the product has few competitors, a skimming price strategy can be used (a high price for [2]_____ which is then gradually lowered). In the Growth phase sales are rising rapidly and profits are high. However, competitors are attracted to the market with [3]_____ . The market is characterized by alliances, joint ventures and takeovers. [4]_____ are large and focus on building the brand.

In the Maturity phase sales growth slows and then stabilizes. Producers attempt to [5]_____ and brands are key to this. Price wars and competition occur as the market [6]_____ . In the Decline phase there is a downturn in the market. The product is starting to look old-fashioned or [7]_____ have changed. There is intense price-cutting and many products are [8]_____ .

7.4 Make phrases and then complete the text below.

1 carrying out   sample of people
2 gaps in the   a survey
3 consumer   of competitors
4 published   needs
5 a representative   market
6 statistically   sources
7 the activity   reliable

Market research is the process by which a company collects information about [1]___*consumer needs*___ and preferences. The information helps to identify market trends and spot [2]_____ . The easiest data to collect is that from existing [3]_____ such as government reports. Other valuable information can be obtained by studying consumer behaviour in more developed markets, or looking at [4]_____ (benchmarking).

Primary data, collected for the first time, is more difficult to obtain. First, [5]_____ has to be carefully chosen – it has to be large enough to be [6]_____ , and also checked for factors such as age, sex, occupation. Common research methods include [7]_____ using a questionnaire, or face-to-face interviews with existing customers.

7.5 Match the words in the box to their definitions below. Be careful – they are very similar.

benefit   characteristic   feature   requirement   specification   USP (unique selling point)

1 something a customer asks for, or needs
   _____

2 something that makes a product special or different from others _____

3 (usually plural) exact technical details, or a detailed instruction about how something should be made
   _____

4 advantage that a customer gets if they buy the product
   _____

5 important, special or interesting part of a product
   _____

6 typical quality that makes a product recognizable
   _____

Now do the same for these words.

budget   estimate   quotation

7 an approximate price that someone will charge you
   _____

8 a fixed price that someone will charge you, often showing different items in detail _____

9 a plan of how to spend money, or the money itself
   _____

7.6 Marketers use a PEST analysis to look at the business environment. Typical items are listed a)–l). Put them into the correct category below.

a) age structure of population
b) changes in the fixed and variable costs of business
c) new production methods
d) national government policy
e) changing tastes and fashions
f) level of consumer spending
g) developments in IT that open new markets
h) the economy, inflation, unemployment
i) EU / WTO regulations
j) lifestyle changes (eg more people living alone)
k) pressure from environmental or fair trade lobbies
l) breakthrough products arising from R&D

1 Political / legal factors: ☐ ☐ ☐
2 Economic factors: ☐ ☐ ☐
3 Social / cultural factors: ☐ ☐ ☐
4 Technological factors: ☐ ☐ ☐

7.7 Study the collocations below. Check any unknown words in a dictionary.

sales	campaign, drive, figures, force, personnel, promotion, staff, team, volume	
disappointing, export, foreign, global, international, overseas, poor, weak, worldwide		sales
bring out, discontinue, improve, introduce, launch, modify, take … off the market, upgrade, withdraw		a product
attractive, exorbitant, fair, high, inflated, reasonable, retail, selling		price
agree on / to, arrive at, bring down, cut, establish, increase, lower, push up, put up, raise, reduce, set, work out		a price
booming, depressed, expanding, flat, growing, healthy, niche, sluggish, specialist, strong, weak		market
be forced out of, break into, corner, dominate, enter, monopolize, take over, withdraw from		the market

Now divide the words in each box into three groups, based on their meaning.

sales	campaign, drive, promotion	figures, volume	force, personnel, staff, team
			sales
			a product
			price
			a price
			market
			the market

Discussion topics

1 I buy many products that I don't need. This shows that I am being manipulated by large, evil corporations.
   ○ Agree   ○ Disagree

2 In relation to consumer products, the 'mass market' is becoming an old-fashioned concept.
   ○ Agree   ○ Disagree

3 Think of **one** well-known product you would buy just for the brand name, **one** you would buy just for the price, and **one** you would buy just for the packaging. Then, for each one, discuss the company's marketing strategy.

4 Brainstorm a PEST analysis for these markets: consumer electronics, automobiles, wind turbines.

8 Distribution and promotion

Half the money I spend on advertising is wasted; the trouble is I don't know which half.
John Wanamaker (1838–1922), American businessman

Distribution

Distribution is the final link in a company's supply chain, and involves getting the right products to the customer at the right time. It includes the physical handling of goods, warehousing, choice of distribution channel (eg wholesaler, retailer, direct to consumer), choice of retail outlet, and order fulfilment (= doing something that is promised).

The mind map opposite lists the main options for retailing. The main trend has been to move away from small family-owned stores (AmE mom and pop stores) to large shopping centres (AmE malls). A variation, common in the US, is a large out-of-town mall where giant 'big box' stores surround a central car park (AmE parking lot). Future trends may include offering more entertainment to attract customers, and developing private label (in-house) brands as cheaper competition to name-brand goods.

The promotional mix

The term 'promotion' is very broad. Look at the mind map to see different elements of the promotional mix. The first item in the bubble, sales promotions, is covered in more detail on another branch of the map. The other items are covered in more detail below:

- Personal selling (= sales): this is the direct face-to-face communication between salesperson and customer. The sales process has various stages:

  1 Prospecting: identifying a potential customer (= a prospect) who has the ability and authority to buy.
  2 Approach: contacting the prospect and preparing for the sales interview.
  3 Presentation: describing the features of the product, highlighting the advantages over competing products, and giving examples of satisfied customers.
  4 Demonstration: if possible, the customer is given a chance to see the product in use.
  5 Answering objections: customers should be given a chance to express their doubts, as they are unlikely to buy unless these are dealt with. At this stage the salesperson stresses benefits rather than features.
  6 Closing: the salesperson asks the prospect to buy. If the customer still has doubts then options include offering an alternative product, offering a special incentive, or restating the product benefits.
  7 Follow-up: processing the order quickly and efficiently, and reassuring the customer about their purchase decision during further conversation.
  8 Long-term relationship: going on to establish regular contact with the customer.

- Advertising: the use of different media such as television commercials, advertisements in newspapers and magazines, direct mail, outdoor (billboards, posters on bus-stops), flyers given to people on the street, Internet.
- Public relations: managing 'publicity' (information that makes people notice a company). The PR function in a company needs to establish good relations with the news media in order to control this information, and PR people issue press releases and hold press conferences.
- Events: memorable occasions (in-store, on the street, in an unusual location).
- Sponsorship of sports teams, music groups, theatre / opera / ballet etc.
- Endorsements by celebrities (eg 'the face of L'Oréal', rap artists wearing a clothing brand).
- Trade promotions to retailers, eg financial incentives to stock a new product or to give more space / visibility to existing products (eg shelf height and aisle position).
- Other: product placement in films, word-of-mouth (= personal recommendations), viral marketing (online through social networking websites and friends emailing video clips). The term 'guerrilla marketing' covers all unconventional techniques – from viral marketing to the distribution of free products on the beach.

Building customer relationships

Today, a major part of promotion is developing long-term relationships with customers so that they make repeat purchases and are open to cross-selling of related products. Tools for developing customer relationships include:

- Building a brand identity that the customer will relate to (eg through sponsorship and endorsements).
- Frequency programmes (eg frequent-flyer programmes on airlines).
- Forming communities of buyers (eg consumer chat rooms on the Internet, or meetings of owners of Harley Davidson motorbikes).
- Affinity marketing (= attracting customers on the basis of their other interests, for example linking a credit card to a favourite charity).
- Individualized advertising based on previous purchases (eg Amazon's book suggestions).
- Co-marketing with another company (eg giving away a toy at McDonalds that links to a new Disney film).
- Using CRM software to give the customer a more personal experience when they contact the company.

 Further information www.consumerpsychologist.com ● www.davedolak.com/promix.htm ● www.marketingteacher.com

Internal

To generate enthusiasm amongst salespeople and other customer-contact staff

B2B products

Trade shows (= trade fairs / exhibitions)

Portfolios of products for salespeople

Deals (eg price reductions)

Catalogues / brochures

Distribution channels

Direct distribution: from the producer or service provider straight to the consumer or business user

Use of an intermediary (= middleman): one or more of agent / broker, distributor, wholesaler, retailer

Physical distribution

Warehousing, inventory control and materials handling

Customer service (= order fulfilment, warranty and repair issues)

Logistics: the work of planning and organizing the movement of materials, goods and people

Transportation (the term 'shipping' is a synonym and does not only refer to ships)

Sales promotions

Consumer products

Special offer: 10% off for a limited time

Bonus: buy one, get one free

Coupons to cut out of a magazine

Free samples

In-store displays

Catalogues / brochures

Games and contests

Promotional items with an imprinted logo

Special events

DISTRIBUTION AND PROMOTION

Non-store retailing

Direct-response retailing: home delivery of goods ordered through catalogues, etc

Internet retailing: online selling through virtual storefronts

Automatic merchandising: sales through vending machines

Direct selling: salespeople go door-to-door

Promotional mix

Sales promotions

Personal selling

Advertising

Public relations (PR)

Events

Sponsorship

Endorsements

Trade promotions to retailers

Other: product placement, word-of-mouth, viral marketing, etc

Retailing

Store retailing

Specialty store (eg bookstore, flower shop)

Convenience store (basic goods, store open until late, higher prices)

Discount store (very low prices, eg Aldi, Walmart)

Supermarket / Hypermarket

Department store (eg Harrods) – aimed at more upmarket (AmE upscale) customers

8.1 Fill in the missing letters.

1 Making sure that the customer gets the right goods at the right time is called 'order fu_ _ _ _ment'.

2 A place where goods are sold to consumers is called a 'retail ou_ _ _t'.

3 A potential customer is a 'pro_ _ect'.

4 A large outdoor sign used for advertising is called a 'bi_ _ _oard'.

5 It is important to develop long-term relationships with customers so that they make 'rep_ _t pur_ _ _ses', and are open to 'c_ _ss-selling' of other related products.

6 A synonym for 'intermediary' is 'the mi_ _ _ _man'.

7 A retailer has a shop (AmE store), while a wholesaler has a 'w_ _ _ _ouse'.

8 The process of selling products connected with a popular film, person or event is called 'mer_ _ _ _ _ising'. In American English this word is also used for 'selling goods' in general.

8.2 Complete each explanation with a pair of words from the box. The words may not be in the right order.

agent / broker   brochure / catalogue
client / customer   commercial / spot
promotion / advertising   sponsorship / endorsement

1 To refer to a buyer, the word _____ is more common where there is a standard product, and in shops and restaurants. The word _____ is more common in the service sector and where there is a degree of personalization.

2 A list of everything that a company sells is called a _____ . If it has lots of colour pictures and looks like a small magazine it is more likely to be called a _____ . The former may have prices as well, the latter would not.

3 A general word that means 'the process of attracting people's attention to a product' is _____ . One specific example of this is _____ , which refers to text and images and sound in media such as television, newspapers, billboards and the Internet.

4 An advertisement on television, radio or film is called a _____ . An informal word with the same meaning is _____ .

5 _____ is when a celebrity uses a certain product as a way of promoting it. _____ is the activity of giving financial support to a sports or cultural event.

6 Both words mean 'a person who does business on behalf of another company'. The word _____ is used where there is a long-term relationship, whereas the word _____ is more common for individual transactions (eg stocks).

8.3 Make collocations by matching a word from each column.

1 brand	channel
2 convenience	mail
3 direct	relations
4 distribution	release
5 in-store	placement
6 press	identity
7 product	display
8 public	store

8.4 Match each stage in the sales process with its explanation 1–7 below.

Answering objections   Approach   Closing
Demonstration   Follow-up   Presentation   Prospecting

1 _____ – identifying a potential customer

2 _____ – contacting the prospect and preparing for the sales interview

3 _____ – describing the features of the product

4 _____ – giving the customer a chance to see the product in use

5 _____ – asking the prospect to buy

6 _____ – dealing with any doubts that the customer has

7 _____ – processing the order quickly and maintaining long-term contact

8.5 The sequence 1–7 in exercise 8.4 is probably not the best. Change the order of two items so that the prospect is more likely to buy.

8.6 Match these advertising media to the advantages (+) and disadvantages (-) below: direct mail, Internet, magazines, newspapers, outdoor, radio, television.

1 _____
(+) good coverage of local markets; ads can be placed quickly; ads can be cut out and saved
(-) ads compete with other text; ads get thrown away (short life span)

2 _____
(+) can target very specific audiences in specialist publications; long life of ad (usually several weeks); ads can be cut out and saved
(-) ads must often be placed months in advance; cost is relatively high

3 _____

(+) uses sight, sound and motion; reaches a wide audience; high attention with no competition from other material

(-) very high cost

4 _____

(+) low cost; can target specific audiences; very flexible; good for local marketing

(-) may have low attention because it is a background medium; audience may not remember ad (only one physical sense involved and nothing to keep)

5 _____

(+) high visibility and repeat exposure; relatively low cost; strong local focus

(-) limited message; difficult to get attention of audience for any one specific ad

6 _____

(+) if linked to a customer database can be targeted at very specific markets; very flexible; ad can be saved

(-) high cost; consumers may reject ad as 'junk'

7 _____

(+) connects a company with its customers at the precise moment they are looking for a product; global coverage at a relatively inexpensive price; interactive

(-) many 'eyeballs' but few 'click-throughs'; click fraud (clicks on your advert arranged by dishonest companies or competitors, not made by potential customers)

8.7 Find a word from the previous exercise which means:

1 how widely information is distributed _____

2 put somewhere, especially in a careful or deliberate way _____

3 try to influence a particular group of people _____

4 something that is not wanted or not healthy (collocates with 'mail' and 'food') _____

5 Internet term referring to those occasions when someone looks at something _____

8.8 Complete the text with the phrases in the box.

~~inbound logistics~~	outbound logistics	materials handling
retail outlets	warehouses	customer returns	end user
ex-works	fob (free on board)	cif (cost, insurance, freight)

The process of planning and controlling the physical flow of materials in the supply chain is called logistics. There are four stages. First, [1] _____inbound logistics_____ is concerned with bringing raw materials, packaging, etc from suppliers to producers. Second, [2] _____ is the movement of goods within a warehouse, from the warehouse to the factory floor, and from the factory floor to the various workstations. Third, [3] _____ manages the flow of finished products through intermediaries to the final consumer. Finally, reverse logistics involves bringing goods back to the premises of the original manufacturer because of defects or other [4] _____.

The whole process is a shared responsibility between marketing and operations, but clearly marketing is more concerned with those areas that impact directly on wholesalers, retailers and the [5] _____.

A key issue in logistics is choosing the right means of transport. Options include rail, road (using trucks with trailers), ships and air. Combinations of these are common.

Another key area of logistics is the storage function. Marketers must have goods available in [6] _____ all over the country, ready to restock [7] _____ or be delivered to customers when ordered.

If import and export are involved, then there is an important issue: who pays for which parts of the transportation? Contracts have to specify this clearly, and use Incoterms (international commercial terms) to do so. There are many Incoterms, but the most common are:

- [8] _____ – the buyer picks up the goods at the seller's premises and arranges all the transport and insurance.
- [9] _____ – the seller delivers the goods onto a ship at a named port; from here all responsibility (including the sea journey) passes to the buyer.
- [10] _____ – the seller has responsibility to a named port of destination, and so pays for the cost and risk of the sea journey as well.

Discussion topics

1 'Sales' sometimes has a bad reputation (selling used cars). But this is wrong. In fact it is creative, challenging and fun.
○ Agree   ○ Disagree

2 Advertising is not so important. A good product with the right price and the right distribution will sell itself.
○ Agree   ○ Disagree

3 Everyone knows that celebrities in their private lives don't actually use the products they advertise. You must be a fool if you are persuaded by endorsements.
○ Agree   ○ Disagree

4 Contemporary trends in advertising, communication and promotion include …

9 Accounting and financial statements

Remind people that profit is the difference between revenue and expense. This makes you look smart.
Scott Adams (1957–), creator of the Dilbert comic strip

Preparation of the accounts

The accounting process starts with inputs, and these are things such as sales documents (eg invoices), purchasing documents (eg receipts), payroll records, bank records, travel and entertainment records. The data in these inputs is then processed by specialized software:

1 Entries are recorded chronologically into 'journals'.
2 Information from the journals is posted (= transferred) into 'ledgers', where it accumulates in specific categories (eg cash account, sales account, or account for one particular customer)
3 A 'trial balance' is prepared at the end of each accounting period: this is a summary of the ledger information to check whether the figures are accurate. It is used directly to prepare the main financial statements (income statement, balance sheet and cash flow statement).

The financial statements of large companies have to be checked by an external firm of auditors, who 'sign off on the accounts' (= officially declare the accounts are correct). They are publicly available, and appear in the company's annual report. Users of financial statements include: shareholders, potential shareholders, creditors (lenders, eg banks), customers, suppliers, journalists, financial analysts, government agencies, etc.

Profit and Loss Account

The profit and loss account (= income statement, or just 'the P&L') summarizes business activity over a period of time. It begins with total sales (= revenue) generated during a month, quarter or year. Subsequent lines then deduct (= subtract) all of the costs related to producing that revenue.

At this point look at the example on page 40, and then return to this text.

Balance Sheet

The balance sheet reports the company's financial condition on a specific date. The basic equation that has to balance is: Assets = Liabilities + Shareholders' equity.

- An 'asset' is anything of value owned by a business.
- A 'liability' is any amount owed to a creditor.
- Shareholders' equity (= owners' equity) is what remains from the assets after all creditors have theoretically been paid. It is made up of two elements: share capital (representing the original investment in the business when shares were first issued) plus any retained profit (= reserves) that has accumulated over time.

At this point look at the example on page 41, and then return to this text.

Note the order in which items are listed:

- Assets are listed according to how easily they can be turned into cash, with 'current assets' being more liquid than 'fixed assets'.
- Liabilities are listed according to how quickly creditors have to be paid, with 'current liabilities' (= bank debt, money owed to suppliers, unpaid salaries and bills) being paid before 'long-term liabilities'.

Figures for 'current assets' and 'current liabilities' are particularly important to a business. The amount by which the former exceeds the latter is called 'working capital'. This gives a quick measure of whether there is enough cash freely available to keep the business running.

Cash flow statement

Companies need a separate record of cash receipts and cash payments. Why is this? Firstly for the reason given above – it shows the real cash that is available to keep the business running day to day (profits are only on paper until the money actually comes in). Secondly, there are many sophisticated techniques that accountants can use to manipulate profit, whereas cash is real money. It's cash that pays the bills, not profits.

There are many reasons why companies can have a problem with cash flow, even if the business is doing well. Amongst them are:

- Unexpected late payments, and non-payments (bad debts).
- Unforeseen costs: a larger than expected tax bill, a strike, etc.
- An unexpected drop in demand.
- Investing too much in fixed assets.

Solutions might include:

- Credit control: chasing overdue accounts.
- Stock control: keeping low levels of stock, minimizing work-in-progress, delivering to customers more quickly.
- Expenditure control: delaying spending on capital equipment.
- A sales promotion to generate cash quickly.
- Using an outside company to recover a debt (called 'factoring').

Cost centres: discrete business units where budgets are spent

Profit centres: units where profits are generated

Variance analysis: comparing planned costs (or income) with actual costs (or income)

Costing methods (eg standard vs marginal costing)

Valuing assets

Ratio analysis (uses): to analyse performance in more depth, to compare companies in the same industry

Ratio analysis (types): liquidity ratios, profitability ratios, leverage (=debt) ratios, activity ratios

Finance and organizational structure

CFO (Chief Financial Officer) is on the Board. 3 senior managers below report to CFO

1. Financial Controller

Planning: preparing forecasts and budgets

Monitoring: comparing planned spending with actual spending

Producing financial data for the senior management team

Analysing major investment decisions

2. Treasurer

Managing cash flow
Raising new funds

3. Chief Accounting Officer

Keeping the company's books

Preparing financial statements

Preparing tax returns

Developing strategies to minimize taxes

Issues in financial management

INCOME

EXPENDITURE

$560,000

$750,000

ACCOUNTING AND FINANCE

Causes of cash-flow problems

Late payments and non-payments

Unforeseen costs

Unexpected changes in demand

Over-borrowing from the bank to finance expansion plans

Debt financing

Short term (trade credit, bank loan)
Long term: issuing bonds

Sources of new funds

Managing cash flow

Equity financing

Reinvested earnings
Sale of assets
Issue of new shares

Solutions

Credit control

Stock control

Expenditure control

Marketing initiatives

Using an outside company to recover a debt

Accounting and financial statements

Study the simplified financial statements for an imaginary retail store. All figures are in €000s. The convention in accounting is that a negative figure is shown by a bracket. To understand the figures, work from the right:

- the right-hand column shows totals for each major category
- the central column shows information that is used in producing the figures to the right
- the left-hand column shows details of the calculations in the central column.

Vocabulary in financial statements is surprisingly non-standard, with many companies using a mixture of US and European terms. See the right-hand column for alternatives, more detail, etc.

Profit and Loss Account (Income Statement) For the Year Ended December 31, 20XX

Revenues			
Gross sales		640	
Less: Sales returns	6		
Less: Sales discounts	4		
		(10)	
Net sales			630
Cost of goods sold			
Purchases		290	
Salaries of manual workers		30	
Transport costs		30	
Cost of goods sold			(350)
Gross profit			280
Operating expenses			
Selling expenses			
Salaries for sales staff	82		
Advertising	18		
Total selling expenses		100	
General expenses			
Salaries for administrative staff	52		
Insurance	6		
Rent	18		
Light, heat and power	10		
Office supplies	2		
Miscellaneous	2		
Total general expenses		90	
Total operating expenses			(190)
Operating profit			90
Non-operating income			5
EBITDA			95
Depreciation			(10)
EBIT			85
Interest paid on bank loans			(6)
Net income before taxes			79
Less: Income tax			(19)
Net income (or loss) after taxes			60
Dividends			(13)
Retained profit			€47

'Revenue' (= income / turnover / sales / the top line)

'Cost of goods sold' (= direct costs) includes manufacturing costs, salaries of manual (= blue-collar) workers etc.

'Operating expenses' (= indirect costs / overhead) include salaries of sales and office staff, marketing costs, utility bills etc.

'Non-operating income' includes profits from investments in other companies.

'EBITDA' stands for Earnings Before Interest, Tax, Depreciation and Amortization.

'Earnings' (= profit / the bottom line)

'Depreciation' and **'Amortization'** are very similar, and are often used in the same way. However, 'depreciation' can refer to the loss in value of a tangible asset (eg a vehicle), and 'amortization' to the loss in value of an intangible asset (eg the purchase of a licence or trademark). This loss over time is treated as a cost and written off (= subtracted from the profit) over several years.

'Interest' refers to money paid to the bank for loans (or received from the bank for cash balances).

'Dividends' is money paid to shareholders.

'Retained profit' is transferred to the Balance Sheet, where it joins the amounts from previous years.

Balance Sheet, December 31, 20XX

ASSETS		
Current assets		
Cash at bank	15	
Accounts receivable	200	
Inventory	<u>180</u>	
Total current assets		395
Fixed assets		
Building and improvements	300	
Less: accumulated depreciation	(90)	
	210	
Equipment and vehicles	120	
Less: accumulated depreciation	(80)	
	40	
Furniture and fixtures	20	
Less: accumulated depreciation	(8)	
	<u>12</u>	
Total fixed assets		262
Intangible assets		
Total intangible assets		<u>20</u>
Total assets		**677**

LIABILITIES AND EQUITY		
Current liabilities		
Bank debt	20	
Accounts payable	30	
Accrued taxes	22	
Accrued salaries	<u>45</u>	
Total current liabilities		117
Long-term liabilities		
Mortgage	100	
Bonds payable (due Mar 2018)	20	
Total long-term liabilities		<u>120</u>
Total liabilities		237
Shareholders' equity		
Share capital (300,000 shares @ €1)	300	
Retained profit	<u>140</u>	
Total owners' equity		<u>440</u>
Total liabilities & equity		**677**

'**Accounts receivable**' is the amount owed to the business by customers (= creditors).

'**Inventory**' is the value of raw materials & stock.

'**Current assets**' may also include 'marketable securities' (= shares intended for disposal within one year).

'**Fixtures**' are part of a building that cannot be moved, such as lights.

'**Fixed assets**' may also include long-term financial investments.

'**Intangible assets**' include patents, trademarks & 'goodwill' (reputation, contacts and expertise of companies that have been bought).

'**Bank debt**' (= loan capital) also includes any overdraft (= temporary negative balance).

'**Accounts payable**' is the money owed to suppliers.

'**Accrued**' items are those where an expense has been incurred, but the money is not yet paid. 'Accrued salaries' typically includes future bonuses.

Another item, '**provisions**', can appear under current liabilities. These are amounts set aside for anticipated one-time payments that are not part of regular operations – perhaps a lawsuit, or a compensation package for employees being laid off.

A '**mortgage**' is a long-term bank loan to buy a property.

With bonds, the '**principal**' (= amount raised by issuing the bonds) is repayable to the bond holders at 'maturity'.

'**Share capital**' (= common stock, AmE) is amount raised at initial flotation on the stock market.

'**Retained profit**' (= Reserves / Retained earnings). The figure showing here is more than the €47,000 transferred from the income statement because it is an amount accumulated over several years.

9 Accounting and financial statements: Exercises

9.1 Fill in the missing letters.

1 On a balance sheet, 'assets' are what you ow_ and 'liabilities' are what you ow_.

2 The loss in value of a tangible asset over time is called 'd_ _ _ _ _ _ _ _ _n'. This loss is 'w_ _ _ _en o_ _' in the accounts over several years. The loss in value of an intangible asset is called 'am_ _ _ _ _ _ _ _ _n'.

3 The term 'debtor' is now often replaced with 'accounts rec_ _ _ _le'. Similarly, 'creditor' is often replaced with 'accounts p_ _ _le'.

4 The total value of raw materials + work-in-progress + unsold stock is called 'in_ _ _ _ _ _y'.

5 Expenses that have been incurred but are not yet paid are called 'acc_ _ _d expenses'.

6 The extent to which a firm relies on debt financing rather than equity financing is called its 'lev_ _age'

9.2 Underline the correct words from those in italics.

The terms 'direct costs' and 'variable costs' are close synonyms. They both refer to things like raw materials costs and the wages of manual (= blue collar) workers. But:

● to emphasize costs which increase in proportion to any rise in output, say [1]*direct costs / variable costs*

● to emphasize costs which can be identified with one particular product, say [2]*direct costs / variable costs*.

Similarly, the terms 'fixed costs', 'indirect costs' and 'operating costs' are close synonyms. They all refer to things like advertising, rent and the salaries of office staff. But:

● to emphasize costs which stay the same at all levels of output in the short term, say [3]*fixed costs / operating costs*

● to emphasize costs which result from the whole business (rent, utilities, etc), not any particular products, say [4]*indirect costs / operating costs*. A synonym here is 'overhead' (BrE overheads).

● to emphasize costs resulting from the day-to-day activities of the business (products and processes), say [5]*fixed costs / operating costs*.

There are many other types of 'costs' referred to in finance and accounting. Two of the most important are:

● [6]*capital expenditure / capitalism expenditure* – the costs of buying or upgrading physical assets like buildings and machinery; often referred to in business as 'capex'

● [7]*mark-up costs / marginal costs* – the costs of increasing output by one more unit.

9.3 Put these words into three groups, so that all the words in a group have a similar meaning: *costs, earnings, expenditure, expenses, income, profit, revenue, sales, spending, turnover.*

9.4 Put the words into the correct column.

accounts payable	cost of goods sold	ledger
shareholders' equity	EBITDA	trial balance	invoices
operating expenses	current assets

Preparation of accounts	Profit and loss account	Balance sheet

9.5 Put the solutions for managing cash flow 1–6 into the correct category below.

1 just-in-time manufacturing
2 making payments to suppliers in instalments (= part payments)
3 leasing fixed assets rather than buying them
4 offering a discount for early settlement (= complete payment) of a bill
5 improving sales forecasting so that the warehouse holds less inventory
6 cancelling the office Christmas party

Credit control: ☐ ☐
Stock control: ☐ ☐
Expenditure control: ☐ ☐

9.6 Put the sources of new funds 1–6 into the correct category below.

1 Issuing new shares
2 Issuing new bonds (note that only large companies do this)
3 Trade credit (asking suppliers if you can pay them later)
4 Reinvested earnings
5 Sale of assets (eg a building, or a part of a company)
6 Bank loan or bank overdraft (= temporary negative balance)

Debt financing (money raised has to be paid back to outside creditors): ☐ ☐ ☐

Equity financing (money raised comes directly or indirectly from the owners of the business, who hope to have it paid back in the form of more profits): ☐ ☐ ☐

9.7 Match topics 1–5 with the conversation extracts a)–e) below.

1 cost centres ☐
2 profit centres ☐
3 variance analysis ☐
4 standard versus marginal costing ☐
5 valuing assets ☐

a) 'How are we going to show the depreciation of our new machinery in the accounts? We could write it off in a straight line over six years, but we're losing most of the value in the early years. I think we should do it on a percentage basis, say 25% every year, so that the book value is more realistic.'

b) 'We allocated a budget of €200,000 for R&D last quarter, but there seems to be an overspend of €25,000. I need to find out what's going on.'

c) 'I'd like to see earnings broken down according to our major product lines.'

d) 'All our marketing activities are shown under one budget heading. In the future I'd like to see separate figures for the different areas of marketing so that we can have more control of spending.'

e) 'Should we accept this order? The profit margins are low. But, on the other hand, the machines will be running anyway, there isn't much extra labour required, and other variable costs are low. So it's probably worth it.'

9.8 Study the collocations below. Check any unknown words in a dictionary.

budgeted, escalating, estimated, increasing, likely, rising, unexpected, unforeseen	costs
bring down, calculate, cut, figure out, lower, meet, pay, reduce, work out	costs
bring in, earn, generate, jeopardize, make, plough back, put at risk, reinvest	profits
accurate, approximate, ballpark, deceptive, dubious, exact, misleading, precise, rough, round	figure
announce, check, cook, doctor, examine, falsify, go over, go through, issue, manipulate, massage, publish, release, study	the figures

Now divide the words in each box into three groups, based on their meaning.

budgeted, estimated, likely	escalating, increasing, rising	unexpected, unforeseen	costs
			costs
			profits
			figure
			the figures

9.9 Match the definitions 1–4 with the examples of financial ratios a)–f) below.

1 Liquidity ratios: these measure ability to turn assets into cash to pay short-term debts. ☐

2 Profitability ratios: these measure ability to generate profits. ☐ ☐ ☐

3 Leverage (Debt) ratios: these measure the degree to which a company relies on borrowed funds. ☐

4 Activity ratios: these measure the effectiveness of the use of resources from an operational point of view. ☐

a) *Debt to owners' equity* = Total liabilities / Total owners' equity

b) *Net profit margin* = Net income before taxes / Net sales

c) *Working capital* = Current assets / Current liabilities

d) *Return on equity* = Net income after tax / Total owners' equity

e) *Inventory turnover* = Cost of goods sold / Average inventory (mid point between inventory at beginning and ending of accounting period)

f) *Earnings per share* = Net income after taxes / Number of shares issued

Discussion topics

1 To some people, finance is a dry and technical area of business. In fact, it's fascinating.
   ○ Agree   ○ Disagree

2 When an auditor looks at an income statement they will be particularly interested in … because …

3 When an auditor looks at a balance sheet they will be particularly interested in … because …

4 Here's what I know about a famous financial scandal that was in the news …

Our favourite holding period is forever.
Warren Edward Buffett (1930–), American stock investor, businessman and philanthropist

Securities

The term 'securities' refers to stocks, bonds and money market instruments. These are explained in turn below.

Individual investors and financial institutions can buy **stocks** (= equities) of companies listed on a stock exchange. The term 'shares' includes both stocks and privately held stakes in small firms that are not publicly traded. A 'basket' of stocks can be picked by a fund manager and put together into a mutual fund (UK: unit trust). Funds may invest in particular countries, or different sectors of the market, or may 'track' (= exactly follow) a particular index. Each fund will have an investment objective, normally either regular income (from share dividends), or long-term capital growth (from an increase in the share price), or a balance between the two.

Stocks are bought and sold on a stock exchange (= bourse). Sometimes this is a physical location, like the New York Stock Exchange on Wall Street. Other times there is no location: the NASDAQ is an electronic exchange. A small selected group of stocks can be brought together to make an index. For example, the Dow Jones publishing organization compiles 'the Dow' (an index of 30 large companies), and Standard and Poor's – a credit ratings agency – compiles dozens of different indices based on company size or market sector.

Why do stocks go up and down in price? When is a stock worth buying? Financial analysts do research on this, using three main tools:

- Analysis of individual companies: their market position and performance.
- Analysis of the national and global economy.
- Technical analysis: using charts and internal market statistics (eg volume and momentum) to identify future trends and turning points.

The **bond market** is about ten times bigger than the stock market. If a government or large company wants to borrow a large sum of money, it issues a bond and receives the money as a loan from the institution or individual who buys it (= the bondholder). The original amount (= the principal) is then paid back over a fixed period of time (= the maturity / the term of the loan). And of course the bondholder also receives interest (= the coupon). The bond market is entirely electronic and does not have any physical exchanges.

US government bonds include the 30-year T-bond (= treasury bond) and the 10-year T-note, while European government bonds include the German bund. These are all considered to be low-risk. Corporate bonds have two grades, depending on the risk, ie the credit rating of the company. Safer corporate bonds are called 'investment grade', while high-risk bonds (the company might go bankrupt or default on its repayments) are called 'high-yield bonds' or 'junk bonds'.

Bonds can be traded on the open market – they don't have to be held by the original buyer until maturity. In particular, their price goes up and down over the term of the loan according to:

- Inflation (the interest repaid on a bond is fixed over its term, so rising inflation will reduce the bond's final value).
- Currency movements (bonds are issued and then repaid in one particular currency – their value changes as that currency fluctuates).

A third type of market, used by investors with spare cash available for a short time period only (under a year), is called the **money market**. Investors can buy T-bills from the US government, 'certificates of deposit' from a bank, or 'commercial paper' from a company. These are all short-term loans that pay interest.

Other markets

The foreign exchange (= forex / currency) market is bigger than all the securities markets combined (around $2 trillion a day). Here, dealers buy and sell currency pairs such as EUR / USD (= euro against the dollar). Players include:

- Commercial banks (representing both themselves and client companies).
- Central banks (representing governments trying to maintain stability of their own currency).
- Pension funds, etc.

There is a huge amount of speculation in this market. If a currency fluctuates in value, there are all sorts of implications for: buying or selling foreign equities and bonds; international trade; inflation (because of payments for imported goods), etc. A lot of dealing is done to protect against (= hedge) such risks.

Finally, there are the commodity markets. Here, dealers trade the future price of such things as:

- Energy: crude oil, natural gas, etc.
- Metals: gold, silver, copper, steel, etc.
- Soft commodities: coffee, sugar, grains (eg corn, wheat, soybeans), livestock (eg cattle, hogs), etc.

U.S: Dow Jones Industrial Average ('the Dow'), S&P 500, Nasdaq

Europe: FTSE (UK), DAX (Germany), CAC (France), MIB (Italy), SMI (Switzerland)

Asia: Nikkei (Japan), Hang Seng (Hong Kong)

Stock index (group of selected stocks)

Owning stocks

Valuing stocks

STOCK MARKETS

Types of investor

Private investors

Financial institutions: investment banks, pension funds, mutual funds, insurance companies, endowments

Funds that hold various, carefully selected stocks

Types of funds:
country fund, or sector fund, or fund based on company size (e.g. a Japanese Smaller Companies fund),

equity or bond (e.g. a UK corporate bond fund),

specialist funds (e.g. biotechnology, natural resources, real estate, tracker, etc)

Investment objectives: current income, future capital growth

Strategies

Investing: buy and hold for the long term

Trading: buy and sell over the short term

Company analysis: performance

Growth, profitability, cash flow, level of debt, etc

Financial indicators: earnings growth, p/e ratio, market capitalization, etc

Company analysis: market position

Barriers to entry (how difficult it is for new players to enter the market)

Price elasticity (to what extent a rise in prices causes a fall in sales)

Ease of substitution (to what extent customers can find similar products from other suppliers)

Capital requirements

Market penetration

Technical analysis

Internal market factors such as volume, breadth, momentum

Chart Patterns: resistance and support, trading channels

Investor sentiment: levels of bullishness or bearishness in the market

The general economy

Growth and productivity of economy

Inflation and direction of interest rates

Consumer confidence: willingness of consumers to spend

10 Financial markets: Exercises

10.1 Write these words in the spaces below: *bonds, equities, money market instruments, securities, shares, stocks.* **Note that three words are near synonyms.**

The general term ^{1}_____ refers to
^{2}_____ (or _____ or
_____) + ^{3}_____ +
^{4}_____

10.2 Fill in the missing letters.

1 Instead of investing in the shares of just one company, you can invest in a m_ _ _ _l fund which holds a basket of stocks.

2 Regular income can be provided by the di_ _ _ _ _ds of shares that you own.

3 The issuer of a bond pays back the original amount (= the pr_ _ _ _ _al) to the bondholder over a fixed period of time (= the t_ _m of the loan).

4 The most traded bond in the world is the 30-year US government T-bond. The letter 'T' stands for 'tr_ _ _ _ _y'.

10.3 Make collocations using an item from each box. Then use the collocations to complete the sentences below.

capital	fixed	junk	risk	~~tracker~~

bond	~~fund~~	growth	management	rate

1 A fund that exactly follows the movement of an index is called a _____ *tracker* _____ *fund* _____.

2 A fund can provide regular income or _____ _____.

3 A bond is a financial instrument where a borrower raises capital and then repays the loan at a _____ _____ of interest over a fixed term.

4 A high-risk corporate bond can be called a _____ _____.

5 'Hedging' is a term associated with _____ _____. It means having a second position in a market, so that if the market moves against your first position your losses are minimized.

10.4 Divide each set of words in italics into two, according to their meaning.

1 a *booming / bear / bull / depressed / falling / rising / strong / weak* market

2 to *acquire / buy / have / hold / own / purchase* shares

10.5 Match the names of the different stock indices to their descriptions.

CAC	DAX	Dow	FTSE	Nasdaq	S&P

1 index of 500 large US companies _____

2 index of 4,000 US companies, many of them in the technology area, and some quite small _____

3 index of 30 large, well-established US companies, chosen by the editors of the Wall Street Journal _____

4 index of 30 large German companies _____

5 index of 40 large French companies _____

6 index of 100 large UK companies _____

10.6 Rank these financial instruments according to their probable risk: from 1 (low risk, low return, low volatility) to 4 (high risk, high potential return, high volatility).

a) an investment-grade corporate bond ☐

b) a UK government bond ☐

c) a fund investing in small biotech companies ☐

d) shares in an individual company listed on the Dow (eg General Electric) ☐

10.7 Choose which of these investment objectives is most suitable for the investors described below: *income, growth, income + growth.*

1 a highly-paid young professional, without a family, who wants to save long-term for a pension _____

2 a newly retired person who wants to supplement their pension _____

3 someone in their fifties who has just received money from an inheritance – they want to save for their pension, but also want help paying for their children's university fees

_____

10.8 Match these financial institutions with their descriptions below: *endowment, insurance company, investment bank, mutual fund, pension fund.*

1 used by large companies to issue bonds, buy and sell currencies, manage their portfolio of shares in other companies, and advise on any potential merger or acquisition _____

2 used to save money during your working life and then have an income during retirement _____

3 used by private investors to hold a basket of stocks

_____

4 used to protect yourself against risks (money is paid out if something bad happens) _____

5 used to generate an income for non-commercial purposes, in particular to run a university or provide for charity (the 'Bill and Melinda Gates Foundation' has one)

_____

10.9 Financial analysts use the terms in the box when trying to value a company and its share price. Match each term to its definition below.

> barriers to entry   capital requirements   ease of substitution
> market penetration   price elasticity

1 how sensitive a company's sales are to changes in the price of its products _____

2 how much money is needed to run this type of business _____

3 whether other companies could offer a similar product _____

4 how much market share a company has, and whether it has strong products in different segments of the market _____

5 difficulties that other companies would face if they tried to compete _____

10.10 The terms in the box are indicators of a company's performance and are listed in financial publications. Match each one to its definition below.

> earnings growth   p/e ratio   dividend yield
> market capitalization   return on equity

1 share price multiplied by total number of issued shares _____

2 earnings per share, compounded over several years _____

3 how much profit is generated in relation to the money shareholders have invested _____

4 current share price compared to its earnings per share _____

5 the annual dividends per share divided by the share price _____

10.11 Which terms from the box in exercise 10.10 are probably being referred to in these comments:

1 'the company is the biggest in its industry'
2 'compared to its competitors, the shares are cheap'
3 'it's a real growth stock – revenues are up year on year'
4 'it's not a growth stock, but you'll get a steady income from the shares'
5 'it's a profitable company'

Discussion topics

1 Financial advice is garbage. If anyone knew how to beat the market they'd be sitting on a beach drinking piña coladas – not trying to sell stocks to other people.
   ○ Agree   ○ Disagree

2 Why invest in the stock market? What goes up must come down. Spend the money today and enjoy it while you can.
   ○ Agree   ○ Disagree

10.12 Investors and traders make much use of 'technical analysis'. Write these terms next to their definitions: *breadth, leadership, liquidity, momentum, resistance, support, trading channel, volume.*

1 a price level which has stopped an advance on previous occasions _____

2 a price level which has stopped a decline on previous occasions _____

3 the total number of shares traded in a market on a particular day _____

4 the number of individual stocks participating in the movement of an index _____

5 the strength of a trend, as measured by speed and length of time _____

6 two parallel lines drawn on a chart that contain all price movements over a time period _____

7 the kind of companies that are moving the market: technology companies or utility companies? large cap or small cap? _____

8 whether there is new money available to invest in the market _____

10.13 Complete this text about the foreign exchange market using the words in the box.

> buyer   seller   Bank   Reserve   exports   imports   rises   raises

All international transactions in goods and services have to be paid for, and the [1]_____ usually pays in the currency of the [2]_____ . So, there will be a high demand for a country's currency if:

a) there is a trade surplus (ie the country [3]_____ more than it [4]_____) – because foreigners need the currency to make their payments

b) foreigners are buying a lot of that country's equities and bonds – they need the currency to make their purchases.

Increased demand for the currency for either reason will make it rise in value.

But over the short term the main factor affecting the forex market is interest-rate differentials. As the central bank of a country [5]_____ rates, the demand for its currency [6]_____ . Why? Simply because currency traders are looking for somewhere to park their cash. If the US Federal [7]_____ is paying 4% and the European Central [8]_____ 2%, then cash will earn more interest held in the US as dollars.

3 Over the next one year / five years (*choose one*) the dollar is going to rise / fall (*choose one*) against the euro / yen / other (*choose one*) because …

4 If I could invest in just one individual stock (or one national stock market) it would be … because …

11 Human resources

By working faithfully eight hours a day you may eventually get to be boss and work twelve hours a day.
Robert Lee Frost (1874 –1963), American poet

Human resource management (HRM)

Up to a few decades ago, the term 'human resources' did not exist. Recruitment, compensation and training were done by individual departments, and there would be a small 'personnel department' that was responsible for clerical jobs such as keeping staff records and processing the payroll. This situation has changed dramatically, mainly because jobs nowadays involve higher levels of knowledge and skill, and qualified labour is in short supply. Increasingly, the modern company sees its human capital – its employees – as one of its most important assets, and most large companies today have an HR strategy. But it is still often true that HRM is seen as having lower status than other areas of management.

Determining staffing needs

The key area of HR is staffing (= manpower planning). There are many issues to consider when trying to find qualified candidates:

- The choice between internal recruitment (less expensive recruitment process, boosts morale) and external recruitment (brings new ideas and skills, wider selection).
- Legal issues such as equal opportunities (no discrimination on the grounds of gender, race, age, disability, etc).
- Finding the right balance between permanent, full-time employees (who provide continuity of knowledge and company culture, as well as stability for families in the local community) and other employees hired on a more flexible basis.

Amongst the flexible staffing options are:

- Part-time staff on permanent contracts. This option can include 'job sharing' – often of interest to a parent with a young child.
- Staff on temporary contracts, perhaps leased from an outside agency (eg secretaries, hotel and catering staff, students working through college, etc). These people 'temp' and are 'temps' (verb and noun).
- Professional freelancers (sometimes called 'consultants') brought in for individual projects. Often these jobs replace ones that were previously done 'in-house' by permanent staff.

Recruitment and selection

Steps in the process for hiring employees are:

1 Identify job requirements, perhaps by drawing up a 'job description' and then a 'person specification'.

2 Choose the sources of candidates: promotion from within, referrals from existing employees, classified ads (AmE want ads), online recruitment, recruitment agencies, executive search (= headhunting), job fairs, walk-ins, etc.

3 Review applications and CVs (AmE résumés). This initial screening process is called 'longlisting'.

4 Interview a number of candidates on the longlist.

5 Conduct employment tests and check references.

6 Decide on a 'shortlist' of strong candidates and hold follow-up interviews.

7 Select a candidate and negotiate the package: compensation and benefits, job performance expectations, etc.

The selection process can be complex and mistakes expensive (for higher level managers there may be a whole relocation package to negotiate). The company needs the best person, both in terms of skills and of fitting in with the company culture. So to avoid making a mistake HR makes use of:

- Assessment centres where groups of people do role plays, take psychological tests etc. This is common for younger candidates without a track record.
- Checks on a candidate's background.
- Trial (= probationary) periods before a permanent contract is offered.

Compensation and benefits

Your basic compensation is your 'salary' (white-collar staff) or 'wage' (blue-collar staff, and used for payment on an hourly or piecework basis). Additional financial incentives include:

- Performance-related bonuses.
- Commission (for staff in the sales area).
- Profit sharing.
- Stock options (= the chance to buy company shares in the future at a fixed price).
- Pay rises for additional skills and qualifications.

Employees can also receive a whole range of other benefits (= fringe benefits / perks) such as: sick-leave and holiday pay, retirement (= pension) plans, health insurance, child care and elder care, training, company car, laptop, mobile device, subsidized canteen, the chance to travel, etc.

 Further information www.opm.gov/lmr/glossary ● www.managementhelp.org (> Human Resources Mgmnt etc)

HUMAN RESOURCES

Worker-management relations

Conduct local negotiations with trade unions

Ensure that agreements are interpreted and implemented correctly

Deal with individual grievances, disciplinary issues, absenteeism, etc

Monitor 'health and safety' issues

Monitor arrangements for 'joint consultation' - areas where workers participate in decision-making

Staffing and recruitment

Determining staffing needs

Selection process involving advertising, CVs, interviewing, etc

Monitoring the rate of staff turnover, and conducting 'exit interviews' to see why people leave

Motivation

Compensation and benefits: basic salary or wage, perhaps rising by increments over time; additional financial incentives; fringe benefits

Motivation through job satisfaction - see unit 4

Initial orientation for new employees

Training and development

On-the-job training

Apprenticeship programs

Coaching and mentoring

Understudy / assistant positions (working closely with the boss and perhaps doing some of their jobs - also called 'shadowing')

Job rotation

Off-the-job training

Classroom instruction

Computer-based training (= e-learning)

Management training through longer, sponsored courses such as MBAs

Appraisal (= evaluation)

Aims

To identify talent and help to align individual goals with company goals

To get direct suggestions for improving work procedures

To provide an input into decisions about promotion, etc

Stages in performance appraisal

1. Establish performance standards

2. Evaluate performance (often annually)

3. Discuss results with each employee, giving corrective feedback and asking for suggestions

4. Use the results to make decisions about promotions, compensation, additional training, job transfers, etc

11.1 Fill in the missing letters.

1 A list of all employees and how much each one earns is called the 'p _ _ _ ll'.

2 'Equal opportunities' means making sure that everyone has the same chance to get a job or get promoted. One of the most common forms of 'disc_ _ _ _ ation' (= treating a certain type of person unfairly) is on the grounds of 'dis_ _ _ _ _ty' (= a physical problem that makes someone unable to use a part of their body properly).

3 Freelancers are often brought in to do jobs that were previously done 'i_-h_ _ _ _' (by employees of the company).

4 The activity of discretely approaching employees of one company and asking them if they want to work for another is called 'h_ _ _ _ _ _ _ing'.

5 A small group of job candidates who have gone through to the final interview stage is called the 's_ _ _ _l_ _ _'.

6 Somebody's work history, and in particular their successes and failures, is called their 'tr_ _k r_ _ _ _d'.

7 The formal process by which an employee's performance is measured and discussed by a supervisor is called the 'a_ _ _ _ _ _al process'.

11.2 Put the HR activities 1–6 into the most appropriate category below.

1 apprenticeship programs
2 dealing with disciplinary issues
3 identifying talent and rewarding performance
4 health and safety
5 coaching and mentoring programs
6 getting suggestions for improving procedures

Appraisal process: ☐ ☐
Training and development: ☐ ☐
Worker-management relations: ☐ ☐

11.3 Complete each explanation with a pair of words from the box. The words may not be in the right order.

| bonus / commission   candidate / applicant   coaching / mentoring |
| employees / staff   retirement / pension   wage / salary |

1 A _____ is paid monthly, but a _____ is paid hourly, or by piecework.

2 A / An _____ is one of the people being actively considered for a job, whereas a / an _____ has sent a completed form and CV but is not necessarily being considered.

3 _____ is where an employee is 'paired' with a more experienced employee who supervises and guides them (and it can take place over a long time period); _____ is a more limited term, and is where someone is trained under active supervision to use a piece of equipment or carry out a particular process.

4 The word _____ refers to all the people who work in an organization; the word _____ can have exactly the same meaning, but it can also refer just to non-managerial workers.

5 If you receive a fixed percentage of every sale you make, you get a _____ ; if you (or your team or your company) performs well, then at the end of the year you might get a _____ .

6 Your _____ is the period of your life after you stop working (eg after 65); your _____ is the money you receive during this time (from the government, your company, or a private plan).

11.4 Match the words in the box to their definitions below. Clue: if the word appears in a definition, it won't be the answer.

| ~~ability~~   aptitude   background   competence |
| experience   knowledge   qualification   skill |

1 something you are capable of doing; also the quality of doing something well _____*ability*_____

2 (formal) the ability to do something well; also (formal) the legal power that a body has to deal with something

_____

3 an ability to do something well, especially because you have practised it _____

4 knowledge and skill you get from being in different situations; also something that happens to you

_____

5 an exam you have passed, especially at school or university; often appears in the plural as a heading on a CV _____

6 the type of education, experience and family that you have; also information about the past that helps you understand the present _____

7 the facts, skills and understanding you have gained through learning or experience _____

8 a natural ability to do something well or to learn it quickly

_____

11.5 Divide the words in italics into one of the three groups below.

| be appointed   ~~be dismissed~~   ~~be employed~~   be fired |
| be headhunted   be hired   ~~be laid off~~   be let go |
| be made redundant (BrE)   be recruited   be sacked   be taken on |

Group A: get a job
be employed _____ _____

_____ _____ _____

Group B: lose a job – you do something wrong
be dismissed _____ _____

Group C: lose a job – for economic reasons
be laid off _____ _____

11.6 Write one of these words in each space: *ability, experience, knowledge, qualification, skills.*

have	a formal a recognized a specialist a professional	1 _____	in something
have gain get	considerable first-hand hands-on practical valuable wide	2 _____	of / in something
have	a detailed an encyclopedic first-hand inside a thorough a working	3 _____	of something
have develop	communication interpersonal marketable transferable	4 _____	
have show	a great a remarkable an outstanding a proven	5 _____	to do something

Continue. Write one of these words in each space: *aptitude, background, competence, experience, knowledge.*

6 These matters fall outside (or come within) the
_____ of this committee.

7 This candidate has a strong _____ in marketing.

8 She has a lack of (or a wealth of) _____ in marketing.

9 I did some research to fill in the gaps in my
_____ .

10 He's got a real _____ for maths (AmE math) and accounting. It's in his genes!

Discussion topics

1 People think that HR requires low-status 'soft' skills. But it's HR managers who appraise, negotiate compensation, fire people and deal with the unions. That's not 'soft'.
   ○ Agree   ○ Disagree

2 Shortlisting and interviewing should be the responsibility of HR. Other people (from the functional department involved) should only have a minimal input. This ensures fairness and equal opportunities.
   ○ Agree   ○ Disagree

11.7 Complete the text about worker–management relations with the words in the box.

> arbitration   boycotts   collective bargaining
> court injunction   individual grievance   layoffs
> legally binding   length of service   mediation
> official dispute   picketing   strikes

The process by which management and unions form an agreement is called 1 _____ Typical issues for discussion are wages, benefits and working conditions. HR and the union may also sometimes discuss an 2 _____ , where someone thinks they have been treated unfairly. And of course negotiations will be necessary if the company is in financial difficulties and has to make 3 _____ . Workers who lose their jobs get a 'severance package' (BrE redundancy package), usually based on their 4 _____ in the company.

In any dispute, the employees' side will initially be led by a union rep (= representative) – a worker who represents the interests of their colleagues on a daily basis. Then, if the conflict escalates and becomes an 5 _____ , there might be involvement of a full-time union official. The union side has various tactics it can use, including 6 _____ (people stop working), 7 _____ (persuading others not to work by standing at the factory gates) and 8 _____ (getting consumers to stop buying the company's products).

The management side will usually be led by someone inside the HR department. Management tactics include hiring replacement workers, and in extreme circumstances obtaining a 9 _____ which directs workers to do (or not do) particular activities.

The procedure for resolving conflict goes through various stages. First, managers and workers will hold direct talks to try to resolve the problem. If these talks fail, then there may be involvement of a third party who can make suggestions and try to find a compromise. This is called '10 _____ '. Finally, if talks break down, the whole process goes to 11 _____ This is where a judge (or perhaps a government-appointed official) makes a decision which is 12 _____ on both sides.

3 Performance-related pay is a horrible invention that creates enormous stress and insecurity in the workplace.
   ○ Agree   ○ Disagree

4 Most training programmes are a waste of time. You just put the handouts in a file and forget about them.
   ○ Agree   ○ Disagree

> *Web users ultimately want to get at data quickly and easily. They don't care as much about attractive sites and pretty design.*
> **Sir Tim Berners-Lee (1955–) British inventor of the World Wide Web**

Management issues

The basic issues in information technology (IT) management are:

a) increasing the stability of the system to reduce down-time

b) ensuring that information is secure and backed-up (use of encryption, firewalls to keep out hackers, viruses, spyware, etc)

Beyond that, the following may be important issues at different times:

- Tension between the IT department and other business units. How are business requirements translated into an IT solution? How is the efficiency of IT spending measured? Do the business people understand the technology?
- Should the software be a commercial off-the-shelf (COTS) package or a tailor-made solution? If the latter, then what degree of customization is needed?
- How well does the new IT integrate with the old (= legacy) systems?
- How good is the documentation? Is training necessary?
- What level of integration is appropriate? Should the organization use just one standard of software (eg SAP/Oracle) and/or hardware (eg IBM/HP)?

Trends

Predicting the future of information and communication technology (ICT) is notoriously difficult, but several trends appear to be happening:

- Computing power is moving away from the local PC to the network (delivered where and when it is needed).
- Software is also moving to the network: companies are leasing it online for a monthly fee instead of buying it.
- Wireless connectivity is becoming possible between more and more devices.
- Bandwidth is increasing.
- Processing power and storage capacity keep increasing, while prices keep going down.
- Open-source platforms (designed and improved by users, owned by no-one) are becoming more common.
- Profitability is becoming an issue for vendors as IT becomes widespread and standardized.
- Integrating and managing IT systems is becoming more important than selling new products.
- Back-office functions (eg payroll) and software development are being outsourced to low-cost countries.

- There is the development of an 'Internet of things' – pervasive computing – where everyday objects have embedded processing power with a connection to the Net.
- There is a convergence between traditionally separate media.

E-business

A business with no online presence is a 'bricks-and-mortar' organization. At the opposite extreme, a few 'virtual' businesses exist only online. But most businesses are 'clicks-and-mortar' – they have some part of their business on the web, but also physical premises.

The phrase 'e-commerce' refers to the part of e-business related to buying and selling. Retailers set up an electronic storefront (BrE shop front) and shoppers place items they want to buy in an electronic cart (BrE trolley). When the shopper is ready, they go to the 'checkout' where their payment is processed.

For customers, key issues include:

- Fraud (the safety of online payment systems).
- Merchandise delivery and returns.
- The difficulty of speaking directly to a customer services representative rather than getting an automated response.

For companies, key issues include:

- The protection of intellectual property (piracy).
- Website costs and maintenance.
- Measuring the effectiveness of the website (click-through rates for ads, traffic counts, conversion rates to show percentage of visitors who make a purchase).

In terms of the technology involved, e-commerce is a good example of the role of dedicated (reserved for a specific use) servers:

1 A database server stores customer data and product information in tables. ↓

2 An application server is responsible for calculations and program logic; it retrieves data from the database server and feeds it to the web server. ↓

3 A web server is responsible for the interface and graphics; it presents the web page to the user. ↓

4 A browser on the user's computer allows the customer to interact with the company's web server.

INFORMATION TECHNOLOGY

Business software

Transaction processing: constant updating of mission-critical data such as orders, invoices, payments, payrolls, inventory, etc

Marketing: CRM (customer relationship management)

Production / Operations: MRP (material requirements planning), CIM (computer integrated manufacturing)

Finance: financial planning and budgeting

Human resources: payroll and employees' records

ERP (enterprise resource planning): manages all stages in the supply chain

Data and knowledge management

1. Raw operational data is kept in databases, eg sales info, inventory info, customer info

2. All the databases and documents from across the organization are collected together in a 'data warehouse'

3. Information from the data warehouse is retrieved by 'management information system' (MIS) software using 'datamining'. MIS software supports decision making, identifies patterns and trends, etc

Network computing

LAN (local area network) allows single-user workstations to share data, eg inside a company building

WAN (wide area network): a geographically dispersed LAN

Intranet (company network)

Extranet (part of intranet with limited access for certain people outside the company)

Collaboration tools (= groupware) that allow users at different workstations to work on the same project (screen sharing, webconferencing, etc)

Teleworking (employee can work at home, from a customer's premises, from a hotel, from the beach)

Mobile and wireless computing

Technology

Wireless LAN provides service within a hotspot

GPS (global positioning system) to determine location of device

Bluetooth to enable short-range connection between wireless devices

Applications

Personal services (content including news and entertainment is aggregated in a mobile portal)

M-commerce (= mobile-commerce): shopping and payments from your phone, person-to-person payments, advertising based on your location

Intrabusiness (support for mobile workers, job dispatch, access to intranet for sales staff to get customer / product info, etc)

E-business

B2B

'Electronic exchange': a marketplace for a specific industry

Supply chain management

Extranet to work more closely with suppliers and partners

B2C

Online marketing

Virtual store with online transaction processing and electronic funds transfer

Online customer service

Major areas include financial services, reservations for travel and holidays, sale of real estate, etc

12 Information and communication technology: Exercises

12.1 Fill in the missing letters.

1 Old IT systems (hardware or software) which are still in use are called 'l_ _ _cy systems'.

2 The written instructions for using IT software / hardware are called 'doc_ _ _ _ _ _ion'.

3 A piece of equipment intended for a particular purpose is called a 'de_ _ _e'. The word usually suggests something portable and electronic.

4 The rate at which data can pass through a communication channel is called its 'ba_ _ _ _th'.

5 A type of hardware and / or software on which application programs run is called a 'pl_ _ _ _rm'.

6 If a chip or wireless device is incorporated physically into an object it is described as being 'em_ _ dded'.

7 A software application used to locate and display web pages is called a 'br_ _ _er'.

8 In knowledge management, a key function is the 'data wa_ _ _ouse' – the place where all the company's data is collected together.

12.2 Complete the sentences using the pairs of words in the box.

accessibility / intranet   aggregate / portal   enable / devices
ensure / secure   measure / efficiency   retrieve / trends
stability / downtime   translate / solution

1 Perhaps the most important task for an IT manager is to increase the _____ of the system to reduce _____ .

2 IT managers also have to _____ that information is _____ and backed-up.

3 It can be difficult to _____ business requirements into an IT _____ .

4 It can also be difficult to _____ the _____ of IT spending.

5 Managers across the company use 'datamining' to _____ data from the data warehouse, and turn it into useful information by identifying patterns and _____ .

6 An extranet provides outsiders with various levels of _____ to the company's own _____ .

7 Bluetooth is a way to _____ short-range connection between wireless _____ .

8 Mobile phone companies charge for downloading content which they _____ on their own _____ .

12.3 Look at the completed sentences in exercise 12.2 and find a word that means:

1 make certain that something happens _____

2 copied (in case the original is lost) _____

3 needs _____

4 find something that is stored in order to use it again _____

5 make possible; often used as a past participle (an Internet-_____ed device is one that can use the Internet)

6 ask someone to pay an amount of money for a service _____

7 taking information from a network and putting it onto your own computer (or other device) _____

8 put together _____

9 a website that gives access to a wide range of services such as news and information, email, online shopping, links to other sites _____

12.4 Complete the text with the words in the box.

encryption   firewall   intranet   LAN
servers   stand-alone PC   WAN   workstations

It used to be common to see a ^{1} _____ sitting on a desk. No more. Now, individual ^{2} _____ inside a company are connected via a ^{3} _____ (= data communication system inside a building) to the company's ^{4} _____ (= high-capacity computers that store data and manage all the network resources). Large, multi-site organizations (eg a national health service) will require a ^{5} _____ (= computer network that covers a large geographical area).

How is all the internal company information accessed by users? Easily, via an ^{6} _____ . This is an internal network that acts just like a website, but is accessible only with a password and is protected by a ^{7} _____ . Further levels of security are provided by ^{8} _____ (= transforming data into a code to protect its confidentiality) and, for large organizations, housing the servers inside a bunker to provide physical security in case of fire, etc.

12.5 Make collocations by matching a word from each column.

1 off-the-shelf   capacity
2 wireless   connectivity
3 processing   functions
4 storage   package
5 back-office   page
6 intellectual   power
7 click-through   property
8 web   rate

12.6 Use the words in the box to make pairs of collocations with a similar meaning.

> ~~application~~   customized   defective   ~~design~~
> ~~develop~~   environment   faulty   the latest
> ~~old-fashioned~~   out-of-date   package   platform
> provide   run   supplier   supply   tailor-made
> up-to-date   use   vendor

Verb + noun collocation

1 to _____design_____ / _____develop_____ software

2 to _____ / _____ software

3 to _____ / _____ software

Noun + noun collocation

4 software _____application_____ / _____

5 software _____ / _____

6 software _____ / _____

Adjective + noun collocation

7 _____old-fashioned_____ / _____ software

8 _____ / _____ software

9 _____ / _____ software

10 _____ / _____ software

12.7 Underline the correct (or best) words.

1 We have IBM machines *running / running on* SAP.

2 We have SAP *running / running on* IBM machines.

3 All your *software / softwares* can run on our servers.

4 Sometimes we have to write *a / some* special software.

5 We need a more powerful and effective system. It needs to be *updated / upgraded*.

6 We need the latest version of the system. It needs to be *updated / upgraded*.

7 The database *updates / upgrades* automatically when new information is entered.

12.8 Read the text about ERP then answer the questions below.

Small companies tend to use separate off-the-shelf software packages to do specific tasks, such as preparing accounts. But larger companies need a solution that provides software on a modular basis – with the possibility of customization – and then integrates all the parts. This solution is called ERP (enterprise resource planning), and the main vendors are SAP and Oracle.

ERP has its origins in manufacturing, where it is used to manage all the stages in the company's internal supply chain. So, using sales data the software can forecast demand, order materials, schedule production, project financial results, etc.

But to this basic package it is possible to add many further modules. For example, to include the upstream end of the supply chain (= suppliers of components and raw materials) the company can add a procurement module. And to include the downstream end of the chain (= customers) there is a customer relations management module (CRM).

CRM – which other vendors sell as a stand-alone package – includes:

● for sales staff: contact management, quote management, customer preferences and buying habits, etc.

● for customer services staff: order fulfilment, complaints, returns, etc.

By keeping all the information on individual customers in one place, a company aims (i) to make cost savings through efficiency and (ii) to present a unified face to the customer, regardless of the communication channel that they use.

Another common ERP application is a management information system (MIS). This is a decision-making tool that allows managers to extract useful knowledge (specific details, key indicators, trends) and present it as graphs, reports, alerts, forecasts, etc.

Find a word from the text that means:

1 available in a standard form, not designed for a particular customer

2 personalization

3 predict (word #1)

4 predict (word #2)

5 the combined activities of sourcing (= finding what you want) + purchasing (= buying it)

6 able to be used on its own (ie without buying other components)

7 the price that a supplier says they will charge

8 delivering goods in the way that is promised and expected

9 on-screen warnings

Discussion topics

1 Business people don't understand IT, and IT people don't understand business.
   ◯ Agree   ◯ Disagree

2 E-commerce is a wonderful thing … until you want to speak to anyone about anything.

3 In five years' time, the biggest change in our lives from ICT will be …

4 Teleworking is the way to go. Who needs an office when everyone is networked?
   ◯ Agree   ◯ Disagree

13 Trends, graphs and figures

Trends

Read the text and then study the bullet points below.

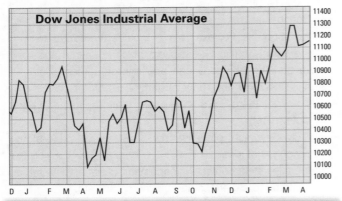

The chart shows the US stock market (Dow Jones index) for last year and the first quarter of this year. **As can be seen from the chart**, last year started on a positive note. The market **rose** until late February when it almost **reached the 11,000 level**. But interest rates **were rising**, and investors decided to take profits. **There was a sharp fall** during the month of March and the Dow **bottomed out** at **just over** 10,000. At that point investors started buying again – strong economic numbers and global liquidity (central banks printing money) offered support to the market. Over the summer the Dow **was flat**, trading **in a range** from 10,300 to 10,700. The market was unable to **break out** of this range, **even though** company profits **were increasing**. What was the reason? It was almost entirely **due to** the price of oil, which **had climbed dramatically** from $42 a barrel at the start of the year to $68 in August. This price rise **was caused by** the hurricane season in the Gulf of Mexico and **increasing tension** in the Middle East.

In mid-October the markets started to **rally strongly**, and went **from** 10,200 **to** 10,900 over just four weeks. This **sudden jump** was **as a result of** comments made by a member of the Federal Reserve, who indicated that interest rates would soon stop rising. This is positive for business **as** the cost of borrowing also stops going up. From November to January the market **remained more or less unchanged**, failing to break through the February **highs**.

Over the last few months the market **has advanced** again. The economic backdrop remains healthy: company profits are good, consumer spending **is up**, and interest rates are close to **reaching a peak**. The only dark cloud is the price of oil, which **has risen** back to the $70 level and looks certain to **go up** further. The next hurricane season is approaching and production worldwide cannot be **significantly expanded**.

- In any text describing trends there will be verbs and nouns of movement. Examples in this text are *fall, bottom out, be flat, increase*, etc.
- The mind map opposite lists verbs of movement. Note that words describing the same type of movement are often used in different contexts. For example, share prices 'rally' whereas profits or economies 'grow'. Use a good dictionary to check on points of usage such as this.
- Note the use of verb tenses in the text: *reached, were rising, had climbed, has risen*, etc. There is a summary of verb forms and uses in the mind map opposite.
- A text describing trends will include many examples of linking words. (See units 20–22.) Examples here are *even though, due to, as a result of* and *as* (meaning 'because').

Transitive and intransitive verbs

When using verbs of movement it is important to know whether they are:

- Transitive – needing an object – shown in the dictionary with a 'T'.
- Intransitive – used without an object – shown in the dictionary with an 'I'.

So the following verbs are transitive and need an object (*the budget*):
We cut / lowered / raised / reduced the budget.

But these examples are wrong (no object):
The budget ~~cut / lowered / raised / reduced.~~

The following verbs are intransitive and are used without an object:
Costs went down / fell / declined / rose.

But these examples are wrong (there is an object):
We ~~went down / fell / declined / rose~~ *costs.*

Many verbs like *increase* and *decrease* can be used both with and without objects.

Adjectives and adverbs of movement

In the text, some nouns are qualified with adjectives (*sharp, sudden*) and some verbs with adverbs (*dramatically, significantly*).

Adjectives used to describe movement include: *slow, slight, gradual, steady, quick, rapid, significant, sharp, substantial, dramatic.*

Adverbs are formed by adding *-ly* to the adjective, and sometimes one or two other letters change as well.

Upward: go up, increase, rise, raise, put up (= raise), climb, pick up, grow, expand, double, show an upward trend

Rapid upward: jump, rocket, soar, take off

Downward: go down, decrease, fall, drop, slip back, reduce, lower, bring down (= lower), cut, shrink, halve, show a downward trend

Rapid downward: plummet, collapse, crash, slump

Highs and lows: peak, reach a peak; bottom out, hit a low

Volatility: fluctuate, be volatile

Stability: stay the same, be flat, be (relatively) unchanged; level off / out

Good and bad: improve (= get better), strengthen, recover, bounce back; deteriorate (= get worse), weaken

Single points: be above / below, stand at

States: be up / down

Verbs of movement

Graph, chart, bar chart, pie chart, table, diagram

Title, row / column (with headings), horizontal axis (labeled with months), vertical axis (showing the values for ...)

Curve, solid line, dotted line, dashed line, segment, shaded area, slope (steep or shallow)

As can be seen from the chart, The graph / My next slide shows ..., Looking now at the figures for the third quarter we can see ...

Referring to visuals:

TRENDS, GRAPHS AND FIGURES

Action in progress

Present: sales <u>are rising</u> strongly at the moment

Past: sales <u>were rising</u> more strongly last year

Verb forms and uses

Approximate figures

A great deal more than, way over

Somewhat more than, well over

Just over, slightly more than

Around, about, roughly, somewhere in the region of, approximately

Almost, nearly, not quite, just short of

Far less than, nowhere near, nothing like as much as

Looking back

From the present to the past: sales <u>have risen</u> by 6% this year

From the past to earlier in the past: sales <u>had risen</u> to a high level, but in 2006 the market began to change

Linking words

See units 20–22.

Looking back at an action in progress

Action in progress up to a point in the past: sales <u>had been rising</u> strongly, but then new competitors entered the market

Action in progress up to the present: sales <u>have been rising</u> in all our major markets

Trends, graphs and figures: Exercises

13.1 Match each phrase on the left with its closest synonym (same meaning) on the right.

1 drop by 50%	a) deteriorate
2 rise by 100%	b) recover
3 get better	c) double
4 get worse	d) raise
5 bounce back	e) expand
6 grow	f) lower
7 put up	g) halve
8 bring down	h) improve

13.2 Match each verb on the left with its closest antonym (opposite meaning) on the right.

1 rise	a) plummet
2 raise	b) be flat
3 take off	c) bottom out
4 expand	d) fall
5 fluctuate	e) lower
6 peak	f) shrink

13.3 Complete each sentence with a phrasal verb from the box.

bounce back	*bottom out*	*bring down*	*level off*
pick up	*put up*	*slip back*	*take off*

1 If your prices are too high, you have to _____ them _____ .

2 If your prices are too low, you have to _____ them _____ .

3 If sales reach their lowest level, they _____ .

4 If sales recover after a period of downward movement, they _____ .

5 If sales go up a little after being flat for some time, they _____ .

6 If sales go up a lot after being flat for some time, they _____ .

7 If profits were going up – or down – and then become stable, they _____ .

8 If profits go down a little after a period of growth, they _____ .

13.4 Underline the correct words in italics.

1 The verbs 'rise' and 'grow' are similar. However, *rise / grow* is more common for longer periods of time, and where there is a total increase in size (eg describing the economy).

2 The phrasal verb 'grow up' refers to the change from being a child to being an adult. It *can also / cannot* be used to refer to things like profits, the economy.

3 The phrasal verb 'fall down' refers to movement towards the ground. It *can also / cannot* be used to refer to things like sales, profits.

4 We can 'raise / lower' prices or 'put up / bring down' prices. However, the *first two examples / last two examples* are slightly more formal, and can refer to a change in the level or standard of something as well as prices.

13.5 Put a tick (✓) if the sentence is possible. Put a cross (✗) if it is not. The answers depend on whether the verb is transitive, intransitive or both.

1 We cut costs by 5%. ☐
2 We fell costs by 5%. ☐
3 Profits cut by 5%. ☐
4 Profits fell by 5%. ☐
5 We raised prices by 2%. ☐
6 We rose prices by 2%. ☐
7 Inflation raised by 2%. ☐
8 Inflation rose by 2%. ☐
9 We increased sales by 4%. ☐
10 Sales increased by 4%. ☐
11 We went up market share by 3%. ☐
12 Market share went up by 3%. ☐

13.6 The -ing form of many verbs can be used as an adjective, eg an increasing demand for oil. Make adjectives from the verbs in the box using the information in brackets.

expand	*grow*	*rise*	*shrink*	*soar*

1 a ___*shrinking*___ budget (decreasing in size)

2 an _____ business (increasing in size)

3 a _____ problem (increasing over a long period)

4 _____ inflation (increasing)

5 _____ costs (reaching a very high level)

13.7 Fill in the missing letters in these adverbs using the information in brackets.

Sales increased …

1 ra___*pid*___ly (quickly)
2 gr_____lly (slowly and by small amounts)
3 st_____ily (in a constant, regular way)
4 sli_____ly (a little)
5 mar_____lly (fractionally)
6 sig_____ly (in a large and noticeable way)
7 sh_____ly (suddenly and by a large amount)
8 dr_____lly (suddenly and surprisingly)

Note that 'dramatically' can refer to both good and bad changes (unlike in many Latin languages).

13.8 Put a tick (✓) if the sentence makes sense. Put a cross (✗) if it does not.

1 Profits have risen steadily over recent years. ☐
2 Sales plummeted marginally in July. ☐
3 The price of oil soared gradually last year. ☐
4 Share prices dropped back slightly last week. ☐
5 Unemployment numbers levelled out sharply. ☐

13.9 Write the nouns for these verbs. Sometimes the form is the same.

1 cut _____   6 improve _____
2 deteriorate _____   7 increase _____
3 fall _____   8 recover _____
4 grow _____   9 reduce _____
5 halve _____   10 rise _____

13.10 Rewrite the 'verb + adverb' sentences as 'adjective + noun' sentences.

1 Sales fell slightly.
There was a _____*slight fall*_____ in sales.
2 Profits rose steadily.
We saw a _____ in profits.
3 The economy improved gradually.
There was a _____ in the economy.
4 We need to reduce costs sharply.
We need to see a _____ in costs.

13.11 Underline the correct words.

1 I'd like you to look at the blue segment on this next *bar chart / pie chart*.
2 I'd like to draw your attention to the *heading / title* at the top of each column of this table.
3 I'm sorry, the *heading / title* of this next slide is off the screen, but at least you can see the graph.
4 The horizontal axis is *marked with / labeled with* the months of the year.
5 Sales growth has been very rapid – as you can see from the *steep / shallow* slope of this graph.

13.12 It is very common to use approximate figures – particularly in speech. Match each approximate figure a)–p) to an exact figure 1–6 below.

a) just over 150
b) around 150
c) just short of 150
d) roughly 150
e) not quite 150
f) almost 150
g) some 150
h) 150 or so
i) far less than 150
j) way, way over 150
k) nowhere near 150
l) slightly more than 150
m) somewhat more than 150
n) 150 give or take a little
o) somewhere in the region of 150
p) nothing like as much as 150

1 90   ☐ ☐ ☐
2 146   ☐ ☐ ☐
3 154   [a] ☐
4 190   ☐
5 240   ☐
6 140 to 160   ☐ ☐ ☐ ☐ ☐

13.13 Fill in the gaps with a preposition where necessary (in <u>one</u> case there is no preposition). Choose from: *at, between, down, from, in, into, of, on, to, with*.

1 Last year sales rose _____ €7m _____ €7.5m. So that's an increase _____ €0.5m.
2 Last year there was an increase _____ sales _____ 8%.
3 Our market share now stands _____ 28%.
4 One _____ five (= one out of every five) of our products never makes a profit.
5 Two million _____ euros were spent on television advertising.
6 Unemployment figures have been relatively stable for some time, fluctuating _____ 4.3% and 4.6%.
7 There hasn't been much movement _____ the unemployment figures for some time.
8 Sales rose _____ line _____ predictions.
9 From January 1st to now, sales have gone up by €0.5m. So that's a year-_____-date increase of 8%.
10 Over the last twelve months, sales have gone up by €0.5m. So that's a year-_____-year increase of 8%.
11 In this pie chart, sales are broken _____ by region.
12 In this pie chart, the whole country is divided _____ five regions.

Speaking / Writing practice

● Prepare two graphs. They could be about your company (sales, profits, costs, etc) or your country (inflation, unemployment, house prices, etc). You could take graphs from an article on the Internet or in print, in English or in your own language. Remember to label the two axes.
● Speaking practice 1. Tell a partner about the graphs. Your partner should ask for more information (eg 'I'm sorry, can you explain that again?' 'What were the reasons for that?').
● Speaking practice 2. Regroup and work with a new partner – you are going to repeat the exercise and explain the graphs again. This time speak slowly and focus on accuracy rather than fluency. Take a moment to review pages 56–57 before you begin.
● Writing practice. Write a short report based on the two graphs.

Presentation styles

Read the two alternative openings for the same presentation and then study the points below.

Opening 1

Good morning, ladies and gentlemen, and thank you very much for inviting me here to speak to you. Let me introduce myself – my name is Carlos Pinto and I am the sales director of Downtown Properties. My objective today is to introduce our company and show you how we can help you find the right office for your business. I have divided my presentation into three parts. First I'll tell you a little about the history of our company, then I'll show you some slides of office space that we currently have available, and finally I'll deal with the question of cost. My presentation will take around twenty minutes, and if you have any questions I'll be pleased to answer them at the end. Okay. Let's start by looking at who we are and how the company has developed over the last twenty years (*shows first slide, which is a timeline of the history of the company*).

Opening 2

I bet you're sick of looking for office space, right? Are you feeling like this? (*shows slide with a cartoon of a stressed businessman in a small room*) Who feels like that? (*everyone laughs*) Wouldn't you prefer to feel like this? (*shows slide with a cartoon of a relaxed executive in a large, modern office*) Now, you all know the importance of location for business success. Well, we can help you. We're called Downtown Properties, and we've been offering rental solutions in this city for more than twenty years. I'd like to find out something from each of you in turn: what is the single most important reason why you want to move from your current offices?

- Opening 1 is more formal, structured and European-style. There are many typical 'key phrases' for presentations. In fact, the whole extract is based on standard phrases for introducing the speaker, introducing the topic, describing the structure of the presentation, telling the audience when they can ask questions, moving to the first point, etc.
- The advantages of a presentation in this style are: it is safe for a non-native speaker; it relies less on personality; it guarantees that all important points will be covered; it makes the structure clear at the beginning; the audience knows when to ask questions.
- The disadvantages are: it might be boring; it might focus on irrelevant information.
- Opening 2 is more informal, spontaneous and American-style. There are no 'key phrases'.
- The advantages of a presentation in this style are: it is lively; it involves the audience; the speaker can respond immediately to the needs / interests of the audience.
- The disadvantages are: it is risky for a non-native speaker; it relies on an extrovert personality; the speaker might lose direction or miss important points.

Most people will use a presentation style that is somewhere between these two extremes, and it depends on many things such as the speaker's confidence and personality, the topic, and the expectations of the audience.

The mind map opposite gives help with key phrases for those occasions when you choose to use them. Units 15, 18 and 20–22 are also very relevant to the language of presentations.

Presentation structure

A possible structure for a presentation is given below. Use it as a planning checklist – you don't have to follow every step, but at least consider all the points. The first letters make an easy-to-remember acronym: ***Bomber B***.

Bang! – something that you say or do at the beginning that gets the attention of the audience: a visual aid, a story, a joke, a surprising fact, a reference to 'here and now' (the audience, the place, etc).

Opening – thanking the organizers for inviting you, a few words about yourself, telling the audience the topic and structure of your presentation, making it clear whether questions should be kept to the end or not.

Message – the main points of your presentation. Decide on just three key points at the planning stage and write them down as three short sentences. This will focus your mind, and more than this will be hard for the audience to remember. Perhaps use these three sentences as the final slide in your presentation.

Bridge – make it clear to the audience how your message connects to their needs / interests.

Examples – use practical, easy-to-understand examples to make your points clear.

Recap – short for 'recapitulation', a summary of your main points.

Bang! – a link back to your first *Bang!* to give a sense of closure.

Good question

That's a very good question.
I'm glad you asked that.

Clarification needed

Let me check that I understand. Are you asking ...?

Could you be a little more specific?

Difficult question

Well, it's a very complex issue. What are your own views?

Would anyone like to comment on that? (Beatrix), can you help me to answer that?

You lack information

I don't have that information with me, but I can find out.

If you leave me your contact details at the end, I'll send it to you.

Control the timing

Okay, I think we have time for one last question

Introduction

On behalf of ...., may I welcome you to ...

For those of you who don't know me already, my name is ...

Before I begin, I'd like to thank (Sue) for inviting me to speak to you.

Purpose and structure

I'm here today to talk to you about...

I've divided my talk into three parts.

My talk will take around forty minutes.

First, I'll look at ...., then I'll show you ..., and finally I'll say a little about ...

Please feel free to interrupt me during the talk if you have any questions.

I'll be happy to answer your questions at the end.

Opening

Main body

Dealing with questions

PRESENTATIONS

First point

Okay, let's start with the first point which is ...

Right, that's all I want to say about .... Any questions so far?

New points

Moving on now to my next point...
Let's turn now to ...

Referring forward

I'll go into this in more detail in a moment.
I'll come back to this later.

Referring back

In the first part of my talk I mentioned ...

Going back for a moment to what I said earlier...

Digressing

Before going on, I'd just like to say a little about ...
If I can just digress (= side-track) for a moment, ...
So, getting back to my original point, you can see that ...

Visual aids

As you can see from this next slide, ...
Have a look at the diagram on the left ...

Handling interruptions

That's an interesting question. I'll come back to that at the end

Yes, thank you, I was just coming to that.

Closing

Summarizing

So, just before I finish, let me summarize the main points again, ...

So, to sum up, I have talked about three main areas. First ..., second ... and third ...

Concluding

Right, let's stop there. Thank you very much for your attention.

Inviting questions

And now, if you have any questions, I'll be pleased to answer them.

14 Presentations – structure and key phrases: Exercises

14.1 Put the words into the correct order to make phrases used in a presentation.

a) Could please your attention, I have?

Could I have your attention, please?

b) I'm here at InfoCom new product responsible for development.

_____

_____

c) For who don't know me those of you already, my name is Nancy Holmes.

_____

_____

d) It's always a pleasure of experienced professionals an audience to speak to like yourselves. I know a long way that of you many have travelled to be here.

_____

_____

_____

e) On the company behalf of, to this presentation may I you welcome.

_____

_____

f) The aim of our new product line is to give some you information about my talk.

_____

_____

g) Please during the talk feel free me to interrupt if you any have questions.

_____

_____

h) Okay, I'd like to slide by at this first looking begin. Can see at the back the people okay?

_____

_____

i) My forty minutes take presentation will around.

_____

j) I've divided into my talk three parts main. First, I'll give you the different models an overview in of the range. Then I'll to describe move on each the key benefits of model. And finally I'll say about prices a little.

_____

_____

_____

14.2 Match the phrases from exercise 14.1 to their uses below.

1 Getting attention [a]   6 Purpose ☐

2 Name ☐   7 Structure ☐

3 Position ☐   8 Timing ☐

4 Greeting ☐   9 Questions ☐

5 Audience / Place ☐   10 First point ☐

14.3 Speaking practice. Exercise 14.1 gives some phrases for opening a presentation and exercise 14.2 gives the correct order. Make your own script:

● Write the phrases again, in order. Writing will help you to memorize the language.

● Use your own name, organization, etc.

● Substitute any other words or phrases to personalize the introduction for you.

When you finish, read it aloud several times. As you speak, think about where and how often to pause, and also which syllables have a strong beat.

14.4 Match the more formal phrases in exercise 14.1 with the more informal phrases below.

1 Okay, let's get started. [a]

2 I'm Nancy Holmes. ☐

3 And I'm in charge of product development. ☐

4 Thanks for coming. ☐

5 It's nice to see so many familiar faces, and I hope you all found somewhere to park! ☐

6 I'm here today to tell you about our new product line. ☐

7 I'm going to cover three areas: first, the different models in the range, then key benefits, and finally price. ☐

8 I'll speak for about forty minutes. ☐

9 If you have a question, please feel free to interrupt. ☐

10 Okay, let's take a look at this first slide. ☐

14.5 Speaking practice. Read aloud the version in exercise 14.4. It is already in the correct order. Again, use your own name.

14.6 Speaking practice. You are going to use the structure in exercise 14.2 to practise a more spontaneous opening. Follow the instructions.

1 Cover all the exercises on this page <u>except</u> exercise 14.2.

2 Give the opening to a presentation:

● Use the headings in 14.2 as a guide while you speak. (Don't worry if you change the sequence a little.)

● Invent any details that you want – it is not a memory exercise.

● Practise several times in a low voice, and then speak with a strong, clear 'presentation' voice.

14.7 Each pair of words can be used in one sentence. Write them in the correct spaces.

as / see   come / later   digress / little
finish / summarize   getting / to   going / moment
let / attention   moving / talk   pleased / answer
right / far   ~~start / looking~~   turn / question

1 Okay, let's _____*start*_____ by _____*looking*_____ at an overview of our new product line.

2 I'll _____ back to this _____

3 _____ , that's all I want to say about the overview. Any questions so _____ ?

4 So, _____ on, I'd like to _____ about the key benefits of each model.

5 _____ back for a _____ to what I said earlier.

6 If I can just _____ for a moment, I'd like to say a _____ about the background to this decision.

7 So, _____ back _____ my original point, you can see that this really is a big improvement on the old model.

8 Finally, I'd like to _____ to the _____ of price.

9 _____ you can _____ from the table in this next slide, our prices are still very competitive.

10 So, just before I _____ , let me _____ the main points again.

11 Right, _____ 's stop there. Thank you very much for your _____

12 And now, if you have any questions, I'll be _____ to _____ them.

14.8 Memory game. Follow these instructions:

- Take one minute to try to memorize all the phrases in exercise 14.7. Repeat them in your head, or aloud in a low voice.
- Cover the whole of 14.7.
- Take a piece of paper. Write down the phrases using the hints 1–12 at the top of the next column. (If you are in class, work with a partner.)

1 Okay / start / looking / overview / product line.

2 I'll / back / this later.

3 Right / all / want / say / overview. / questions / far?

4 So, / moving / like / talk / key benefits / each model.

5 Going back / moment / what / earlier.

6 If / just digress / moment, / like / say a little / background / decision.

7 So, / getting back / original point, / can see / is / big improvement / old model.

8 Finally, / like / turn / question / price.

9 As / see / the table / this next /, prices / very competitive.

10 So, / just / finish / let / summarize / main / again.

11 Right, / stop there. / Thank / much / your attention.

12 And now, / if / questions, I'll / pleased / them.

- When you finish, compare with the original phrases.

14.9 Match the beginning with the end of each phrase. They are used for dealing with questions.

1 I'm glad ——————— complex issue.

2 Leave me your one last question.

3 Could you be ————— you asked that.

4 Well, it's a very contact details and I'll send it to you.

5 We have time for a little more specific?

6 Let me check own views?

7 What are your the top of my head.

8 I don't know that off that I understand.

14.10 Match the phrases from exercise 14.9 with their uses below.

a) Reply to a good question   [1]

b) Clarification needed   [ ] [ ]

c) Reply to a difficult question   [ ] [ ]

d) You lack information   [ ] [ ]

e) Control the timing   [ ]

Speaking practice

Give a short presentation. Follow these instructions:

1 Decide on a topic. Here are three suggestions:
- You are the Director of Tourism for a city or region in your country. Give a presentation about why people should come to visit.
- Choose an object that you have with you, or that is in the room. Give a sales presentation about why it is the best of its kind and why everyone should have one.
- Choose a topic that is similar to real-life presentations that you make.

2 Plan your presentation. **Make a few very short notes on the main points.** However, do not write a full script. You want to look at the audience, not at a piece of paper.

3 Look back briefly at the mind map and the exercises to review some phrases.

4 Give your presentation. Remember to ask for questions at the end.

(If you are working in class, your teacher will set a time limit. If you are working alone, use a colleague / friend / domestic animal as your audience.)

15 Presentations – being lively and persuasive

The ancient Greeks

The ancient Greeks were famous for their love of arguing and debating in public places – people like Plato and Aristotle gave the best presentations of their day. They thought that the best form of argument was reason, but they recognized that because of human weakness two further techniques would always be used: appeal to a person's good character and appeal to the emotions. These three techniques together they called 'rhetoric', and nowadays we use the expression 'rhetorical language' to refer to language that is deliberately intended to persuade and influence.

You will see a summary of the most common rhetorical techniques in the mind map opposite. Some would be recognizable to the ancient Greeks, others are more associated with the language of advertising or public relations. All are useful in business presentations – they add a bit of colour to what would otherwise be a rather dry and boring talk. But use them with care: they can sound false and manipulative if used too often or too obviously.

A persuasive presentation?

Below is a short presentation that uses many of the techniques opposite. How many of them can you spot? Check afterwards with the Answer Key, then read it aloud, emphasizing the rhetorical techniques.

This year marks our fiftieth anniversary as a life insurance company. And over those fifty years, we've seen a lot of life. We've seen anger and joy. We've seen bad times and good times. Social change has been dramatic. But over that time one thing has been constant: our commitment to innovation, quality and value.

That's why we're still here, and growing. We understand our customers. We know what our customers want. They want financial security – for now, and for the generations who follow. In these changing times, they want a solid future.

What about you? Perhaps you want to build funds to pay for your children's college education? We have a plan that's right for you. Perhaps you want to provide for your children in the event of you having an accident – or worse? We have a plan that's right for you. Perhaps you want to turn your regular savings into a guaranteed retirement income for your golden years? We have a plan that's right for you.

All that is for families. But families aren't the only ones to benefit from our products. We also provide business owners with financial incentives to offer their employees. With our products, you can give your staff pension plans, health plans, and life insurance. Those are the things that really count in a compensation package, those are the things that make a worker feel valued. And we all know: a happy worker is a productive worker.

I encourage individuals, families and business owners to take time today to create financial peace of mind tomorrow. Thank you.

A key element in 'persuasion' is effective use of your voice. Above all, this means using pauses for emphasis and dramatic impact. Try reading aloud the above presentation again. Do it several times in different ways. Experiment with pauses, volume changes, and intonation. Exaggerate for fun; create a sense of drama.

Other issues in presentations

In a presentation it is essential to transmit self-confidence and build trust. To achieve this, key issues are:

● Good eye contact. Looking directly at the audience is vital – it is always a mistake to read from notes, or have your back to the audience.
● 'Being yourself'. This means using your strengths and not trying to be something that you are not. If you are normally funny, then use humour, otherwise don't. You want your natural personality, and your natural interest and enthusiasm for the subject, to come across to the audience. This won't happen if you are thinking all the time about presentation tricks and techniques.

If you begin to feel nervous at any time, the best advice is: stop, breathe, smile, and look around the room. One slow, deep breath will give you a sense of calm and help to lower your voice and reduce its speed. Smiling and looking around the room will give you and the audience some human contact.

Another useful technique – good at any time, not just when you are nervous – is to throw the presentation back to the audience. Ask them a question, or ask them if they have any questions to ask you.

Finally, planning is everything. *Fail to prepare and prepare to fail.* This means:

● Be clear about the 3–5 points you want the audience to go away with.
● Know your audience (especially their level of background knowledge).
● Prepare your notes (key words – perhaps on numbered cards).
● Think of ways to present the information visually (but keep slides clear and simple).
● Get to the room early to practise with the technology and check the seating.

BEING LIVELY AND PERSUASIVE

Emotional language

Imagine that your car breaks down on a lonely country road. It's the middle of the night. Our car recovery service with GPS tracking means that we'll be there within an hour.

Metaphor

This proposal is pointless. It's like rearranging deckchairs on the Titanic.

Idiom

Don't worry, there is light at the end of the tunnel.

Anecdote

It reminds me of the time I ...

Rhetorical question

You don't expect an answer

Can we really get involved in this project when our resources are so limited?

You give the answer yourself

What's the solution? You can see it right here on this next slide.

Being lively

The 'rule of three'

Use words / structures in groups of three

It's economical, reliable, and easy-to-clean.

I ask you: 'Is this reasonable? Is this good business practice? Is this what our customers expect?'

Make three key points

This presentation will cover three main issues. First, ... Second, ... and Finally

Do you want high safety at low cost?
Global reach – local solutions

Contrast

Repetition

Sounds

Beginning of word:
Software for leisure and learning

Stressed syllable in middle of word:
And we call our shop: Planet Organic.

End of word:
We need negotiation, not confrontation.

Words

We deliver on time, every time.

This device is powered by a tiny battery. It's a battery that lasts 40% longer than the one in our previous model. Yet this same battery weighs less than a paper clip.

Sound + Structure

Beat the rest – choose the best.

You'll feel happy and healthy, relaxed and refreshed.

Words + Structure

Saving time is good, saving money is better.

Wherever you are, whenever you need us, we'll be there.

Stop-and-start repetition

What's the problem? The problem is ...

Just take a moment to look at our results. Results that have made us a leading player in the financial services industry.

15.1 Complete the rhetorical questions with the pairs of words in the box.

How + do	When + expect	Why + keep on
Where + go	How much + is	What + waiting

1 The opportunities are there. We've got the staff.
_____ are we _____ for?

2 Our production costs are going up and we're losing market share. There's one question on everyone's mind.
_____ do we _____ from here?

3 We went from a small office in Bratislava ten years ago to be market leader in Central Europe today.
_____ did we _____ it?

4 We've invested €5 million in new plant and machinery. I know what you're thinking. _____ can we _____ to see a profit?

5 Product development times went way over schedule and we were late to market. Again. _____ do we _____ making the same mistake?

6 We spend a lot of money on TV advertising at all hours of the day and night. _____ of that _____ wasted?

15.2 Replace one key word in each sentence with a close synonym from the box. Your aim is to produce repetition of sounds for dramatic impact.

boom	effective	glorious	major	~~progress~~	variety

1 We're 100% focused on technological innovation – we
progress
believe in the power of ~~improvement~~.

2 You don't want just any knowledge management system – you want a system that is efficient and helpful.

3 Choose us as your local partner, and watch your business grow!

4 As well as value, we also offer choice.

5 Congratulations to all members of the sales team – results this year haven't just been good, they've been wonderful.

6 Invest in Rubovia – we have easy access to important markets.

15.3 Replace one word each time with a word that has already been used. Your aim is to produce repetition of words for dramatic impact.

1 You have a lot of information on your databases. But can
information
you mine that ~~knowledge~~ to get what's really useful?

2 Our new range of shoes features tiny diamonds set into the leather. It's the most exclusive line that we have ever produced.

3 What's the reason that we keep going over-budget? The explanation clearly is that we lack good financial control.

4 The issue of energy conservation is becoming increasingly important – it's the topic that's at the top of the agenda in the construction sector.

5 We have a global presence, with offices in every major centre from Berlin to Beijing. But being international doesn't always help – sometimes you need a local strategy as well.

15.4 Underline five contrasts in this presentation extract. (Remember, one contrast will have two words.) The first one has been done for you.

Our exclusive new watch makes its own electrical power by the movements of your hand. Wear it for <u>one</u> day to get energy for at least <u>two</u> weeks. It is made of titanium – a light material, yet strong and kind to your skin. The styling is superb, combining classical elegance with modern design. As you know, our watches are not cheap. But people who wear our watches are not looking for a cheap product. They are looking for something special. They want a quality timepiece – to celebrate their success today, and pass on to their children tomorrow.

15.5 Complete each sentence with the three most appropriate words or phrases from the box.

clean	commitment	customer needs
distribution channels	drive	future	maintain
highly profitable	well-run	running costs
time-to-market	vision

1 Take a look at our new machine. It's easy to _____ , easy to _____ , and has very low _____ .

2 It gives me great pleasure to introduce to you our new CEO. She's a woman with _____ , _____ and _____ .

3 Why should you invest in this company? Because it's _____ , _____ and has a great long-term _____ .

4 Sales are flat. What can we do? We need more accurate identification of _____ , more efficient _____ and faster _____ .

Metaphors and Idioms

● Here is an example of a metaphor:
It's like rearranging deckchairs on the Titanic.
(= It's just making small changes that will do nothing to stop the big disaster that's coming.)

● Here is an example of an idiom:
There is light at the end of the tunnel.
(= Finally there is a solution in sight after a long period of difficulties.)

● A metaphor is where you describe one thing in terms of another. An idiom is a fixed expression whose meaning is different to the meaning of the individual words. In practice, they are often very similar.

● Metaphors and idioms add colour to a presentation or discussion. But use them with care: other non-native speakers may find them difficult to understand. Also, you have to get every single word right, otherwise they sound ridiculous.

15.6 Complete each phrase with the correct word/s in the right-hand column.

a) make a	ground
b) corner the	fire
c) get off the	market
d) cook the	killing
e) come under	books
f) keep an eye	of the action
g) get a piece	like water
h) put my	on things
i) spend money	the red
j) be in	foot in it
k) sell like	black and white
l) be a real high-	your buck (AmE)
m) see it in	hotcakes
n) get more bang for	in a small pond
o) be a big fish	flyer

15.7 Match the phrases in exercise 15.6 with the meanings below.

1 accidentally say or do something embarrassing or that annoys someone ☐
2 be important, but only in a small field of activity ☐
3 be criticized ☐
4 be destined to go to the top of a profession ☐
5 become involved (in something exciting and profitable) ☐
6 be over budget; have a negative bank balance ☐

7 dominate (or even monopolize) the market ☐
8 falsify the accounts ☐
9 get more value for the money you spend ☐
10 have written confirmation, not just a verbal agreement ☐
11 look after things (while someone is away) ☐
12 make a large, sudden profit ☐
13 sell very well ☐
14 spend a lot of money without any control ☐
15 start a project and make it successful ☐

15.8 Complete each example by writing the letter of a phrase from exercise 15.6 in the gap.

1 Our main competitor has just gone bankrupt! If we offer a job to their marketing director and get access to their client list, we'll ___a___

2 We're losing money fast. If we go on like this, we'll _____ by the end of the year.

3 I have an apology to make. I went out for a drink with some colleagues after work yesterday and I _____ . I told them you were applying for a new job.

4 I'll be away for a few days, but Isabel will _____ .

5 It's an interesting project, but I don't think it will ever _____ – it's too expensive.

6 On balance I think it's the right thing to do. But it's a big risk, and we're going to _____ from the shareholders for taking it.

7 City Hall has plans to build a huge out-of-town industrial park. There's going to be a lot of contracts for the construction work, and we need to make sure we _____

8 Profits were up 28% last year. And don't worry – we didn't ask our accountants to _____ !

9 It's the World Cup next year. If we put the national flag on our t-shirts they'll _____ .

10 We have to set a tight budget – with corporate hospitality it's very easy to _____ .

11 Thank you for that kind introduction, but I'm not really as famous as you say! My area of research is very specialized and it's quite easy to _____ .

12 All three candidates have good CVs. I think we should choose the one with real leadership potential, the one who's going to _____ .

13 This is a very innovative product in a very specialized field. I think we can _____ .

14 They were making a lot of promises at the meeting, but we need to _____ before we can go ahead.

15 Value-for-money is important to many people. We need to give a clear message: shop with us and you'll _____ .

Speaking / Writing practice

● Write the script for a short presentation that you might give as part of your job or university course. At the planning stage, refer to units 14 and 15.

● Practise speaking the presentation, using the script.

● Now write down the key points (max 20 words in total) on a piece of paper. Practise again using just these key points to guide you – not the full script.

● Practise again. Be lively and persuasive.

16 Discussions

Managing a discussion

Read this dialogue in a real estate agency and then study the points below.

A: Can you help me? **I'd be interested to know something about** property prices in this area.

B: Yes, of course. But first, **could you tell me a little more about** your present situation?

5 A: I've been living in rented accommodation for several years. Now I'm wondering whether it's a good time to buy somewhere for myself.

B: Okay. **What sort of price were you thinking of?**

A: Oh, you know, nothing too expensive.

B: **Could you be a little more specific?** We have some small one-
10 bedroom apartments that start at around €120,000. **Was that the kind of thing you had in mind?**

A: Possibly. But I'm not ready to think about individual properties just yet. I wanted to know more about the market in general. There are a lot of stories in the newspapers about house prices, and they worry me.

15 B: Okay. **If I understand you correctly,** your worries are probably these: you don't want to buy at the top of the market and see your house fall in value, but equally you don't want to miss the chance if prices are going to continue to rise.

A: **Yes, exactly.**

20 B: This is of course a concern for all our clients, but you know it's very difficult to time the housing market. Newspaper stories can make forecasts, but no-one really knows.

A: **I see what you're saying, but** you must have some idea. I read one article that said that house prices are going to crash.

25 B: **I don't think that's true.** Prices have stabilized recently, but they're not going to crash.

A: **Really? Do you think so?** My friend bought an apartment near here last year for €165,000, and now other apartments in the same block are going for less than €150,000.

30 B: **Well, of course, it all depends.** There are many factors that can cause these short-term changes. But **there is another way of looking at this**. If prices have dropped temporarily, then now is a good time to buy.

A: But **going back to what you said earlier**, have prices stabilized,
35 or are they actually falling? I **disagree with you about** now being a good time to buy if they are still falling.

B: In certain areas they are still falling. But **I think we're losing sight of the main point**. You're living in rented accommodation, and the rent you pay could be going to repay a mortgage. And you would
40 have your own home.

A: **That makes sense. But it's a difficult issue**.

B: **You're absolutely right.** But while you're here, **why don't I give you an idea of** what's available in your price range?

A: Okay.

45 B: Right. **I'd like to start by** writing down one or two personal details, and **then we can move on to** looking at some of the properties we have on the market.

● Look at the words in bold above. Underline:
  – five phrases asking for more information.
  – one phrase showing the speaker is going to check using their own words.
  – three phrases for full agreement.
  – one phrase using *Yes, but ...* for half agreement.
  – one phrase using two open questions to show polite disagreement.
  – two phrases for simple disagreement.

How many of these can you find in the mind map opposite?

● At lines 7 and 10 you will see the phrases: *What sort of price were you thinking of?* and *Was that the kind of thing you had in mind?*

These questions are interesting for two reasons:
  – first, they use 'vague' language: *sort of, kind of*.
  – second, they use past tenses (*were / was / had*), even though the time reference is present.

The past forms create an indirect, distant feeling. They combine with the vague language so that the client feels that he / she is under no pressure.

● Look back at lines 30–42. There is a battle for control of the topic:
  – at line 31 B tries to change the focus: *... there is another way of looking at this.*
  – but at line 34 A resists: *... going back to what you said earlier, ...*
  – at line 37 B deals briefly with this resistance: *In certain areas ...* but then tries to block further discussion with: *I think we're losing sight of the main point.*
  – at line 42 B manages the conversation so that they move on from the opening to begin a sales conversation about specific properties. For B, this is the main topic.

Now look at the 'Topic management' branch of the mind map.

Other language for discussions

In discussions you are likely to use a lot of linking words and phrases. (See units 20–22.)

Full agreement

That makes sense.
You're absolutely right.
Yes, I would agree with that.

Half agreement

I see what you're saying, but ...
I agree with you up to a point, but ...

Polite disagreement

Well, of course, it all depends.
I'm not sure I agree with that.
I've got mixed feelings about that.
Really? Do you think so?
Don't you think that ...?

Simple disagreement

I don't think that's true.
I disagree with you about ...
That's not how I see it.

Beginning the main topic

Right, let's get down to business.
Why don't I give you an idea of ...?
I'd like to start by ... (-ing)

Moving from point to point

So that's decided, then. Shall we move on?
Okay, let's go on to the next point.

Changing the focus

There is another way of looking at this.
Perhaps we should also consider ...

Returning

Going back to what I / you said earlier ...
Let me back up. (AmE).

Interrupting

Could I just interrupt for a moment?

Blocking

I think we're losing sight of the main point.
Sorry, if I can just finish, I was saying that ...

Buying time

It's a difficult issue.
I'll have to think about it.
Could I get back to you on that?
Why don't we come back to that later

Agreeing and disagreeing

Topic management

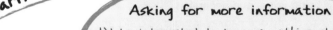
Clarification

DISCUSSIONS

Asking for more information

I'd be interested to know something about ...
Could you tell me a little more about ...?
Could you be a little more specific?
What (exactly) do you mean by ...?
What sort of price were you thinking of?
Was that the kind of thing you had in mind?

Asking for repetition

Could you go over that again, please?

Checking by using your own words

So, if I understand you correctly, ...
So basically what you're saying is ...

Checking the other person's understanding

Does that answer your question?
Does that make sense?

Responding

Yes, exactly.
Yes, that's right.
Not exactly.
Well, let me put it another way.
No, that's not what I meant.
No, what I'm trying to say is ...

16 Discussions: Exercises

16.1 Without looking back at the mind map, think of just one word to fill each gap.

a) There is another _____ of _____ at this.

b) Right, let's get down to _____ .

c) _____ back to what you said earlier.

d) I think we're losing _____ of the main _____ .

e) Could I _____ interrupt for a _____ ?

f) Could you be a little more _____ ?

g) What exactly do you mean _____ 'more expensive'?

h) Sorry, if I can _____ finish, I was saying that …

i) Could I _____ back to you _____ that?

j) Was that the _____ of thing you had in _____ ?

k) Does that make _____ ?

l) Well, let me _____ it another way.

16.2 Match each phrase in exercise 16.1 with one of the uses 1–12.

1 You want to change the focus. [a]

2 You want to block the other person's change of focus and return to the main issue. ☐

3 You want to interrupt. ☐

4 You want to block an interruption and continue. ☐

5 You want to begin the discussion. ☐

6 You want to return to an earlier point. ☐

7 You want to buy time after a question. ☐

8 You want more detailed information because the other person is being vague and general. ☐

9 You want to clarify one particular word or concept. ☐

10 You want to clarify what you just said by saying it again more simply and clearly. ☐

11 You want to clarify what the other person wants, using vague language to avoid putting them under pressure. ☐

12 You want to check the information you gave was clear. ☐

16.3 Cover exercise 16.1 with a piece of paper. Then fill in the gaps using the prepositions in the box.

about	at	back	back	down	in	of	of
of	of	on	on	over	to	to	to	to

1 Right, let's get _____ _____ business.

2 Okay, let's move _____ _____ the next point.

3 There is another way _____ looking _____ this.

4 Going _____ _____ what you said earlier.

5 I think we're losing sight _____ the main point.

6 Could I get _____ _____ you _____ that?

7 Could you tell me a little more _____ it?

8 What sort _____ price were you thinking _____ ?

9 What exactly did you have _____ mind?

10 Could you go _____ that again please?

16.4 Find a phrasal verb (eg take off or look forward to) in exercise 16.3 that means:

1 start doing something seriously _____get down to_____

2 stop doing one thing and begin doing another

_____

3 return to a subject _____

4 speak to someone at a later time _____

5 repeat something in order to understand it

_____

16.5 Match the beginning with the end of each phrase.

a) You're absolutely   a point, but …

b) Yes, I'm in favour   I see it.

c) That might be worth   right.

d) I agree with you up to   agree to that.

e) I can see one or two   so?

f) I'm sorry, I can't   of that.

g) Really? Do you think   problems with that.

h) That's not how   trying.

16.6 Write each phrase letter from exercise 16.5 in the grid below.

	with someone	about something
Agreement	1 _____a_____	5 _____
Half agreement	2 _____	6 _____
Polite disagreement	3 _____	7 _____
Disagreement	4 _____	8 _____

16.7 Complete each mini-dialogue using the phrases in the box.

> Can I get back to you on that?   Yes, exactly.
> I think we're losing sight of the main point.
> Shall we move on?   Let me put it another way.

1 A: Yes, I think that would work very well.
  B: So that's decided, then. _____

2 A: Are we going to have a hot buffet at the product launch or just finger food?
  B: _____ Some major issues are still unresolved – like the advertising campaign.

3 A: The price is okay, but what about shipping times? Can you deliver by the end of April?
  B: I don't know right now. _____

4 A: So are you saying you want me to transfer to the Madrid office?
  B: _____ It would be a great opportunity for you.

5 A: So are you saying I have to transfer to the Madrid office?
  B: Well. _____ You don't have to, but it would be a great opportunity for you.

16.8 The words *offer, suggestion* and *proposal* are often misused. Match each with an explanation:

1 _____ – an idea or plan, perhaps quite tentative and vague

2 _____ – an idea or plan, more formal and definite, and usually one that a group has to consider

3 _____ – a statement saying you will give something to someone (used mainly in negotiations)

16.9 Match each item on the left with one on the right that has a similar meaning.

1 put forward	take up (a suggestion)
2 accept	think of (a suggestion)
3 reject	make (a suggestion)
4 come up with	dismiss (a suggestion)

5 take part in	tackle (an issue)
6 come to	bring up (an issue)
7 raise	be involved in (a discussion)
8 deal with	open it up for (discussion)
9 reconsider	reach (a decision)
10 throw it open for	reassess (a decision)

11 a sensible	feasible (suggestion)
12 a sensitive	reasonable (suggestion)
13 a realistic	ridiculous (suggestion)
14 a minor	difficult (issue)
15 an absurd	side (issue)

16 a constructive	in-depth (discussion)
17 a hard	fruitful (discussion)
18 a detailed	initial (discussion)
19 an easy	tough (decision)
20 an exploratory	straightforward (decision)

16.10 Cover exercise 16.9 with a piece of paper. Then fill in the missing letters.

1 She was the only person to c _ _ _ u_ w _ _ _ a fea_ _ _le suggestion.

2 I think we should ta_ _ u_ his suggestion – it sounds very rea_ _ _ _le to me.

3 He p_ _ fo_ _ _ _d a ri_ _ _ _ _ous suggestion about going to the CFO and asking for a bigger budget.

4 I need to b_ _ _g u_ a rather sen_ _ _ _ _e issue.

5 It's a difficult issue, but we'll have to t_ _ _le it one day.

6 I've been inv_ _ved i_ the expl_ _ _ _ _ry discussions, and now we're ready to call a formal meeting.

7 I thought the conference was going to be a waste of time, but in fact I t_ _k p_ _ _ i_ some very fr_ _ _ _l discussions.

8 You've all read my summary, so now I think we can o_ _ _ it u_ f_ _ a more in-d_ _ _h discussion.

9 We finally r_ _ _ _ed a decision, but it was a t_ _gh one to make.

10 It should be a relatively str_ _ _ _ _ _ _ _ _ _rd decision.

16.11 Put a tick (✓) if the sentence is grammatically correct. Put a cross (✗) if it is not.

1 I suggested a different idea. ☐
2 I suggested him a different idea. ☐
3 I suggested a different idea to him. ☐
4 I suggested using another approach. ☐
5 I suggested to use another approach. ☐
6 I suggested we should look at alternatives. ☐
7 I suggested it we should look at alternatives. ☐

(Note: *propose* and *recommend* have the same patterns)

16.12 One item in each group does not collocate with the verb. Cross it out.

1 hold	a meeting / all the cards / an opinion / a proposal / sb responsible for sth
2 take	part in a discussion / an effort to do sth / a decision / up a suggestion / another approach
3 reach	an agreement / a compromise / a dead-end / a decision / a demand
4 raise	awareness of the issue / a difficult challenge / the matter later / an important objection / an interesting question
5 meet	a challenge / a deadline / an issue / a need / an objective

---

Speaking / Writing practice

● Work in small groups. Have a discussion on one of the topics below.

– Computer games and children
– Fast food
– Genetic engineering
– Clean energy
– Working from home
– The future of Russia (or China)
– Euthanasia
– Transport issues in my city
– My favourite leisure technology
– UFOs
– Destruction of the environment
– Immigration
– Global warming
– Emotional intelligence
– The uses of location-based (satellite) technology
– Save the tiger! Save the panda! Why? We manage OK without the dinosaur.

or any current general / business news item

● When you finish, write the script for a part of the discussion that was interesting. Feel free to add other points – it is a language exercise, not a memory exercise.

17 Social English and cultural awareness

Social English

The mind map opposite shows some phrases for typical social situations, and the exercises on pages 74–75 refer to these. The remainder of this page gives an introduction to the closely-related topic of 'cross-cultural awareness'.

Diversity and tolerance

Here is a question: *Do you think that Americans are more outgoing and informal while Brits are more private and reserved?* We feel instinctively that there is some truth in this. However, having made a generalization, our next reaction is usually: *But wait, that's a stereotype, and anyway it depends on so many other things: age, ethnic group, regional differences, not to mention the individual person.* Everyone will have their own views. The point is simply this: to recognize that the way we think and behave is not the only way. When dealing with people from other cultures, and especially when actually doing business in another country, we need to observe and listen and show respect. That doesn't mean we have to abandon our normal way of doing things – we are also entitled to respect and tolerance from others, and we cannot just change our personalities. But if we want to have successful friendships and business relationships in an international context, then we have to understand and accept the differences.

National differences

Writers in the field of cross-cultural awareness look for opposing behaviours (or values) and then place different cultures at different points along the scale. Here is a simplified version of some well-known cultural differences; many are closely related. Notice how the descriptions are all neutral. There are no positive or negative connotations.

- **outgoing / informal** (share feelings easily with a wide circle of acquaintances) vs **private / reserved** (share feelings with care, and only with close friends and family)
- **live to work** (status comes through professional achievement) vs **work to live** (living a full, rounded, stress-free life is more important than just having money)
- **order** (the rules are the rules – society suffers if you break them) vs **flexibility** (sometimes we can ignore rules – the context, your conscience and friends are more important)
- **hierarchical** (we need clear direction from above to do our jobs properly) vs **democratic** (power should be distributed – everyone's opinion is important)
- **loose time** (deadlines are guidelines) vs **strict time** (delay is failure)

- **formality in names** (using *Mr X, Doctor X, Professor X* when speaking directly to someone) vs **informality in names** (moving quickly to first names, even for your boss)
- **expressive body language** (people wave their arms, move chairs around freely in meetings, look each other in the eye) vs **restrained body language** (small, subtle facial expressions carry significant meanings, physical contact in public or lingering eye contact is uncomfortable)
- **large personal space** (people stand at a distance when talking) vs **close personal space** (people stand near to each other)
- **self-determination** (we make free choices and control our lives) vs **fatalistic** (our lives are determined by god or destiny or the government)
- **personal fulfilment** (individual initiative and achievement are valued) vs **group fulfilment** (group harmony is valued – Who needs initiative when duties are fixed by tradition, leaders or team needs?)
- **merit** (respect is given to those who have earned it) vs **standing** (respect is given to those with the right age / social class / rank)
- **relationship** (if we can get along well, we can do a good job) vs **task** (if we can do a good job together, we might get closer as people)
- **welcoming risk** ('go for it!') vs **avoiding risk** ('better safe than sorry')
- **innovative** (new is exciting and always best) vs **traditional** ('if it isn't broken, why fix it?')
- **open disagreement** (competition between ideas is necessary to make the best decision) vs **subtle disagreement** (no-one must 'lose face' by being proved wrong in public, and consensus must be built slowly, so disagreement is signalled using code such as *Really?* or *I'm not sure about that.*)
- **multi-tasking** (people handle several things at the same time) vs **linear tasking** (people do one thing properly, and then move on)
- **lunch is a snack** (business and food do not mix) vs **lunch is a pleasure** (and the restaurant is a place to consolidate a business relationship)
- **pride in your country** (more than just football) vs **foreign is best** ('the grass is always greener on the other side of the fence')

Discuss these points, using your own national culture and others as examples. You can refer to the scale below. '1' means the culture is an extreme example of the behaviour / value mentioned first. '10' means it is an extreme example of the one mentioned second.

1	2	3	4	5	6	7	8	9	10

Preparing to go

Is that the time? I ought to make a move. > Oh, so soon? You don't have to rush off just yet do you?

Going

Well, I'd better be off now.
Well, I really must be going now.
It's been really nice meeting you.

Thanking

Thank you so much for ... I really appreciate it.
It was really kind of you to ...

Goodbye

Have a safe trip!
Say 'hello' to (Isabel) for me.
Give my regards to (Michael).
Best of luck for ...
Keep in touch!

Introductions

Formal: Allow me to introduce (Klaus Neuberger).

Informal: (Klaus), this is (Stefania). (Stefania), (Klaus).

Visitors

Hello, it's (Ruth Taylor), isn't it?
It's very nice to meet you, (Ruth).
Do have a seat.
Did you find us OK?
How was the flight?
Is this your first time in Cologne?

Ritual

How are you? > Fine, thanks, and you?
> Fine.
Nice / Pleased to meet you. >
Nice / Pleased to meet you, too.

Real question

How's it going?
How's life?

Saying 'hello'

Really?
Really!

Leaving

SOCIAL ENGLISH

Showing interest

Preparing for difficult news

Have you got a moment?
I have an apology to make.
There's something I've been meaning to tell you.

Action

Just bear with me for a moment.
I'll see what I can do.
Don't worry, I'll deal with it.
I'll do my best to sort it out.

Big requests

I was wondering if you could ...
Is there any chance you could ...
Would you mind ...? > No, not at all.

Apologies and Replies

I do apologize, I didn't mean to ...
I'm so sorry, I didn't realize that ...
That's quite all right.
Don't worry, it happens all the time.

Problems

Reacting to good news

You must be delighted!
Wow, that's fantastic

Reacting to bad news

How awful!
What a nightmare!
What a pity!
Poor you!

Reacting with surprise

You're joking! (UK)
You're kidding! (US)
That's strange!
Really?

Active listening

Mhm.
Uh-huh.
Right.
Really!

Add a follow-up question

So what happened next?
Why was that, then?
How come?
(= Why / How did that happen?)
What for? (= Why?)

Social English and cultural awareness: Exercises

17.1 Underline the words that a native speaker would probably say in the introductions and greetings below.

1 Diana, *here* / *this* is Steve.

2 Nice to meet you. ➡ Nice to meet you, *also* / *too*.

3 *Pleasure* / *Pleased* to meet you.

4 Hi, (Kristina), how are you *going* / *doing*?

5 How's it *going* / *doing*?

6 How's *life* / *the life*?

7 May I *present* / *introduce* myself?

8 You *must* / *should* be Chris Wood, is that right?

9 How are you? ➡ *Fine* / *Well*, thanks, and you?

10 Hi, (Peter), *good* / *I'm happy* to see you again.

11 Thank you so much for coming. I really *appreciate* / *appreciate it*.

12 Can I *have* / *take* your coat?

13 Did you find *us* / *here* okay?

14 Water? *With gas or without gas?* / *Still or sparkling*?

17.2 Tick (✓) the responses that are both possible <u>and</u> appropriate in a business context. Cross (✗) the ones that are not. More than one may be correct.

1 Allow me to introduce Petra Reinhart.
  a) Pleased to meet you. ☐
  b) How are you? ☐
  c) How do you do? ☐

2 Hi! How's it going?
  a) Nice to meet you. ☐
  b) Fine, fine. And you? ☐
  c) Actually, I'm having one or two personal problems at the moment. ☐

3 Did you arrive last night?
  a) Yes, of course. ☐
  b) Yes, that's right. ☐
  c) Yes, certainly. ☐

4 Could you bring me a glass of water?
  a) Yes, of course. ☐
  b) Yes, that's right. ☐
  c) Yes, certainly. ☐

5 Would you mind opening the window?
  a) Yes, of course. ☐
  b) Yes, I mind. ☐
  c) No, not at all. ☐

6 Do you mind if I open the window?
  a) Please do. ☐
  b) I do. ☐
  c) I'd rather you didn't, actually. ☐

7 Wonderful food!
  a) Yes, I think so. ☐
  b) Yes, certainly. ☐
  c) Yes, 'antastic. ☐

17.3 Put the lines of this dialogue into the correct order 1–9. You are introducing Leon to Teodora at a conference coffee break.

☐1 a) **You:** Do you two know each other?

☐ b) **You:** Let me introduce you, then. Leon, this is Teodora. Teodora, Leon.

☐ c) **You:** Leon is at UBS – we used to work together in Zurich.

☐ d) **Teodora:** No, we've never met.

☐ e) **Teodora:** Yes, you too.

☐ f) **Teodora:** Ah, so you're at UBS. That's interesting. I work in the area of security for online banking.

☐ g) **Teodora:** Of course, I'd be happy to explain. Perhaps we could have lunch together?

☐ h) **Leon:** Hi, Teodora. Nice to meet you.

☐ i) **Leon:** Really? That's a very important field for us. I'd like to find out more about what you do.

Notice in this dialogue how the person doing the introductions (*You*) gives some personal information in line c) to help the conversation to continue.

17.4 Make phrases by matching words from the first column with words from the second.

1 Wow, that's	kidding, right? ('joking' in BrE)
2 You're	change.
3 How	be delighted!
4 Poor	fantastic!
5 You must	news! Congratulations!
6 Yes, of	done!
7 What a	you.
8 That makes a	awful. I'm so sorry.
9 Well	course. Sure.
10 That's great	nightmare!

17.5 Look at how B shows interest in this dialogue:

A: *Mary went into hospital again.*

B: *Did she? Poor her. Which hospital?*

B replies in three stages. First with an 'echo question', then with a personal response, and finally with a follow-up question to keep the conversation going.

Respond to each piece of news below in the same way. First use a phrase from Box A below, then Box B, and finally Box C.

1 I'm going to France next week for a holiday.

_____

2 Hey, guess what. I got that job I wanted.

_____

3 Apparently, hundreds of people were made homeless when the Danube flooded.

_____

4 My car is being repaired – again. It's going to be three days before I get it back.

_____

5 Dave arrived an hour late this morning.

_____

Box A

| Are you?   Did he?   Did you?   Is it?   Were they? |

Box B

| Three days – what a nightmare!
Lucky you, I wish I was going!   How awful for them.
That's not like him.   Congratulations – you must be delighted! |

Box C

| What are your responsibilities going to be?
What did the boss say?   Can I give you a lift anywhere?
Which areas were affected?   Whereabouts? |

17.6 Complete the two dialogues by using the words in brackets to make whole phrases.

Dialogue 1

Naomi: Frank, ¹ _____*have you got a moment?*_____
(have / got / moment?)

Frank: Just ² _____ (bear / me) while I close down this program on my PC. Okay, what's the problem?

Naomi: I ³ _____ (wondering / if / help me). I tried to import a file into Excel and now the whole spreadsheet just looks like a big mess.

Frank: I'm not an expert, but I'll
⁴ _____ (do / best / sort / out).

Dialogue 2

Emil: Oh no! How stupid of me!
Roberta: What's up?
Emil: I ⁵ _____ (have / apology / make). I've put cream in the soup. I completely forgot you were allergic to dairy products. I'm really sorry, I
⁶ _____ (do it / purpose).
Roberta: Don't worry, that's quite alright. It
⁷ _____ (happens / time).

17.7 Complete the explanations by writing *Sorry* or *Excuse me*.

1 _____ is used: i) <u>before</u> you inconvenience sb; ii) to ask sb to repeat sth (in AmE)

2 _____ is used: i) <u>after</u> you inconvenience sb; ii) to ask sb to repeat sth (in BrE)

17.8 Complete these three conversation extracts in a restaurant.

Alice: Is that the time? I ought to ¹m_ _ _ a m_ _ _.
Pavel: Oh, ²s_ s_ _ _? You don't have to ³r_ _h o_ _ just yet, do you? ⁴H_ _ a_ _ _ _ some more coffee?
(10 minutes later …)
Alice: Well, I really ⁵m_ _ _ be g_ _ _ _ now. My flight leaves at 8:30 in the morning. It's been ⁶r_ _ _ _ _ n_ _ _ m_ _ _ _ _ _ you. And ⁷th_ _ _ you s_ m_ _ _ for showing me round Prague. I ⁸r_ _ _ _ a_ _ _ _ _ _ _ _ it.
Pavel: Don't ⁹me_ _ _ _ _ it. It was ¹⁰m_ p_ _ _ _ _ _.
(5 minutes later, outside the restaurant …)
Pavel: Have a ¹¹s_ _ _ tr_ _! And ¹²s_ _ 'h_ _ _ _' to Isabel f_ _ me.
Alice: I will do. And ¹³b_ _ _ of l_ _ _ for the presentation next week. Bye!
Pavel: Bye! ¹⁴K_ _ _ in t_ _ _ _!

Speaking practice

1 Exercises 17.2, 3, 5, 6 and 8 can be read aloud with a partner. Practise them, taking the other role when you finish. Think about intonation: sound friendly and interested.

2 Work in pairs.
a) You meet a colleague during the coffee break at an international conference. You have not seen each other for four years.
   ● Greet each other and make small talk.
b) Find another pair. One person in each pair knows the other (decide who).
   ● Make introductions.
   ● Make more small talk.
   ● Arrange for all of you to meet in the bar this evening.

c) Now you are in the bar.
   ● First, each of you tell a short story about something interesting / funny that happened to you recently. The others show interest.
   ● Then continue the conversation by talking for a short time about some of the following topics:
     – interests / sports / home
     – current affairs and the economy
     – business travel
     – cultural differences
d) Now it is the end of the evening.
   ● Prepare to go and then leave the bar together.
   ● Say goodbye.

18 Style – clarity and emphasis

Clarity and simplicity

In contexts like presentations or meetings there is a tendency for advanced learners of English to switch to a style which is too complicated and too formal. You might hear something like this in a presentation:

> "Consumer tastes and fashions are always in a process of change in the global marketplace, and for this reason in the near future I think it will be necessary for us to look at the possibility of making some modifications to the design of our range of products – in the manner which I have indicated in this next slide, which shows some of my initial ideas on the subject."

The extract above would be better like this:

> "Consumer tastes are always changing. Because of this, I think we'll have to make a few changes to the design of our products. Have a look at this next slide, which shows some of my ideas."

Here are some other examples of how to simplify language:

You have the possibility to … ➝ *You can …*
There is a chance that it will … ➝ *It might …*
It will be necessary for us to … ➝ *We need to …*
the price of commodities ➝ *commodity prices*
a document that shows you have insurance for sports that you practise in the winter ➝ *a winter sports insurance document*

There is a strong trend to clarity and simplicity in business communication. Simpler constructions and shorter sentences are easier to understand and have more impact. Business people value directness, and complex language can sound indirect or worse (perhaps you are trying to hide something).

However, complex formal language is not necessarily 'wrong'. In some contexts (eg legal documents, formal reports) it may actually be valued and expected. You always have to bear in mind the company culture, the expectations of the audience, etc.

Clarity in emails and letters

Read the different versions of the same email and then study the points below.

Version 1

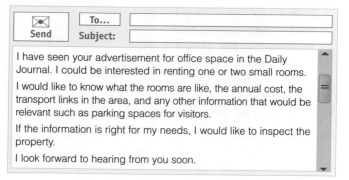

I have seen your advertisement for office space in the Daily Journal. I could be interested in renting one or two small rooms.

I would like to know what the rooms are like, the annual cost, the transport links in the area, and any other information that would be relevant such as parking spaces for visitors.

If the information is right for my needs, I would like to inspect the property.

I look forward to hearing from you soon.

Version 2

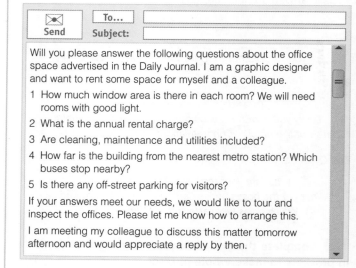

Will you please answer the following questions about the office space advertised in the Daily Journal. I am a graphic designer and want to rent some space for myself and a colleague.

1 How much window area is there in each room? We will need rooms with good light.
2 What is the annual rental charge?
3 Are cleaning, maintenance and utilities included?
4 How far is the building from the nearest metro station? Which buses stop nearby?
5 Is there any off-street parking for visitors?

If your answers meet our needs, we would like to tour and inspect the offices. Please let me know how to arrange this.

I am meeting my colleague to discuss this matter tomorrow afternoon and would appreciate a reply by then.

- Version 1 begins slowly. The writer gets to the point in the second paragraph but there are no clear, direct questions. The requests for information are listed together in one sentence and do not stand out. The close is friendly, but in this context a standard phrase is perhaps a little old-fashioned.
- Version 2 begins directly by stating the purpose of the email (to ask for information). The explanation is brief but a little more complete than Version 1. The questions, with an explanation included where needed, are numbered. Each starts a new line. This makes answering easy. The close gives a sense of urgency without being rude.

Emphasis

There are many individual words that can be used before adjectives, adverbs, nouns and verbs to intensify the meaning. Try reading aloud the following presentation extract two ways: first **without** and then **with** the words in bold. Both ways make sense, but the words in bold give emphasis.

> "Our business is going **extremely** well, but it could be going **even** better. The **whole** Chinese market is opening up, and I'm **absolutely** sure that there are **many** opportunities for us in that part of the world. It's **such** a huge market. We **really** can't pretend that we are a global company unless we **significantly** raise our profile in South East Asia."

Be careful: if you use too much of this kind of language it sounds like you are exaggerating and being insincere.

CLARITY AND EMPHASIS

Emphasis of ideas in an argument

above all, in particular
mainly, mostly, principally, predominantly
particularly, especially
specifically

Complicated / formal language > simple / conversational language

It will be necessary for us to ... > We will need to ...

Our expectations are that ... > We expect...

on an official basis > officially

You have the possibility to determine your own preferences. > You can choose.

verify > check

requirements > needs

inform > tell

in spite of the fact that > even though

Impact

Short, simple sentences call attention to their content.

Long, complicated sentences take time to understand.

Separating points

In writing, use numbering or bullet points.

In speech, say first of all, ..., secondly, ..., third, ... and finally ...

Position

The beginning and end carry more emphasis: this applies to a paragraph of text, an email, or a whole presentation.

✓ Good quality
✓ Good value
✓ Good Customer Support

Clarity

Emphasis by intensifying the following word

very, extremely (eg extremely successful)

far, considerably, much, significantly, even (eg much cheaper)

fully, totally, completely, absolutely (eg I'm fully aware that ...)

the whole, the entire (eg the whole process)

actually (eg It actually reduces our costs by 5%.)

(absolutely) no ... at all (eg There's absolutely no hope at all of ...)

really (eg We really can't ...)

such a ... (eg It's such a complex issue.)

so (eg The issue is so complex.)

Choice of language depends on context and audience

Report or email?

Formal or informal presentation?

Level of English of the readers / listeners?

18.1 Rewrite each sentence 1–6 using the words in brackets below. The number in bold shows the maximum words for the new sentence.

1 It will be necessary for us to request additional assistance. (need, ask for, more help – **8**)
We will need to ask for more help.

2 You have the possibility to determine your own preferences in relation to the colour. (can, choose – **6**)
You

3 These days the labour unions have a declining influence on governmental operations. (less, government – **9**)
These days the unions

4 My boss terminated Claudia's employment as a consequence of her ineffective performance. (fired, because of, poor – **9**)
My boss

5 Our expectations are that the price of commodities will go up in value. (expect, to rise – **6**)
We

6 In view of the fact that their requirements are so specific, I suggest that we verify all the details with exceptional care. (because, needs, let's check, very carefully – **13**)

18.2 Continue as in exercise 18.1. There are some bigger changes to make, but the meaning of the two versions is always the same.

1 I have an idea in mind for how we can utilize better credit control to make improvements to the situation regarding our cash flow. (know, use, improve – **14**)

2 The new regulations state that we have an obligation to stop using the PCs of the company for emails of a personal nature. (rules, say, must not, personal emails – **14**)

3 During the time we were talking she asked a great number of questions with regard to the recent modifications in our range of products. (while, lot, about, changes, product range – **18**)

4 Your line manager will make an appropriate decision about your bonus, in spite of the fact that the HR department has the responsibility for this on an official basis. (decide, even though, officially responsible – **15**)

18.3 Read this extract from a report.

> Although we have not definitely determined the causes for the decline in sales volume for March we know that during this period construction work on the street limited the number of customers who entered the store and also that because of staff changes in the advertising department promotion efforts were reduced.

It would be clearer if it was broken down into shorter sentences. Put in all the capital letters, commas and full stops in the version below.

> we have not definitely determined the causes for the decline in sales for March we know however that during this period construction work on the street limited the number of customers who entered the store in addition we know that promotion efforts were reduced as a result of staff changes in the advertising department

18.4 A customer writes an email asking for more time to pay an invoice. Here is a formal, old-fashioned reply.

✉ Send	To...	
	Subject:	

In reply to your email of April 4, we are pleased to inform you that permission is hereby granted to delay payment of your invoice ref D970 until May 15.

However, we are sure that you will understand our considerable concern in this matter. Should you have any further difficulties in the payment of an outstanding amount, kindly advise us at an early date.

Take a separate piece of paper. Write a simpler version by putting the phrases below into the correct order. Put in capital letters and full stops, but no extra words are needed.

> *regarding invoice D970 / your email / until May 15 / thank you for / to pay / we will give you / contact us immediately / the outstanding amount / any further problems / if you have / please*

18.5 Compare versions 1, 2 and 3 of a paragraph from a business report. Before you read statements a) and b) below, think carefully about the differences between the versions (clarity? simplicity? formality?).

Version 1

> Business activity started to get better in Q1 and we expect the improvement to continue. Our forecasts show that in Q2 sales for the whole company will go up – perhaps to about €1.2m. This is an increase of 8% from the same time last year.

Version 2

> The upturn in business activity that began in the first quarter should continue. In fact, it might even accelerate. Sales forecasts show that total sales from all business units should rise to around €1.2m in Q2. This is an 8% year-on-year increase – much higher than the corresponding figure for Q1.

Version 3

> The upturn in business activity that began in the first quarter of the year (Q1) is expected to continue, and indeed might even accelerate. Sales forecasts indicate that the total revenue from all business units combined should climb to a figure of approximately €1.2m in Q2, representing an 8% annualized increase, which is significantly higher than the corresponding figure for Q1.

Which statement below do you agree with: a or b? There is no 'right' answer!

a) Version 1 is okay. Everything is simple, clear and easy to understand. **Version 2 is the best** – a little more complexity and formality is right for a business report. Version 3 is too complicated. Non-native speakers might find it difficult to follow, and it lacks impact because it takes time to understand.

b) Version 1 is too conversational and fragmented for a report (although it would be okay in an email summary). It creates a bad image. Version 2 is better. But **version 3 is the best** – it shows the high standards of formal writing that international companies expect. If some non-native speakers find it difficult, that is their problem – they should improve their English.

18.6 Add the words in brackets at an appropriate place to give emphasis.

       really   *such*

1 We ∧ can't afford to ignore ∧ a good opportunity.
   (really, such)

2 I'm certain that we're in a better position now.
   (absolutely, far)

3 It's cheaper to use an outside firm for the graphic design work.
   (actually, much, all)

4 There is no truth in what they are saying – their story is lies.
   (absolutely, at all, whole, complete)

5 It's a risky project – I recommend that we take care.
   (highly, strongly, the greatest)

6 It's difficult to know whether the advertising campaign is going to work.
   (just so, actually)

7 I support the Board – they are doing an important job.
   (fully, entire, extremely)

8 I hope we see a rise in sales at Christmas – more than last year.
   (really, significant, even)

9 We can't decide quickly – the issue is too important.
   (really, so, far)

10 I agree – upgrading our computer network will take us over budget.
   (completely, entire, way)

Practise speaking the sentences to give maximum emphasis and impact.

Writing practice

- Collect some documents that you or your colleagues have written: business reports, academic writing, work-related emails, etc. Study them. How could they be clearer and simpler?
- Choose one of the documents (written by you or someone else). Rewrite it, starting from scratch.

Politeness in speech

Read this dialogue at a reception desk.

> A: Good morning, how can I help you?
>
> B: Oh, good morning. I **was wondering** if I could have a quick word with your Finance Director?
>
> A: Do you have an appointment?
>
> B: **Actually**, I don't.
>
> A: I see. That's **not** going to be **easy**. Mr Rodriguez is a very busy man.
>
> B: Of course, I understand that. I **just wanted** to speak to him for a couple of minutes, that's all.
>
> A: **Could you tell me** what it is about?
>
> B: Yes. **There seems to be** a mistake on an invoice you sent to my company. I thought it **might** help if I **spoke** to someone in person about it. I **would** be really grateful.
>
> A: May I see the invoice?
>
> B: Yes, here it is.
>
> A: **Why don't you** phone Mr Rodriguez about this? **As far as I know** he is in a meeting until 10:30, and you **would** have to wait.
>
> B: Yes, I **could** call him. But if there **was** a chance to speak to him at 10:30, I**'d** prefer that.

The words in bold help to make the language more polite and diplomatic. There are two opposing arguments on this subject:

1 So-called 'polite' language just sounds false to me. Why don't people just speak clearly and directly? If you are indirect then people won't know what you mean.

2 People value politeness, and it is worth adding a few extra words to improve your self-image. It allows the other person to 'save face' – it gives them an easier way to say 'no' or to suggest an alternative.

Each speaker of English has to decide for themselves when, and how much, polite language to use. The mind map opposite gives you a range of techniques to choose from. Here are some typical situations where they might be useful:

- You need to ask for a big favour.
- You do not know the other person very well.
- There is a formal context like a large meeting.
- You want to show respect to someone (because of their status, age, etc).
- The other person is from a culture where formality and politeness are valued and expected.

Softening a bad-news email or letter

Read the two different versions of the same email – which one do you prefer, and why?

Version 1

✉ Send	To...	
	Subject:	

We regret to inform you that the software pack you require is not in stock.

We are selling more of this item that we expected, and our suppliers are unable to meet the demand. We are hoping to receive more of these packs in the near future, and will contact you as soon as they arrive.

We apologize again for the inconvenience this has caused.

Version 2

✉ Send	To...	
	Subect:	

Thank you for ordering the new software pack – we are sure that it will make a big difference to the productivity of your business.

Many other companies have seen the advantage of using this software, and we have had a very high number of orders. New stock is expected within the next few days, and you can be sure that we will ship it to you as soon as it arrives.

If we can be of further help, please contact us quoting the reference above.

Now read one point of view below. Think about it, even if you don't agree with it.

- Version 1 states the bad news at the beginning and includes the negative words *regret* and *not in stock*. This immediately creates a bad feeling in the mind of the reader. The explanation that follows is clear, but includes the negative word *unable*. There is a promise to send the goods, but it is vague and unlikely to reassure the customer. The closing words leave the reader with a reminder of the bad news, and no suggestion for how to take follow-up action.

- The general problem with version 1 is that it states the facts without seeing things from the reader's viewpoint.

- Version 2 begins with a positive first sentence and reinforces the idea that the purchase decision was a good one. The explanation of why shipping is delayed uses no negative words. The message continues to be positive and reassuring. The closing words offer the reader a way to take follow-up action.

- The style of version 2 is generally more modern. It is more informal, more friendly, and is written from the reader's viewpoint.

Indirect questions

I need to know ... > Could you tell me ...?

Negative question
(becomes a suggestion)

It would be better to ...
> Wouldn't it be better to ...?

Present > Past

How much do you want to spend?
> How much did you want to spend?

Simple > Continuous

I hope you can ... > I'm hoping you can ...

Past + Continuous
(gives two levels of distancing)

I wonder if I can ... > I was wondering if I could ...
I hope you will ... > I was hoping you would ...

Using the passive to de-personalize an issue

You promised us ... > We were promised ...

First conditional > Second conditional

If there's a chance to ..., I'll be very grateful.
> If there was a chance to ..., I'd be very grateful.

Distancing

Giving an opinion

POLITENESS AND SOFTENING

Softening

Introducing a polite refusal or bad news

I'm sorry but ...
I'm afraid ... (BrE)
Unfortunately, ...
Actually, ...

can > could, will > would / might

We could try to ...
We would have to ...
That might be difficult.

seem

There seems to be/It seems that there is a misunderstanding.

a small / a slight + noun

There may be a slight delay

a bit / slightly + adjective

The price is slightly higher than last year

just

Could I just interrupt for a moment?

Negative-sounding adjective > not + opposite

That's wrong. > With respect, that's not quite correct.

Your products are expensive.
> Your products aren't cheap.

You said ... > I understood ...

I understood that the discount was 4%.

Use of vague language

Did you read my email? > Did you have a chance to read my email?

There are two things I need to discuss with you. > There are a couple of things I need to discuss with you.

It's getting late. I have to leave. > It's getting kind of late. I guess I should leave soon.

Making it personal rather than general

I think...
I suppose ...
I reckon ... (informal)
In my view / opinion, ... (formal)

Information may not be true

Apparently ...
It seems that ...
As far as I know ...
To the best of my knowledge ...

Reformulating something too strong or too definite

Or rather, ...
I mean ...
That's to say, ...
At least, ...

Style – politeness and softening: Exercises

19.1 Make the sentences below more polite or 'soft'. Use the words in brackets.

1 We have a problem. (seems / slight)
   It seems we have a slight problem.

2 Can I interrupt? (could / just / for a moment)

3 There'll be a delay. (might / just / small)

4 You said you can deliver by the end of March.
   (understood / could)

5 Our competitors are expensive. (I'm afraid / not very)

6 It would be better to ship to Rotterdam.
   (wouldn't / Rotterdam?)

7 There are three things I want to discuss.
   (one or two / wanted)

8 I assume that the paperwork is okay. (am)

9 We're unhappy with the quality of this repair.
   (I'm sorry / not very)

10 We expected a more flexible response.
   (hoping for / slightly)

11 Please show me round your factory.
   (I / grateful for the chance / have a look round)

12 Please show me your designs for next season.
   (was wondering / I could / a quick look at)

13 You don't understand how important this is.
   (With respect / don't seem)

14 You must give us more time.
   (We / appreciate it / if / could / a little more)

15 I can speak to my boss about it, but I don't promise
   anything. (suppose / could / but / not promising)

16 Their business is going very badly.
   (apparently / not / well)

17 There are some technical problems to sort out.
   (far / I know / just a couple of)

19.2 The first sentence below is too definite – or just wrong. So the speaker reformulates it in the second sentence. Make a phrase using the letters in italics.

1 He doesn't seem very experienced. *aelmn*
   _____I mean_____ he hasn't been in the company very long.

2 The project is not going to finish on time. *aAelstt*
   _____ , I don't think it will.

3 I'm meeting her on Tuesday. *aeOhrrrt*
   _____ , Wednesday.

4 I'm not working for them again. *aaoh'ssTtty*
   _____ , not unless they pay me more.

19.3 Read the dialogue below.

A: I think you have the old price list. The prices quoted there are not current.
B: But your sales consultant gave this list to me just last month[1].
A: We've had some big increases in our costs recently. Raw materials are becoming a lot more expensive. We had to raise all our prices by 4% from the beginning of this month[2].
B: I see. Is there any way to avoid the increase?
A: Well, you could switch to another product with a lower performance[3]. If you do that, you'll save money[4].
B: No, I don't want to do that. What about if we increased our order?
A: I see what you're saying. But that's going to be difficult[5]. You already have a very generous quantity discount.
B: But is it possible?
A: How many more units are you thinking of[6]?
B: Perhaps another 500 units a month.
A: I'm sorry, but an increase of that size will not be enough to give you a bigger discount[7].

The small numbers come at the end of a sentence that is going to be changed. Make a script by writing a new version on a separate piece of paper:

1: change an active to a passive, leaving out who does the action

2: add the word *unfortunately*

3: add the word *slightly*

4: change a first conditional (*If* + present) to a second conditionals (*If* + past)

5: change a negative-sounding adjective to *not* + the opposite

6: change a present continuous to a past continuous

7: change *will* to *would*

Practise reading aloud the new version. If possible, work with another person and change roles at the end.

19.4 Read this email. It is saying 'no' to a request for a refund for an unwanted product.

> To...
> Send   Subject:
>
> I am writing in relation to your request for a refund for the shoes that you ordered from our website. Thank you for returning the shoes, which we received this morning.
>
> Unfortunately, we are unable to send you a refund. We examined the shoes and found that they had been used outside. This means that we cannot resell the item to other customers. We will return the shoes to you, and you should receive them within ten working days.
>
> We trust that you will understand our position and we regret any inconvenience caused.

The email below is a more positive and friendly alternative. First make phrases by matching an item from the left column with one from the right. Then use the phrases to complete the email.

consider the sale	conditions
in the	stated
suitable for	final
terms and	days
with the relevant	circumstances
this is clearly	to do
we are willing	resale
within ten working	section highlighted

> To...
> Send   Subject:
>
> You have a right to expect the best possible service from Shoes4U, and ¹_____ as much as we reasonably can to make things right.
>
> With returned items, we generally give refunds. Of course, all returned items must be in new condition and ²_____ . You will notice that ³_____ in the '⁴_____' section of our online order form. I attach a copy of this form ⁵_____ .
>
> We examined the shoes you returned to us and found that they had been used outside. ⁶_____ , we must therefore ⁷_____ .
> We are returning the shoes to you, and you should receive them ⁸_____ .
>
> We look forward to serving you.

19.5 First read the email below. It is a refusal to a request to speak at a conference.

> To...
> Send   Subject:
>
> I am sorry but I am unable to accept your invitation to speak at the annual conference of the National Association of Small Businesses (NASB). I am going to be very busy during that period and cannot clear the time in my schedule.
>
> In any case, thank you for your invitation and I wish you every success in the organization of your conference.

The email below is a more positive and friendly alternative. Put the sentences into the correct order, and into paragraphs.

Paragraph 1: [b] [ ]
Paragraph 2: [c] [ ] [ ] [ ]
Paragraph 3: [ ] [ ] [ ]

a) Unfortunately, my time is already fully committed over that period, and so I must suggest that you get someone else.

b) Thank you for your email inviting me to speak at the annual conference of the National Association of Small Businesses (NASB).

c) As you know, presenting a paper to an audience of such experienced professionals requires a good deal of thought and planning.

d) Anyway, thank you again for the invitation, and if I can help you further in your efforts to get a speaker, please get back to me.

e) It is a great honour to be asked to speak at this event, as the work of NASB in promoting small businesses is well known.

f) I'm sure the conference will be a great success.

g) Martha is an outstanding speaker and an expert on financing issues for small businesses.

h) May I recommend Martha Ballard, a colleague of mine?

i) Good luck with everything!

19.6 Look back at the second (more friendly) email in exercise 19.5. Tick (✓) the statements below that are true about this email.

1 the writer shows he / she values the request [ ]
2 the writer gives a reason for refusing the request [ ]
3 the writer uses no negative words [ ]
4 the writer makes a helpful suggestion [ ]
5 the writer ends formally as a sign of respect [ ]

Speaking / Writing practice

- Brainstorm two typical situations where one person has to be polite to someone else. You can have a mixture of business and non-business situations.
- Write the script for each conversation.
- Practise reading the script with a colleague / friend.
- If you are working in a group, practise reading other people's scripts.

20 Developing an argument – linking words 1

Linking words

Read the text and then study the bullet points below.

How do multinational companies operate in today's global economy? Vietnam gives us a clue. **Although** infrastructure is poor **and** there is a shortage of skilled workers, Intel has opened a plant in Ho Chi Minh City. The reason is clear: wage levels are
5 low. **In fact**, they are about a third of those in China. Intel continues to produce chips at its fabrication plants in Ireland and the US, **but** these chips are then exported to Vietnam for the labour-intensive work of
10 test and assembly. From Vietnam, they are re-exported to other countries in Southeast Asia. **As regards** the domestic market in Vietnam itself, current sales are low – most people can only afford a cheap desktop PC using unbranded components. **However**, with a
15 population of over 80 million and information-hungry youths filling the Internet cafés, there is a lot of potential.

    In addition, Intel gains by the fact that its outsourcing operations are more diversified. If there
20 are any problems at its other plants in Shanghai, Malaysia or the Philippines, it can simply switch production. There is also a certain degree of competition between the different facilities, and **as a result** there is downward pressure on wages at them
25 all. **Even so**, it would be a mistake to assume that these workers see themselves as exploited. **In most cases**, workers in developing countries want to work for multinationals, **and** the pay and conditions are better than at local companies.

Look back at the sentence beginning *Although* (line 3). There are actually three separate clauses:

Infrastructure is poor (in Vietnam).
There is a shortage of skilled workers.
Intel has opened a plant in Ho Chi Minh City.

- The writer has used the linking words *and* and *although* to join these clauses together and produce a more complex sentence. With the linking words, the text is easier to read. The relationship between the ideas is clearer.

- Also, with the linking words the style changes. It becomes more formal, typical of a presentation, a meeting or a report. In an everyday conversation or an email it would be normal to use much shorter clauses.

Look at the words *although* (line 3), *but* (line 8) and *however* (line 14) in the text. Are they the same? Think about any differences in meaning and use before you read the next three bullet points.

- *Although* makes a contrast within one sentence. It introduces information that is less important, or surprising. It can come at the beginning or in the middle: *Intel has opened a plant in Ho Chi Minh City,* **although** *infrastructure is poor and there is a shortage of skilled workers.*

- *But* makes a simple contrast within one sentence and comes in the middle. There is a trend for writers to use *but* at the beginning of a sentence to contrast with the previous sentence, but some people think this is not good style.

- *However* comes at the beginning of a sentence and is followed by a comma. It makes a contrast with the previous sentence, or even the previous paragraph.

Other linking words and phrases in the text are written in bold. Study them now.

- Several linking words in the text start a sentence and are followed immediately by a comma. How many like this can you find?

- Look at the phrase *as a result* on line 23. The writer could also have used it at the start of a sentence followed by a comma:
There is also a certain degree of competition between the different facilities. **As a result***, there is downward pressure on wages at them all.*

But the writer decided that in this particular case it was better to put *and as a result* in the middle of a longer sentence. Perhaps it seemed less fragmented.

In general, linking words show a clear connection between clauses, sentences and paragraphs. They show the structure and logic of an argument. Using them effectively is a powerful communication tool.

Types of linking words

The mind map opposite shows how *but, although* and *however* represent three categories of linking words. In advanced grammar books they are given separate names ('coordinating conjunctions', 'subordinating conjunctions' and 'discourse markers'). To avoid these complicated terms many books just use 'linking words and phrases' for everything.

Note: a 'clause' is a grammatical unit that has a subject and a verb (and often an object as well) and forms a simple sentence on its own.

Adding another point
Also
As well as that
In addition
Besides
Furthermore (slightly formal)
Moreover (formal

Emphasizing a contrast
However
Even so
In spite of this
(slightly formal)
Nevertheless
(slightly formal)

Balancing with an equal, contrasting idea
In contrast
On the other hand

Giving a result
Therefore
As a result
For this reason
Because of this
Consequently (formal)

Giving a cause
Because of
As a result of
Owing to
Due to

Listing points
First / Firstly
First of all
To begin with
Secondly
Then
Next
Finally

Talking generally
In general
On the whole
Broadly speaking
In most / many cases
To a great extent

Giving examples
For example
For instance
such as

Expressing reality
In fact
As a matter of fact
Actually
In reality
To tell the truth

Linking words (used like 'but')

and, but and yet
(but expresses equal, contrasting ideas; yet expresses something more surprising)
so
or
nor

DEVELOPING AN ARGUMENT 1

Linking words (used like 'however')

Linking words (used like 'although')

although, though, even though,
in spite of the fact that (formal)

whereas (slightly formal),
while (slightly formal)

despite, in spite of

if, even if, whether, on condition that, unless

after, before, as soon as, while, until

because, since, as

to, so as to, in order to,
in order that, so (that)

Developing an argument – linking words 1: Exercises

20.1 Match one item in each column according to meaning.

informal	formal	formal
1 and	however	as
2 but	furthermore	consequently
3 so	since	nevertheless
4 because	therefore	moreover

20.2 For each word or phrase in bold, underline the one word or phrase in brackets below that is most similar in meaning.

1 **Because** it has above-average sales and earnings growth, Glaxo is a favourite on Wall Street.
   (Since / Due to / Therefore)

2 **Because of** its above-average sales and earnings growth, Glaxo is a favourite on Wall Street.
   (Since / Due to / Therefore)

3 Apple needs to constantly update its product line, **in order to** stay ahead of other consumer electronics companies like Sony and Samsung.
   (so that / so as to / owing to)

4 Apple needs to constantly update its product line, **in order that** it can stay ahead of other consumer electronics companies like Sony and Samsung.
   (so that / so as to / owing to)

5 **Although** the core rate of inflation rose only 0.2% in January, analysts are concerned about higher energy costs.
   (In spite of the fact that / In spite of / So that)

6 **Despite** the low rise in the core rate of inflation in January, analysts are concerned about higher energy costs.
   (In spite of the fact that / In spite of / So that)

7 Nokia is strong in Europe, **whereas** Motorola is strong in the US.
   (as / though / while)

8 Nokia is strong in Europe, **although** Motorola is giving it very strong competition.
   (as / though / while)

20.3 Underline the correct words in italics to make grammar rules. The answers to exercise 20.2 will help you.

1 *Because / Because of* is followed by a clause (subject + verb), while *because / because of* is followed by a noun or noun phrase (no verb).

2 *In order to / In order that* is followed by subject + verb, while *in order to / in order that* is followed immediately by the infinitive form of a verb.

3 *Although / Despite* is followed by a clause, while *although / despite* is followed by a noun or noun phrase.

4 *Whereas / Although* introduces something surprising, while *whereas / although* just compares two facts of equal importance and emphasizes the difference between them.

20.4 Write words and phrases with a similar meaning.

1 because: as / s_ _ _e
2 because of: d_ _ t_ / as a r_ _ _ _ _ of / ow_ _ _ to
3 in order to: to / s_ a_ to
4 in order that: so / so that
5 although: though / e_ _ _ though /
                 in s_ _ _ _ o_ the f_ _ _ that
6 despite: in spite of
7 whereas: wh_ _ _

When you finish, substitute these words into the sentences in exercise 20.2 and read them aloud. This will help you to remember the variety that is available.

20.5 Complete the conversation extract below with the words in the box. Look carefully at the logic of the argument.

also   because of   but   so

❝Yes, people say there's been a lot of damage to US industries because of China. [1]_____ , if you look at the figures carefully, the situation isn't so bad. Jobs have been lost in manufacturing, that's true, but new jobs have been created in the service sector. [2]_____ , the US trade figures with East Asia aren't that bad. When you look at the whole region, the deficit has stayed more or less the same for several years. Surprised? I'll tell you the reason – it's [3]_____ globalization. Yes, China has been growing, but a lot of that growth is because it assembles goods that were previously made in other Asian countries. [4]_____ , at the end of the day, the US is importing the same amount of stuff from Asia, but now it's all made in China.❞

20.6 Compare the version of the same text below. It is more formal, and typical of a written report. Complete it with the words in the box.

consequently   due to   furthermore   however

It is widely thought that there has been substantial damage to specific US industries as a result of competition with China. [1]_____ , if you look at the new service jobs created as a result of trade with China, the actual net loss in American jobs is marginal. [2]_____ , the US trade imbalance is not as bad as many commentators claim. In fact, when we consider the East Asia region as a whole, the deficit has remained basically the same – around 30% – for several years. What is the reason for this relatively stable trade deficit? It is [3]_____ increased economic integration within the Asian market. China's exports have risen dramatically, but that's largely because Japanese, Korean, Taiwanese and Singaporean companies have been moving their own production to the Chinese mainland. [4]_____ , the US is importing a similar amount of goods from Asia as before, but the trade has a different pattern. Much of the business is done with pre-existing non-Chinese trading partners who have simply relocated their operations to China.

20.7 Complete each example with the best pair of linking phrases from the box. Look carefully at the logic of the argument.

| As a matter of fact / For instance | ~~Broadly speaking / Therefore~~ |
| In fact / To a great extent | On the whole / However |

1 _____Broadly speaking_____ , sales and marketing are not coordinated very well. _____Therefore_____ , we should reorganize the department.

2 _____ , open source software like Linux is making a big impact in the world of IT. _____ , it is unlikely to threaten Windows' dominance in the mass market.

3 _____ , she has quite a lot of experience in the sales area. _____ , she worked as a rep in France for two years, going to all the trade fairs and speaking directly with customers.

4 _____ , quality is not just a technical and production issue. _____ it is also a design issue: products have to appeal to a customer's aesthetic sense.

20.8 Look at the box in exercise 20.7 and find:

1 two phrases that mean the same as 'Actually':

_____

_____

2 two phrases that mean the same as 'In general':

_____

_____

20.9 Complete this text by writing the best word or phrase from those in the box. Look carefully at the logic of the argument.

| as | as a result | ~~due to~~ | even if | finally |
| in fact | in spite of | on the other hand | | |

In coming decades, a key challenge for countries in the euro zone is going to be its ageing population. [1] _Due to_ low fertility rates and a lower mortality rate amongst older people, the share of the working-age population will fall from around 67% now to just 56% in 2050. This will create problems for the tax systems of the countries concerned. [2]_____ , some people think this is the greatest long-term challenge that Europe faces. The reason is as follows: governments will have to raise taxes on the working population to fund pension systems, otherwise elderly people will vote them out of office. This rise in taxes can only come from company profits and employees' salaries. [3]_____ , companies will have less money to invest in their businesses and the purchasing power of consumers will fall. This will create a vicious cycle [4]_____ it means lower economic growth and therefore, in turn, less profits and taxes.

What options do governments have? [5]_____ more women and long-term unemployed people take jobs, it will not be enough to solve the problem. It seems that there are three answers. First of all, workers will have to retire later. Next, private pension schemes will have to become far more widespread. And [6]_____ , economies will surely depend much more on immigration to sustain economic growth. It is true that increased immigration has caused social problems in many countries. But, [7]_____ , immigrants have been prepared to do work that natives won't do, working for long hours and low pay. And immigrants are young, and young people are what Europe increasingly needs. So, [8]_____ the problems, their numbers are likely to grow.

Writing practice

- Choose **one** of these texts: *How do multinational companies operate in today's global economy?* (page 84) or *In coming decades, a key challenge for countries in the euro zone is going to be its aging population.* (page 87).

- Read the text again several times, then write the first sentence at the top of a separate piece of paper.
- Write another text beginning with the same first sentence. Use your own ideas. Feel free to refer to the mind map as you write.

Developing an argument – linking words 2

Developing an argument

Read the dialogue and then study the bullet points below.

> A: Have you seen this article about 'peak oil'? It **seems that** most of the oil in the ground has already been discovered, and production in the Middle East is slowly declining. It's quite worrying if you stop to think about it.
>
> B: **Obviously** you're a pessimist. What about the ability of markets to come up with a solution? Look, **for one thing**, as the price of oil goes up, all sorts of other energy sources will become economically viable. **And for another**, I'm sure that technology will help us – it always has in the past.
>
> A: But it's different this time. **To begin with**, China and India are growing so fast – just imagine the oil consumption if they all had cars like in the west. **And then** there's global warming – we can't just go on releasing greenhouse gases like we do now. **We must** do something about it, **otherwise** it'll be a disaster.
>
> B: **As far as** China and India **are concerned**, there's plenty of new technology to replace oil: wind, solar, tides, bio-fuels, natural gas, Canadian oil sands, fuel cell technology, not to mention nuclear. When the cost of energy rises enough, they'll all get developed. And **it's true that** there may be a problem with global warming, **but** what can we do as individuals? The temperature of the world has been changing since time began – think of the ice ages.
>
> A: **To be honest**, I don't think you're aware of how serious things are. **Of course** there's always been climate change, **but even so** all scientists agree that this time it's because of human activity, and the situation is getting worse. **Unless** we do something, **we** just **won't** be able to have the same lifestyle that we do now. And there are lots of things that individuals can do. **Firstly**, we can all reduce our energy consumption by driving smaller cars and flying less, **and secondly** there are ways to conserve energy in the home – better insulation, that kind of thing.
>
> B: **Ironically**, you are the one who flies all over the world on exotic holidays. But **as regards** energy conservation, yes I do agree with you. **In general** we should try to consume less energy, **although** I still think it's higher prices that will make people do that, not their green conscience.
>
> A: **By the way, on the subject of** 'green conscience', have you heard that there's a new vegetarian restaurant near the university? **Apparently** it's quite good.

- In the dialogue there are linking phrases that allow the speaker to make a personal comment. Examples are: *it seems that, obviously, to be honest, ironically* and *apparently*. Find these words in the text and check their use in the mind map.
- There are also linking phrases in the dialogue that allow the speaker to make two related points. One example is: *for one thing … and for another*. Can you find two more examples?
- Another important technique for developing an argument is to first concede a point (*yes …*), and then dismiss it (*… but not in this case*). One example in the dialogue is: *it's true that … but …*. Can you find one more?
- A related technique is to first generalize, and then qualify (limit) your generalization. There is one example – can you find it?
- There are also two examples of structures that a grammar book would call 'conditionals', in other words saying what will happen in certain circumstances. Can you find them?
- In relation to formality, all the language listed in the mind map under 'Making a personal comment' is informal (conversation and emails) and everything else is slightly more formal (careful speech, meetings, presentations, reports, etc).

Contradictory points

Any speaker or writer who is developing an argument has to show that they have considered several points of view, including those that go against their own argument. In real life things are not black and white and there are exceptions to any general rule. By dealing with these contradictory points you demonstrate more complex thought, and the listener is more likely to be impressed and persuaded. In a business report or university paper this style is expected.

In the dialogue above you saw some examples of this kind of language: the phrases for 'Conceding a point but then dismissing it' and 'Generalizing and then qualifying'. There is an additional branch of the mind map that lists eight common lexical structures for discussing contradictory points. They are all fixed expressions: use them exactly as they are here.

On the one hand ...
but on the other ...

At first ... but in the end ...
At the time ... but in retrospect ...
In theory ... but in practice ...
On paper ... but in reality...
On the surface ... but deep down ...

Under normal circumstances ...
but in the current situation ...

In the short term ...
but in the long term ...

Contradictory points

Making a personal comment

You heard something, but are not sure
It seems that, Apparently

Something is true, but surprising
Actually, In fact, Strangely enough,
Believe it or not

Something is obvious or already known
Clearly, Obviously

Good / Bad fortune
Fortunately, Luckily, Unfortunately, Sadly

Saying what you really think
To be honest, Frankly

Saying something confidential
Between you and me,
Please don't repeat this but ...

Other phrases
Hopefully, Amazingly,
Ironically, Understandably,
Predictably, Presumably

DEVELOPING AN ARGUMENT 2

Saying what will happen in certain circumstances (conditionals)

Linking words 2

Making two related points
Firstly ... and secondly ...
To begin with ... and then ...
For one thing ...
and for another ...
In the first place ...
and then on top of that ...

Conceding a point, but then dismissing it
It's true that ... but ...
Of course ... but even so ...
Certainly ... however ...
Admittedly ... but nevertheless ... (formal)

Generalizing and then qualifying
In general ... although ...
On the whole ... but ...
In most cases ... however ...

Announcing a change of subject in advance
As regards ...
Regarding ...
As far as ... is concerned
In relation to ... (slightly formal)
With reference to ... (formal)

Changing the topic
By the way,
Incidentally, (slightly formal)
Talking about ...
On the subject of ...

If ..., it'll probably mean that ...
We must ..., otherwise ...
Unless ..., it will...

Developing an argument – linking words 2: Exercises

21.1 Study a)–e), noticing the phrases in italics.

a) *For one thing* it's too expensive, *and for another* the design is quite old-fashioned.

b) *As far as* the press conference *is concerned*, we need to reassure everyone that the situation is under control.

c) Yes, all our jobs are going to be at risk if the merger goes through. *Incidentally*, did you manage to get any tickets for the game on Saturday?

d) *In general* her decisions about marketing strategy are very good, *although* on this occasion I think she has overlooked the importance of the Internet.

e) *Of course* Silvia has a lot of experience in this field, *but even so* I think the project is too big for just one person.

Now match each phrase in italics above to the one below with the closest meaning. Write the sentence letter in the box.

1 By the way, … ☐

2 As regards … ☐

3 Admittedly … , but nevertheless … ☐

4 On the whole … , but … ☐

5 In the first place … , and then on top of that … ☐

Say sentences a)–e) aloud with both alternatives.

21.2 Fill in each gap with a word from the box. Several answers may be possible, but one solution uses all the words in an appropriate way.

Actually	Amazingly	Presumably	Clearly
Frankly	Ironically	Predictably	Unfortunately

1 A: Can you help us with this email? It's written in Spanish.
    B: _____ *Actually* _____ I'm Brazilian, so I speak Portuguese not Spanish. But I'm sure I can help you.

2 The trend in IT is for software and data to migrate from the individual PC to the network. _____ , this is quite like the situation with mainframe computers in the seventies and eighties.

3 _____ , we can get the information quite easily from Google. But I haven't actually looked for it yet.

4 _____ , the original 19th-century London Bridge is now in the Arizona Desert! It was sold in 1962 to an American oil millionaire, dismantled, and then reassembled brick by brick. It is now a major tourist attraction.

5 Hello? Is that Melanie Bryant? Yes, it's about your order. _____ we're having some problems processing your payment. Can you check at your end to make sure it's been authorized?

6 A: They say they can deliver the materials by the end of the month.
    B: _____ , I don't care. We've already had one bad experience with them and I think we should look for another supplier.

7 _____ , if they want a tailor-made version, they'll have to give us detailed specifications. I'm sure they know that.

8 Cadbury Schweppes announced a cut in its expected earnings on Monday. _____ , the whole food and beverages sector saw lower share prices following the announcement.

21.3 Complete the text with the structures in italics. Note that they all need two gaps.

As far as … is concerned …	*Firstly … Secondly …*
Unless … it will …	*In most cases … but …*
It is true that … however …	

[1]_____ Spain represents only 2% of global GDP, _____ it has produced some multinationals that are major players on the global stage. What are the reasons for this success? [2]_____ , they have focused on what they do best: large-scale operations. Examples include Telefónica (telecommunications networks), Repsol and Iberdrola (energy) and Ferrovial (infrastructure). _____ , they have made significant moves into Latin America, taking advantage of the common language and culture. Banks like Banco Santander and BBVA have been very active in these markets. [3]_____ these success stories have been large, publicly listed companies, _____ some family-owned firms have also done well. Examples include Freixenet, the leading exporter of sparkling wines to the US, and Inditex, the owner of the Zara clothing brand. [4]_____ the future _____ , competition is going to get tougher. By concentrating on Latin America, Spanish companies have already picked the 'low-hanging fruit'. There are some major challenges ahead, especially in terms of top management. [5]_____ these companies develop more senior executives with international experience, _____ be difficult to expand into the rest of the world.

21.4 Review some conditional structures. Fill in the gaps with these words: *in case, otherwise, provided that, unless, whether.*

1 _____ we have managers with international experience, we won't be able to compete in the global marketplace.

2 _____ we have managers with international experience, we will be able to compete in the global marketplace.

3 We need managers with international experience, _____ we won't be able to compete in the global marketplace.

4 Our ability to compete in the global marketplace depends on _____ or not we have managers with international experience.

5 We need to start recruiting some senior managers who speak Spanish, _____ one day we want to enter the Latin American market.

21.5 Answer these two questions, choosing from the words and phrases in italics in exercise 21.4:

1 Which one means the same as all of these: *on condition that / as long as / if and only if*?

2 Which one is used in almost the same way as *if*, but (i) it is more common when there is a choice between two possibilities, (ii) it is more common when the word *or* is also used and (iii) it is used before an infinitive (so not *I can't decide ~~if~~ to go to the conference*)?

21.6 Look at the sentence in the box, and in particular the form of the words in italics.

> If we *recruit* some Spanish-speaking managers, we *will be* able to operate in Latin America.

Now follow these instructions:

1 Make the sentence in the box less certain – it is just a hypothetical idea in the mind of the speaker.
If we _____ some Spanish-speaking managers, we _____ able to open an office in Mexico.

2 Make the sentence in the box about the past. The speaker is expressing regret because they didn't recruit any Spanish-speaking managers.
If we _____ some Spanish-speaking managers, we _____ able to open an office in Mexico.

3 Make the sentence about the past again. This time the speaker is expressing relief – they did recruit Spanish-speaking managers and because of this they were able to open the office.
If we _____ any Spanish-speaking managers, we _____ able to open an office in Mexico.

● Remember that all modal verbs are possible in conditionals. For example, *may / might* could be used in 1 above to make the result less certain than *would*.

21.7 Choose a phrase from the box to complete each sentence below. Several answers are possible each time, but one solution uses all the words in an appropriate way.

> ~~On the one hand ... but on the other ...~~
> At first ... but in the end ...
> At the time ... but in retrospect ...
> On paper ... but in reality...
> On the surface ... but deep down ...
> Under normal circumstances ... but in the current situation ...
> In the short term ... but in the long term ...

1 _____On the one hand_____ the quality is good, _____but on the other_____ the price is quite high.

2 _____ she was quiet and shy, _____ she knew what she wanted and was determined to get it.

3 _____ Hong Kong Disneyland looks like it should be a great success, _____ it will be a challenge to adapt the Disney formula to such a different culture.

4 _____ I found my MBA course very difficult, _____ I got used to the workload and started to really enjoy it.

5 _____ we need to establish our presence in the market and increase the visibility of the brand, _____ profitability will of course be the number one objective.

6 _____ I would agree with you, _____ I just don't think we can afford to take any risks. Let's put your suggestion on hold and discuss it again in six months.

7 _____ it was difficult to leave my job at 28 and invest time and money in an MBA, _____ it was the best career move I ever made.

● Note: *in the end* (#4 above) means 'finally' or 'eventually', while *at the end* refers to the last part of something.

Writing practice

● Choose a topic for a short report. If you are a student, choose an academic topic related to your course. If you are working, choose a typical report from real life. In either case, think of something where the issues and arguments are quite complex.

● Write the report. Feel free to refer to the mind map.

Developing an argument

Read the text and then study the bullet points below.

Never before has business ethics been such a hot topic. A succession of scandals at major corporations like Enron, WorldCom and Tyco caused the US Congress to pass the Sarbanes-Oxley Act in
5 2002 – a major piece of anti-fraud legislation. **Some people argue that** a combination of anti-fraud and equal opportunities laws is enough to ensure ethical practices, and **up to a point**, they may be right. **After all**, American business does seem cleaner and fairer
10 these days. But on the other hand, these laws only come into play after a crisis has occurred, and are **predominantly** concerned with areas like financial reporting, contracts and discrimination. **What companies really need is** a set of standards and codes
15 that describe what is ethical and unethical in the wider sense of society and the environment, and that prevent problems from happening. Moreover, these standards and codes have to be **considerably more** effective than in the past. For example, high-level
20 managers need to take personal responsibility for detecting and preventing misconduct. **Likewise**, whistleblowers lower down in the organization who report misconduct must be protected.

    From a financial point of view, having a strong
25 ethical policy can be good for business. Consumers dislike companies that exploit cheap labour in poor countries or harm the environment, and 'corporate social responsibility' has become a key part of brand image. Of course a company's social audit is still
30 **relatively less** important **than** its financial audit. But it is **in a sense** a victory for ethical campaigners when, for example, the annual report of a company needs to list its contributions to society in order to keep the shareholders happy.

35   **Taking all this into consideration, I am convinced** that ethical considerations will have a growing importance in the company of the future. It is true that government legislation already exists in many areas, but certain core values like integrity,
40 honesty, fair play, commitment to diversity and involvement in the community need extra support. They are too general to be created or defended by laws, **yet** strong leadership in these areas can set an example to employees all through the organization.

- Look at the words in bold above, and the mind map. Find:
  - three structures in the text listed in the mind map under *Opinions*.
  - three structures listed under *Focusing*.
  - one word listed under *Emphasizing*.
  - one phrase listed under *Concluding*.
- Notice the linking phrase *after all* on line 8. It means 'we mustn't forget that'. It does NOT mean 'finally'/'at last'/'in the end'.
- Notice the linking word *yet* on line 43. It is the same as 'but despite this'. There is more sense of surprise than simply 'but'.
- There are five other linking structures that are not in bold because they have already been mentioned in previous units. Find:
  - one for making a contrast.
  - one for adding another point.
  - one for giving an example.
  - one for saying something already known.
  - one for conceding a point, but then dismissing it.
- Study the *Opinions* section of the mind map. Notice how you can vary your language (instead of always writing *I think* or *In my opinion*).

Focusing structures

At line 13 you can see the phrase *What companies really need is ….* Look under *Focusing* in the mind map to find more examples of this structure.

At line 1 you can see a phrase beginning with a negative frequency adverb: *Never before **has business ethics** been….* When you focus on *never* by putting it at the beginning you invert the normal subject/auxiliary word order (***Business ethics has** never before been …*). See the mind map for other phrases that can be used in this way.

Adverb + comparative adjective

Look at line 18 *considerably more effective* and line 30 *relatively less important*. Why add the words 'considerably' and 'relatively' when the sentence is okay without them? The answer is that it makes the comparison more measured – it sounds like you have considered the comparison more carefully. Adverbs used in this way are:
- *far / much / considerably / significantly / substantially* (more effective).
- *relatively / somewhat* (more effective).
- *slightly / marginally* (more effective).

Emphasizing

Above all, In particular
Particularly, Especially
Mainly, Mostly, Principally, Predominantly
Specifically

Comparison

In comparison with, Compared to

Similarity

Similarly, Likewise, In the same way

Exception

Apart from, Except for

Explaining

in other words, to put it another way,
that is, ie
To put it simply

Summarizing

Basically (informal), To sum up,
In short, In summary

Concluding

All in all (informal),
All things considered (informal),
On balance, In conclusion,
Taking all this into consideration

Personal opinion

In my opinion / view …
I really believe that …
I am convinced that …

Less certain:
To my way of thinking …
It seems to me that …

Limited knowledge:
As far as I know …
To the best of my knowledge …

Qualified opinion

Some people argue that …
People often claim that …
People tend to believe that …
This (will) may cause …
(All) The majority of managers …

Partially true statement

Up to a point, In a sense,
In a way, To some degree / extent,
To a limited degree / extent

Opinions

Linking words 3

DEVELOPING AN ARGUMENT 3

Adverb + comparative adjective

What / The thing … is

What companies really need is …
What we want from you is …
What I will do first is …

The thing that impressed
me most was …

The one thing that
worries me is …

Negative frequency

Never before has …
Under no circumstances can we …
On no account must we …
At no time have I …
On no condition will we …
Only in some respects do I …
Only on rare occasions have we …

Field of relevance

From a technical / financial /
commercial / administrative /
ethical point of view
Technically speaking
Financially speaking

Focusing

Far / Much / Considerably / Significantly /
Substantially (more effective)

Relatively / Somewhat (more effective)

Slightly / Marginally (more effective)

22.1 Put these phrases in order, from 1 (most careful and measured) to 4 (most certain).

a) I believe that … ☐

b) I firmly believe that … ☐

c) It would seem to me that … ☐

d) It seems to me that … ☐

Now do the same for this group of phrases, again from 1 (most careful and measured) to 4 (most certain).

e) I tend to think that … ☐

f) I feel it is possible that … ☐

g) I am convinced that … ☐

h) I would argue that … ☐

22.2 In formal writing you often qualify a general opinion so that it sounds more measured. Tick (✓) the phrase from each pair that is more typical of formal writing.

1a Everybody knows that … ☐
1b Many people believe that … ☐

2a Companies tend to … ☐
2b Companies always … ☐

3a All managers … ☐
3b The majority of managers … ☐

4a Not everybody believes that … ☐
4b Nobody believes that … ☐

5a People always say that … ☐
5b Some people argue that … ☐

6a This may cause problems because … ☐
6b This will cause problems because … ☐

22.3 Fill in the missing letters.

1 _ _ _ _ a point, this is true.

2 _ _ a sense, this is true.

3 _ _ a certain e_ _ _ _t, this is true.

4 _ _ a limited d_ _ _ee, this is true.

5 _ _ the b_ _ _ of my knowledge, this is true.

6 _ _ far _ _ I k_ _ _, this is true.

22.4 Rewrite the sentences using *What … is …* to focus on the topic. The first example has been done for you.

1 Companies need a set of standards.
What companies need is a set of standards

2 I'm talking about a completely new approach.

3 We want good quality at competitive prices.

4 I would like to have a chance to speak to him.

(Be careful with the next three examples – a form of *do* is also needed.)

5 I will first give you the history of the project.
What I will do first is give you the history of the project

6 We mustn't go over budget.

7 We should employ more local staff.

22.5 Rewrite the sentences starting with the underlined words.

1 Business ethics has <u>never before</u> been such a hot topic.
Never before has business ethics been such a hot topic.

2 We can <u>under no circumstances</u> accept this deal.

3 This information should <u>on no account</u> be shown to the press.

(Be careful with the next two examples – a form of *do* is also needed)

4 I agree with you <u>only in some respects</u>.

5 We do business without a bank guarantee <u>only on rare occasions</u>.

22.6 The phrases in italics are all in the wrong sentences. Put them back into their correct places.

1 From *a commercial point of view*, it is now possible to prevent the body's organs from deteriorating. It requires very large doses of controversial dietary supplements such as human growth hormone, DHEA, antioxidant vitamins, glucosamine, Omega-3 and more.

2 From *a technical point of view*, anti-aging drugs are going to be big business as the 'baby boomer' generation passes through retirement.

3 From *a legal point of view*, having anti-aging drugs cheap and freely available is going to be very popular – retired people make up a high proportion of the voting population.

4 From *a political point of view*, anti-aging drugs raise important questions. For example, should patients first get a DNA test to make sure that they will benefit? And who tells them if this test shows they have a high probability of dying within the next few years?

5 From *an ethical point of view*, anti-aging drugs need careful regulation so that they do not expose their manufacturers to lawsuits by making false claims.

22.7 Match an informal phrase from Group A with a more formal phrase from Group B.

Group A

1 it's a bit more expensive ☐
2 it's more expensive – but not much more ☐
3 it's far more expensive ☐

Group B

a) it is considerably more expensive
b) it is somewhat more expensive
c) it is slightly more expensive

22.8 Study the position of *particularly* and *in particular* in relation to a noun phrase:

*Business ethics is a hot issue, **particularly** <u>fair trade</u>.*

<u>Fair trade</u> ***in particular*** *has become a hot issue in business ethics.*

Which <u>one</u> of the above could also be used at the beginning of a whole sentence?

_____ , fair trade has become a hot issue.

22.9 Look at these two sentences:

*The software is designed **particularly** for classroom use.*
*The software is designed **mainly** for classroom use.*

1 Which **two** of the formal adverbs in the box below mean the same as *particularly*?
2 Which **two** of the formal adverbs in the box below mean the same as *mainly*?

especially   principally   predominantly   specifically

22.10 Fill in the gaps using these prepositions: *for, from, in, in, into, on, to, with*. Then match a structure from the left column with one from the right.

1 apart _____	to put it briefly
2 _____ comparison _____	except _____
3 _____ short	likewise
4 _____ balance	compared _____
5 similarly	taking everything _____ consideration

22.11 Complete the text using the linking words from the <u>left-hand</u> column in exercise 22.10. Think carefully about the logic of the argument.

¹_____ the issue of blocking access to certain Internet sites by governments, the topic of 'intellectual copyright' is probably the key ethical issue for the Internet age. Intellectual copyright refers to the ownership of a creative work. If you pay for and download an mp3 music file for personal use, that is legal, but what about if you then place it on your hard disk for peer-to-peer sharing? In the first case, the musicians get paid, in the second they don't. ²_____ , an author doesn't get paid if you photocopy their book, and a software writer doesn't get paid if you distribute a pirate copy of their program. What about the movie industry? ³_____ the music and publishing industries mentioned above, they have been considerably more successful in protecting their intellectual property. However, as Internet download speeds increase, file sharing of movies will surely increase. ⁴_____ , it looks like all the creative industries are at risk from digital technology. Does this matter? The answer is yes. If musicians, authors, actors, film makers, software writers and others don't receive an income, they won't continue to work to produce high-quality products. In theory, it is easy to see that this situation is wrong, but in practice it is difficult to persuade yourself to pay for something that you can get for free. ⁵_____ , it is probably better to have some sort of regulation so that everyone pays, otherwise the creative industries will enter a slow decline.

22.12 Match these initials to their meanings: *eg, ie.*

1 for example _____   2 in other words _____

You can also write these with full stops: *e.g.* and *i.e.*

Now complete each sentence with *eg* or *ie*.

3 Scandinavian countries (_____ Norway, Sweden, Denmark and Iceland) tend to be early adopters of mobile communication technology.
4 Scandinavian countries (_____ Norway and Sweden) tend to be early adopters of mobile communication technology.

Speaking / Writing practice

● Re-read the texts *Never before has business ethics been such a hot topic* (page 92) and *Apart from the issue of blocking access to certain Internet sites by governments, the topic of 'intellectual copyright' is probably the key ethical issue for the Internet age* (page 95). This will remind you about some issues in business ethics.

● Do some Internet research. Type the words 'corporate social responsibility' into a search engine.
● Now write a short report with the title 'Corporate social responsibility'.
● When you finish (if you are working in a group), read each others' reports. Have a discussion.

23 Writing paragraphs

Topic sentences and unity

Here are some facts about trends in the consumer goods market:

> High-end products: growth in market share
> Mid-range products: decline in market share
> Low-end products: growth in market share

Study the short texts below; they are alternative ways of presenting the facts above.

Version A

> [1]Consumers at the high end are 'trading up', paying a premium price for highly branded, luxury products. [2]And at the low end they are 'trading down', spending as little as possible on basic, functional products. [3]This is happening all over the world – leaving the middle in decline. [4]Between the two poles lies a vast range of ordinary, boring products that are rapidly losing market share.

Version B

> [1]All over the world, consumer markets are dividing into a high end and a low end – leaving the middle in decline. [2]At the high end, consumers are 'trading up', paying a premium price for highly branded, luxury products. [3]And at the low end, they are 'trading down', spending as little as possible on basic, functional products. [4]Between the two poles lies a vast range of ordinary, boring products that are rapidly losing market share.

Version A is not so easy to follow. Why?
- Sentence 1 presents an idea, but we have not been prepared mentally with any context and so the paragraph begins too suddenly.
- 2 follows well, giving a contrasting idea.
- 3 is strange: instead of continuing the argument, it introduces a new idea ('the middle') half-way through the paragraph.
- 4 is strange after 3 (which made no reference to two poles).

Version B is better. Why?
- Sentence 1 introduces the main idea of the paragraph in a short, simple way. Further sentences develop this main idea rather than adding new ideas.
- There is a logical movement in the paragraph: the sub-topics in 2, 3 and 4 ('the high end', 'the low end', 'the middle') appear in the same order as they are mentioned in the first sentence.

The introductory sentence in Version B is called a 'topic sentence'. It provides a context and summarizes what will follow in the paragraph.

All the sentences in a paragraph should relate to one main idea. This is called 'unity'. Unrelated ideas in the same paragraph produce confusion or complexity. A typical error might be discussing advantages and disadvantages in a single paragraph, or even discussing more than one advantage in the same paragraph.

Movement / Logic

Version B has movement: the ideas flow clearly and logically. In this case, it is because the topic sentence sets up the paragraph structure very clearly. Another typical way to give movement to a paragraph is by using linking words. The left-hand branch of the mind map opposite reviews this language area, which is covered in more detail and practised in units 20–22.

Substitution and repetition of key words

Read this paragraph taken from the same text.

> [1]Consumer behaviour at the bottom end of the price range is changing as well. [2]In the past, low-end products were associated exclusively with low-income groups and poor quality. [3]But nowadays people of all social classes feel satisfaction when they find a bargain. [4]It allows them to feel that they are in control of their finances. [5]Interestingly, as a result of the money saved, they typically then feel able to afford a few high-end luxuries.

- The idea 'the bottom end of the price range' (sentence 1) is a key one, and will be referred to again in the paragraph. Using similar words could be monotonous, and so the writer substitutes the phrase *low-end products* in the next sentence. Equally, *income groups* (sentence 2) is substituted later by *social classes*, and *a bargain* (sentence 3) by *money saved*.
- But repetition can often work well. It can tie the paragraph together, give emphasis, and be stylistically effective. Note how the words *low-end* in sentence 2 are echoed by the words *high-end* in sentence 5. This produces a sense of closure.
- Note the topic sentence at the beginning that summarizes the whole paragraph.
- Note the movement: *as well* linking to a previous paragraph (not given here); time sequencing (*in the past* ➔ *but nowadays*); *interestingly* to make a personal comment.

Topic sentence

One main idea per paragraph, with a topic sentence at the beginning

The topic sentence introduces and summarizes the paragraph.

The topic sentence can occasionally come at the end of the paragraph as a conclusion (in which case the first words will be something like Therefore or The result of all this is that ...).

You may not need a topic sentence if the paragraph has a strong logical connection with the previous paragraph. But in this case use a linking phrase at the beginning to make the logic clear, eg In addition, However.

Paragraph length

4-6 sentences is a reasonable length.

If the paragraph is too short, it may mean that the main idea is not sufficiently developed.

If the paragraph is too long, there may be excessive detail which hides the main idea.

Consider taking out the detail and putting it in a separate paragraph (or a footnote).

A very short paragraph – even just one sentence – can be effective in situations such as introductions, summaries and conclusions. It can give impact and highlight the idea.

Movement

'Movement' means taking the reader from one sentence to the next in clear, logical steps

Achieving movement:

1. Use the first sentence to mention sub-topics, which are then picked up in sequence by further sentences

2. Use time sequence, contrast, list of related points (First, Second, Finally), etc.

3. Use linking words: see opposite branch (and units 20-22).

Emphasis

Starting with the same facts you can emphasize different points and present different arguments. You do this with linking words and the paragraph structure.

(See exercise 23.3 on page 98 for an example.)

Give examples

There are several reasons for this, such as ...
For instance
In particular

Give the reason

The reason for this is ...
This is the result of...

Give the result

Therefore
This would mean that ...
As a result ...
This will lead to ...

Give more than one example, reason or result

Firstly, Second, Finally
Furthermore, In addition

Explain

In other words,
By ... I mean ...

Make a contrast

However,
On the other hand

Give evidence

This argument is supported by ...
Research suggests that ...

Give the consequences

Provided that / If ...,
then ...
Unless

Emphasize

It should be noted that ...
I would like to stress that ...

Show you understand the other side to the argument

Although, Despite

Reject an idea

I do not believe that ...
The main disadvantage (drawback) is ...

Make a personal comment

Obviously, Interestingly, Clearly, Surprisingly

Paragraph design: general points

Movement using linking words

WRITING PARAGRAPHS

23.1 Read the paragraph and then answer the questions.

¹A good example of 'trading up' from the middle market is Olay made by Proctor and Gamble. ²In the 1980s, Olay had just one form and sold at an everyday price in a standard bottle. ³But today it occupies a whole section of the store and sells at a premium price. ⁴P&G have developed the brand in two ways. ⁵Firstly, by product diversification (face or body, cleansing or moisturizing, vitamins, sun protection, anti-ageing, etc). ⁶The act of deciding which item in the range is right for you takes you one step closer to a decision to purchase. ⁷Secondly, by using a huge advertising budget to associate the brand with positive feelings. ⁸When a woman is applying the product, she feels she is going to be beautiful today.

Write the sentence number/s which show:

a) the topic sentence for the whole paragraph: ☐ 1

b) another sentence, like a topic sentence, that introduces the second part of the paragraph: ☐

c) movement by using a time contrast: ☐ ☐

d) movement by listing points: ☐ ☐

e) using a follow-up sentence to develop the idea in the previous sentence: ☐ ☐

Finally, read the two opinions below and decide which one you agree with. There is no 'correct' answer – the aim is just to think in detail about paragraphing.

Opinion 1 At eight sentences, this paragraph is too long. It is difficult to follow the argument. It would be better to start a new paragraph at sentence 4 – after all, this is like a second topic sentence.

Opinion 2 The length is not a problem as the paragraph shows 'unity' – all the sentences relate closely to the main topic introduced in the first sentence. Making a new paragraph at sentence 4 would be a mistake – it would break up the movement and logic of the argument.

23.2 Read the paragraph. The topic sentence (a question) is missing.

_____ ? At first sight, this would seem impossible. High-end shoppers and low-end shoppers are rarely seen in the same store, and the strategy certainly is risky and difficult. But a small number of retailers are making it work, and examples are Costco in the US and Aldi in Europe. These are 'treasure hunt' stores. The money you save on the majority of your purchases you can spend on a luxury treat – like a nice bottle of wine or a special cake.

Now tick (✓) two good topic sentence from 1–3 below. One follows the principle of 'substitution to avoid monotony' and one of 'repetition for stylistic impact'.

1 Is it possible to combine all segments of the market under one roof?

2 Is it possible to be a success in the mid-market?

3 Is it possible to sell to high-end shoppers and low-end shoppers in the same store?

23.3 Here are some figures for sales increases last year:

France 4.5%	Hungary 8%
Germany 4%	Poland 7.5%
UK 3%	

These basic facts can be described in different ways. Look at topic sentences a)–c). They set up the movement in the paragraph in different ways.

a) Sales were strong across all key European markets last year.

b) Sales increases last year were significantly lower in established markets than in the new markets of Central Europe.

c) Sales increases last year were much more impressive in the new markets of Central Europe than in established markets.

Now write one of the letters a–c in each box below. The text after the arrow shows how the paragraph continues.

1 ☐ → Poland and Hungary both had significant increases, with 7.5% and 8% respectively. However, in the rest of Europe the figures were disappointing, at 4.5% in France, 4% in Germany and just 3% in the UK.

2 ☐ → Hungary and Poland had the highest increase, with 8% and 7.5% respectively. But other markets also showed positive growth. France had gains of 4.5%, Germany of 4%, and the UK of 3%.

3 ☐ → The poorest performance was seen in the UK, with growth of only 3%. Germany and France were also weak, with increases of just 4% and 4.5%. However, in Poland and Hungary gains were far more impressive, with increases of 7.5% and 8% respectively.

When you have checked your answers, note:

● There is a difference of emphasis in all three paragraphs (different countries, positive vs negative, etc).

● The idea 'lower' in topic sentence b is a key one. It is referred to again later in the paragraph with the words _poorest_ and _weak_. This is an example of 'substitution to avoid monotony'.

23.4 Here are some facts:

- Soybean prices will stay high.
- China and India import a lot of soybeans.
- The cultivation of soybeans needs hot summers and a lot of water.
- Soybean farming in Brazil is destroying the rainforest.

Write in the boxes the sentence numbers that form a paragraph to describe the facts above.

1 Soybean prices are likely to stay high for years to come. There are several reasons for this.

2 Then, on the supply side, it will be difficult to increase worldwide production much beyond current levels. Why is this?

3 On the demand side, both China and India buy large quantities of soybeans on world markets, and this is certain to continue in the future.

4 In addition, there is pressure on land use in Brazil, the biggest producer, because of the potential impact on the rainforest if more land is converted to soybean farming.

5 First, the cultivation of soybeans requires a combination of hot summers and the availability of water, and not many countries can provide this.

When you have checked your answers, note:

- There is movement in the paragraph – the contrast between *the demand side* and *the supply side*.
- There is also some secondary movement – the listing of two supply side factors.
- The word *cultivation* is substituted later with the word *farming*. This is an example of 'substitution to avoid monotony'.

23.5 Repeat the exercise: write the sentence numbers to form a paragraph. The paragraph refers to the same facts as in exercise 23.4.

1 Over recent years China and India have been buying large quantities of soybeans on world markets, and this is certain to continue in the future. Demand will stay high.

2 The result of all these demand and supply pressures is that soybean prices are likely to stay high for years to come.

3 First, the cultivation of soybeans requires a combination of hot summers and the availability of water, and not many countries can provide this.

4 Second, there is pressure on land use in Brazil, the biggest producer, because of the potential impact on the rainforest if more land is converted to soybean farming.

5 At the same time there are supply side problems: it will be difficult to increase worldwide production of soybeans much beyond current levels. Why is this?

When you have checked your answers, note:

- The topic sentence in this paragraph comes at the end as a conclusion, not at the beginning as an introduction.

Finally, note that all the examples in this unit have been written text. But the 'facts' in the boxes in exercises 23.3 and 23.4 could be PowerPoint slides, and in this case the text would be a spoken presentation.

Writing practice

- Review exercise 23.3, including the notes in bullet points at the end. Then cover the second part of the exercise with a piece of paper so that only sentences a)–c) are showing. Write three separate paragraphs, beginning with a)–c).
- Uncover the original at the end and compare. But it is not a memory exercise – your version may be quite different, and perhaps better!

- Review exercise 23.4, including the notes in bullet points at the end. Then cover 2–5 with a piece of paper, so that only the box of facts and sentence 1 are showing. Write a paragraph beginning with sentence 1.
- Again, uncover the original at the end and compare.
- Review exercise 23.5. Cover 2–5 with a piece of paper so that only sentence 1 is showing. Write a paragraph beginning with sentence 1.
- Again, uncover the original at the end and compare.

24 CV (résumé) / Job interview

Below you will see an American-style résumé /ˈrezjuːmeɪ/ (*résumé*). Its key features are: one side of A4 only, focus on achievements (what you have actually done) as well as skills and responsibilities, no 'personal' information. European-style CVs are longer, and can include other things such as personal interests, courses/conferences attended. After looking at the résumé, refer to the mind map.

PERSONAL DETAILS

Name: Paulo Cannara

Address: Via Carlo Scarpa 51, 20425, Milano, Italy

Home telephone number: +39 12345678

Mobile telephone number: +39 9876543210

Email: paulo.cannara@yahoo.com

Nationality: Italian

Summary: I have a degree in Economics from Bocconi University, Milan and am looking for a position in the Corporate Finance department of an international company. Since graduating I have been working in a small company in Milan offering financial advice to private clients. I am now looking for new challenges to develop my career in the financial area.

PROFESSIONAL EXPERIENCE

June 20XX – now. Assistant Portfolio Manager, Studio Bartolini, Milan

Since finishing my studies at university I have been working in a small Milan stockbroker firm. I assist the Portfolio Manager in a wide range of tasks, including doing research into different financial instruments to reduce the risk of customers' positions. My responsibilities also include handling telephone calls from clients and writing monthly reports.

Key achievements:

– As a result of the financial instruments I recommended, our clients' portfolios grew by an average of 8% last year, despite the fall in equity markets.

– I helped to develop a new E-trading platform at Studio Bartolini. This was given a customer satisfaction rating of 'Excellent' or 'Very good' by 84% of clients.

EDUCATION

Nov 20XX – May 20XX. Postgraduate Diploma for Financial Operators, Bocconi University, Milan

This course covered fundamental analysis, technical analysis and pricing techniques for equity, bond and derivatives markets.

Sep 20XX – June 20XX. Degree in Economics and Business Administration, Bocconi University, Milan

I graduated with a final mark of 78%. My specializations were in Corporate Finance and Financial Markets. My final dissertation was on IPOs in the Italian market.

Key achievements:

– I was a member of the university basketball team. We won the Italian University League in 20XX.

SKILLS

Languages: fluent in English and good level in French.
IT: good knowledge of all components of Microsoft Office.

REFERENCES

Available on request

Responsibilities

Of the main priorities in this role, which ones are well understood and measurable, and which ones are not?

Market environment

I'm aware that it's a very fast-moving market. How is this affecting the priorities and demands of the job?

Job development

In comparison with now, what major changes in this role are you looking for? For example, in terms of customer relations? organizational development? market development?

Internal

What are the key relationships inside the company in this role? Have these always worked well in the past? If not, what have been the issues?

Examples of good questions to ask in an interview

CV/RESUME AND JOB INTERVIEW

Preparing a CV/Resume

Consider putting a one-paragraph 'Summary' at the top.

Normally, put 'Professional Experience' before 'Education'. If you have very little employment history, then 'Education' can come first.

Start with the most recent job/course (reverse chronological order)

For names of universities, courses, etc, use a mix of the original words and English words. Provide a translation in brackets if necessary.

When referring to marks and grades, translate into %. The reader might not understand the marking system in your country.

Use short sentences and bullet points. Leave a lot of white space. Be brief and direct. Avoid jargon.

Use action verbs to describe your responsibilities: see list on page 102.

Use real results to describe your achievements: I increased sales by X%, I made savings of €Y.

University graduates can consider attaching a separate report about official work experience during the course.

Non-work achievements

University graduates without much employment history can still think of 'experiences' with 'achievements'.

For example ...

... voluntary work, committee membership of societies and clubs, organizing events, teaching and helping people, creating things (eg art, writing, photography), sports and fitness, travel, computers, becoming expert in any skill, etc.

Job interview

Prepare by asking a friend to ask you typical questions. In particular, practise talking about your strong points using concrete examples from your current job.

Keep your answers short, simple and relevant. If the interviewer wants more information, let them ask for it.

Be enthusiastic and positive at all times. Never contradict, argue or interrupt. Never criticize previous employers.

Treat the interviewer with respect, but don't be afraid to occasionally take the initiative during the conversation.

Typical mistakes in a CV/Resume

Focusing on skills and responsibilities, and forgetting achievements

Including irrelevant information

Going over the limit (résumé – 1 page; CV – 2 pages)

Brightly coloured paper, too many font styles

Spelling and grammar mistakes. Check very carefully, and if possible show to a native speaker before sending off.

24 CV (résumé) / Job interview: Exercises

24.1 Study the list of personal qualities below. You can use some of these ideas in your CV, or in an interview.

active and dynamic approach – gets things done
comfortable with demanding sales targets
creative problem-solver
critical thinker – strong analytical skills
detailed and precise; conscientious and thorough
determined and decisive
effective project coordinator
emotionally mature and confident – a calming influence
entrepreneurial and proactive
excellent interpersonal skills – good communicator
financially smart – good knowledge of accounting systems and principles
focused on quality and optimizing performance
good researcher – creative and methodical
good team-player – adaptable and flexible
high level of technical competence in …
high standards of honesty and personal integrity
innovates and makes things happen
methodical approach to planning and organizing
positive attitude – seeks and finds solutions to challenges
proactive – anticipates and takes initiative
reliable and dependable in meeting objectives
results-oriented – all decisions are determined by how it affects the bottom line
self-aware – always seeking to learn and grow
self-motivated and self-reliant
strong drive – energetic and positive outlook which often inspires others
task-oriented – good at identifying problems, finding solutions and implementing them
uses initiative to develop effective solutions to problems
well-organized; good planner; good time-manager

Which of these qualities would you use to describe:
a) a real person who has recently been your boss?
b) a real friend or colleague who you admire?
c) yourself?

Can you add any other personal qualities?

24.2 Study the list of action verbs below. You can use some of these ideas in your CV, or in an interview.

analyse (sales data)
carry out (processes and procedures)
complete (projects on time and on budget)
control (quality)
coordinate (complex projects)
deal with (customers, both internal and external)
deal with (suppliers, partners and associates)
design and develop (new procedures)
determine (direction, policy and strategy)
develop and coach (other people)
increase (sales, website hits)
initiate (changes in work practices)
investigate (reasons for customer dissatisfaction)
listen to, understand and help (colleagues)
make decisions (and implement them)
monitor, record and report (sales data, test results)
negotiate (deals)
operate (equipment and tools reliably and safely)
plan (budgets)
research and explore (new markets)
solve (problems and challenges)
supervise and direct (staff working under you)
work effectively (in a team)
work under pressure (and meet demanding deadlines)
write (reports)

Which of these activities have you done:
a) in your previous job?
b) in your current job?
You can include part-time work.

24.3 Prepare a CV / résumé.

- Use the ideas in this unit to help you prepare a one-page résumé or two-page CV.
- Show it to a colleague / friend and ask them how it could be improved.

24.4 First read these typical interview questions.

1   Tell me a little about yourself.

2   Why do you want to leave your current job?

3   What attracted you to this company?

4   What qualities or experience do you think you would bring to this job?

5   What would you find most difficult about this position? How would you handle that challenge?

6   As you look back on your life and career so far, what achievement has given you the most satisfaction?

7   How would other people in your present company describe you as a colleague?

8   What are your strong points?

9   And what are your weak points?

10 How do you deal with criticism and direction?

11 In career terms, where do you want to be in five years time?

12 So, finally, why should we hire you rather than one of the other candidates?

Now choose one of the questions above to match with each reply below. Write the question number in the box.

a) ☐ ➡ 'It doesn't allow me to grow professionally and I want more challenges.' (also practical things like distance from home, job security.)

b) ☐ ➡ Don't talk too much: it's a warm-up question. Cover your origins, education, work history and recent career experience.

c) ☐ ➡ 'Maybe I am a little too perfectionist.' / 'Perhaps I worry too much about deadlines.'

d) ☐ ➡ 'I welcome it and listen carefully, particularly if it allows the team to operate more effectively and produce better results. It is necessary in order to learn and develop.'

Speaking practice

In exercise 24.5 and 24.6 you are going to prepare and then practise a job interview. This is useful for everyone – even if you are not thinking about applying for a new job right now.

24.5 Prepare the roleplay.

1   Think of a job that you might apply for in the future and write it below. If you cannot think of anything, then imagine that you are applying for the position of your current boss (even if you only do part-time work).

_____ (position)

_____ (company)

2   Fill in the gaps in the box below with <u>your own</u> information. You will be asked these questions.

Education

I see that you have a degree in _____ (subject) from _____ (name of institution).

● Which part of the course did you enjoy most? Why did you like that subject?

● Did you do a project in your final year? Can you tell me about that?

Current job

(Use a part-time job if necessary, and use a recent job if you are a student or unemployed.)

I see that you work as a _____ (position) in _____ (company).

● Can you tell me a little about the company? What exactly do you do there?

● What personal and professional skills have you developed?

● What was your most important achievement?

● How have you kept up-to-date with new developments in your field?

● Why do you want to leave?

---

3   Review the questions in the box above and the twelve questions in exercise 24.4. Plan how you personally will answer these questions. Your replies should be natural and comfortable for you, and may be very different to other people's replies.

24.6 Roleplay

Give this book to a colleague / friend and ask them to interview you. The interviewer should follow this sequence:

● 'Tell me a little about yourself.'

● The questions in the box above.

● Questions 3–12 from exercise 24.4.

Interviews

1 Interview with a venture capitalist

Exercises

1 You are going to listen to an interview with Karl, a venture capitalist. How do you think he answers the questions below?

1 What kind of start-up is a venture capital firm looking for?

2 What role does a venture capitalist have in the management of a start-up?

3 Suddenly a start-up is bought by a larger company. How do people react? Are they happy?

2 🌐 Now listen to the interview and compare your ideas with the real answers.

3 🌐 Are these statements true (T) or false (F)? Try to remember what Karl said, then listen again to check.

1 Venture capitalists are usually interested in long-term investment. T / F

2 When a VC sells a start-up to a larger company, it is called a 'trade sale'. T / F

3 Venture capitalists are typically interested in firms in the IT and biotech sectors. T / F

4 In the pharmaceutical sector most start-ups want to become stand-alone companies. T / F

5 It's easier to take a technology start-up to an IPO in Europe than in America. T / F

4 Read the listening script (page 109) and make notes on what Karl says about the following topics (maximum ten words each). When you finish, discuss the general issues with some colleagues.

● the kind of start-up company that a VC is looking for

● why large companies are interested in buying successful start-ups

● why it's difficult in Europe to do a technology IPO

Glossary

break-through innovation important discovery / new product
culture shock negative feelings of surprise when people move to a different environment
exit strategy way to end involvement in something
founders people who establish a start-up
growth potential opportunity or ability to get bigger
IPO (Initial Public Offering) process of issuing shares for the first time (when a privately-owned company becomes listed on the stock market)
milestones important events in a company's development
road map plan for moving from the present situation towards one or more key objectives
serial entrepreneurs founders of several start-ups
stake amount of investment
stand-alone independent, not part of something else
start-up new company, often with higher risk and higher potential return on investment
venture capitalist (VC) outside investor who provides money for financing start-ups. *VC* can also mean *venture capital*.

2 Interview with a CEO

Exercises

1 Read statements 1–4. What is your opinion? Write 'Agree' or 'Disagree' in the column headed 'My opinion'.

	My opinion	Lara's opinion
1 Having a 'Suggestions Box' at work is a good idea.	_____	_____
2 Email has made communication at work much easier.	_____	_____
3 Positive feedback should be given publicly as well as privately.	_____	_____
4 Workers in the public sector are lazy.	_____	_____

2 🌐 Now listen to an interview with Lara about managing people. What does she think about the same statements? Write 'Agree' or 'Disagree' in the final column above.

3 🌐 Read the questions below. Try to remember what Lara said, then listen again to check.

1 What are the three channels of communication according to Lara?

2 What name does Lara give to the kind of skills that are important for teamwork?

3 Apart from giving positive feedback, what other thing does Lara think is important for motivation?

4 What change does Lara want to make in the public sector?

5 What kind of person has vision and sees the big picture?

6 What role does Lara compare to an Admiral?

4 Read the listening script (page 110) and make notes on what Lara says about the following topics (maximum ten words each). When you finish, discuss the general issues with some colleagues.

● top-down communication

● bottom-up communication

● what a CEO should do in meetings

● the relationship between employees and their leader (the CEO)

Glossary

acknowledgement recognition
annual review summary of company's results from previous year
cc send a copy of an email to a third party
cover for sb to do someone else's work on a temporary basis
drive ambition and determination
face-to-face in person
humble with low social status
incentive something that makes you work harder
mingle mix informally
shop floor area in a factory where products are made

3 Interview with a project manager

Exercises

1 Read the stages in a typical construction process below. Put them in the right order 1–7.

a) Project managers make a retention until they have checked the suppliers' work. ☐

b) Put out a tender to suppliers. ☐

c) Select the suppliers. ☐

d) Discuss with the client the number of buildings and the layout. ☐1

e) Suppliers hand over the work to the project managers. ☐

f) Suppliers start work. ☐

g) Receive proposals from suppliers. ☐

2 🎧 Now listen to an interview with Anton, a project manager in the construction industry, and check your answers.

3 🎧 What aspects of engineering does Anton mention? Try to complete the table, then listen again to check.

MECHANICAL ENGINEERING	ELECTRICAL ENGINEERING
Climate services	**Electrical supply**
heating	transformers to reduce the
ventilation	high ^{5}vo _ _ _ _e coming
^{1}a _ _ c _ _ _ _ _ _ _ _ _g	into the factory
Utility services	**Lighting**
water supply	level of light
drainage	the mix of ^{6}ar _ _ _ _ial light
refuse ^{2}h_ _ _ing	and daylight
Mechanical transportation	the position of the windows
lifts	**Telecommunications**
^{3}esc _ _ _ _ _s	^{7}c_ _ling
Safety	
sprinkler system	^{8}A _ _ _ _ICS
^{4}f_ _ -r_ _ _ _ _ _t materials	noise levels

4 Read the listening script (page 111) and make notes on what Anton says about the following topics (maximum ten words each). When you finish, discuss the general issues with some colleagues.

- the tendering process
- contractors unable to work and claiming compensation
- making a retention

Glossary

compensation money to cover a loss caused by sb else
crane large machine used to lift heavy things
drainage pipes that take away water and waste liquids
greenfield site rural land not previously built on
knock-on effect indirect result
layout the way in which objects are arranged
local authority governing body of a city, town or district (UK)
penalty clause part of contract that imposes punishment if certain conditions aren't satisfied
refuse waste, rubbish
retention money owed but not paid until work is approved
tender formal process by which suppliers bid for a contract

4 Interview with a design engineer

Exercises

1 Read the stages in the engineering process below. Put them in the right order 1–7.

a) The assembly company checks and assembles the parts. ☐

b) The customer supplies a specification. ☐1

c) The design engineer tests a virtual, CAD-generated piece. ☐

d) The manufacturer machines the parts. ☐

e) The assembly company tests the prototype. ☐

f) The design engineer does initial concept sketches on paper. ☐

g) The design engineer constructs a virtual piece in CAD. ☐

2 🎧 Now listen to an interview with Alex, a design engineer, and check your answers.

3 🎧 Alex explains some technical terms. Read each definition 1–7 and try to remember the term, then listen again to check.

1 The piece has to fit into a specified space – we call that the 'w_____ e_____'.

2 The design is 'i_____'. That means repetitive and cyclical.

3 'D_____ f_____ m_____' means that the piece can be made easily and cost-effectively.

4 'O_____-d_____' is when you end up with a piece that's much too expensive in every respect – materials, manufacturing costs, design time.

5 'Co_____ Nu _____ Co_____' (CNC) means that the machine tool is driven by a computer program as it is making the components.

6 'T_____' means the amount of permitted variation.

4 Read the listening script (page 112) and make notes on what Alex says about the following topics (maximum ten words each). When you finish, discuss the general issues with some colleagues.

- CAD
- design and quality vs cost
- building and testing a prototype

Glossary

batch a group of things that are made together or arrive together
CAD computer-assisted design
constraint limitation
mil short form of millimetre
nut small piece of metal with a hole in the middle used to fasten things together
screw thin pointed piece of metal that you turn to fasten things together
seal something that stops air or liquid entering or leaving
sketch drawing that is made quickly and without many details
slot long, narrow opening in a surface
trade-off acceptable balance between two different things
welding joining two pieces of metal by heating them and pressing them together

5 Interview with a marketing director

Exercises

1 Imagine you are the marketing director of a company that sells domestic appliances, eg fridges, ovens. Think about the following questions and make a few brief notes.

1 Who are your two main types of customer?
2 How can you use existing customers to do market research?
3 How can you get a list of potential new customers?

2 ⊕ Now listen to an interview with Louis, a marketing director of a company that sells domestic appliances. What does he say about questions 1–3?

3 ⊕ Are these statements true (T) or false (F)? Try to remember what Louis said, then listen again to check.

1 Americans are more interested in design than functionality. T / F
2 His company is going to stop providing appliances for holiday flats because the profit is zero. T / F
3 A facelift happens more often than a restyling. T / F
4 In Europe your social status is judged by your kitchen. T / F
5 If you fill in a questionnaire, people will use your name and address to send you junk mail, whether you like it or not. T / F

4 Read the listening script (page 113) and make notes on what Louis says about the following topics (maximum ten words each). When you finish, discuss the general issues with some colleagues.

● why companies need a wide product range
● quality in relation to price
● the effectiveness of advertising in increasing brand awareness

Glossary

appliance piece of electrical equipment that you have in your home
built-in forming part of something and cannot be separated
drum circular container in a washing machine
facelift superficial changes that make something look newer or better
fitted made to fit a particular space in a building
free-standing not fixed to a wall or other support
junk mail advertising that is sent to you, but you did not ask for
opt in decide to be part of something; (direct marketing) give permission to be sent mail or email
stale old and no longer fresh
status social position
straightforward clear and easy to understand

6 Interview with a communications consultant

Exercises

1 Match the communication tools 1–8 with the definitions a)–h).

1	lobbying	a)	producing printed material
2	Internet advertising	b)	organized occasion involving many people
3	outdoor	c)	when a specific brand is used in a movie or TV show
4	viral marketing	d)	associating a brand with a famous person
5	event	e)	trying to influence important people
6	publishing	f)	using social networks to increase brand awareness
7	product placement	g)	using billboards, posters on bus-stops etc
8	endorsement	h)	banner ads, pop-ups, pay-per-click

2 ⊕ Now listen to an interview with Angelika, a communications specialist. Which six of the eight tools in exercise 1 does she mention?

3 ⊕ Listen again. What does Angelika say about the following topics? Complete her sentences.

1 *Events* 'We've got a big events department, because more and more companies want to create _____ with their end-users.'
2 *Endorsements* 'One way to build a brand is to associate it with famous people that consumers believe in and trust. You pay for an endorsement and you buy _____ of that celebrity – it transfers to your product.'
3 *Communication* 'You need inspiration more than market research. You need to understand how to speak to the _____ side of people's brain.'

4 Read the listening script (page 114) and make notes on what Angelika says about the following topics (maximum ten words each). When you finish, discuss the general issues with some colleagues.

● the benefits of events
● how communication channels have changed
● market research

Glossary

attention span period of time a person is able to concentrate
brand recognition how well the public knows your company / products
end-users last customers in the supply chain
fragmentation when something breaks into smaller pieces
in-store displays stands used in shops to promote a product
outcomes results
peanuts colloquial term meaning 'very cheap'
tour operator company which combines components to create a holiday, eg a flight plus car hire plus hotel
trade customers people in a supply chain who buy from a supplier and then sell to another customer or the end-user
video clip short video extract

7 Interview with an auditor

Exercises

1 What is the role of an auditor? Match 1–6 with a)–f) to make a list of auditors' responsibilities.

1 State that financial statements give _____
2 Audit the way _____
3 Look closely at big fluctuations _____
4 Check that the company values _____
5 Make sure that internal accounting processes _____
6 Check that the amount for provisions _____

a) on the income statement.
b) comply with government regulations.
c) is reasonable.
d) a true picture of the accounts of the business.
e) the figures are collected.
f) its inventory properly.

2 ⊛ Now listen to an interview with Claudia, an auditor. Which one of the above does she not mention?

3 ⊛ Read the questions below. Try to remember what Claudia said, then listen again to check.

1 Who do auditors now have to interview?
2 Why might a high price from a supplier be suspicious?
3 What is 'stock taking'?
4 Why do auditors send out letters to customers to ask them how much money they owe the company?
5 Why might a company want to put some of its profit into 'provisions'?

4 Read the listening script (page 116) and make notes on what Claudia says about the following topics (maximum ten words each). When you finish, discuss the general issues with some colleagues.

- the main change to auditors' responsibilities since the Enron scandal
- how to pay less tax (two ways)
- her proposals for controlling the 'big four'

Glossary

alleged stated but unproven
auditor sb who makes an independent assessment of a company's financial condition
comply (with) obey a rule or law
depreciation loss in value of a tangible asset
discrepancy variation
kickback bribe or illegal commission (informal)
offset balance two opposite effects
outgoing soon to leave a position of authority
provisions money set aside for a specific reason
receivables money owed to the business by customers
sourcing finding supplies such as components and raw materials

8 Interview with a portfolio manager

Exercises

1 Investment banks use different types of analysis to decide which companies and sectors to invest in. Put the key factors in the correct column.

> key price points   macro trends   a company's balance sheet
> a company's product pipeline   the economy
> support and resistance levels

Bottom-up analysis	Top-down analysis	Technical analysis
_____	_____	_____
_____	_____	_____

2 ⊛ Now listen to an interview with Jo, a portfolio manager in an investment bank, and check your answers.

3 ⊛ Are these statements true (T) or false (F)? Try to remember what Jo said, then listen again to check.

1 Jo's investment bank manages all the capital in the clients' pension funds. T / F
2 Jo only manages investments in Japanese companies. T / F
3 Jo, as portfolio manager, has a broader view of the market than the analysts. T / F
4 If a company issues a profit warning, you should sell all your shares very fast. T / F
5 Issuing new shares dilutes the value of the existing shares and so always makes the share price go down. T / F

4 Read the listening script (page 117) and make notes on what Jo says about the following topics (maximum ten words each). When you finish, discuss the general issues with some colleagues.

- the liaison between client and portfolio manager
- what gives Jo's investment bank a competitive edge
- headaches for a portfolio manager

Glossary

asset management a service offering advice on investments
bonds long-term debt sold to investors by companies
commodities products such as oil, coffee or metals
diluted made less strong by the addition of something else
diversify (risk) reduce risk by spreading it over different types of investment
drivers key factors that cause a situation to change
emerging (markets) markets in a transitional phase between 'developing' and 'developed'
equities stocks / shares (which represent ownership of a company)
investment bank bank that helps companies by arranging new share issues and providing advice
metrics parameters / criteria used for measuring
P/e ratio used to measure how cheap share prices are
portfolio collection of investments
price-to-book ratio ratio used to compare a stock's market value to its book value
product pipeline products in preparation, but not yet launched

9 Interview with an HR director

Exercises

1 Line managers and HR managers both play a role in the recruitment and appraisal processes. Write 'LM' or 'HR' next to the responsibilities.

Recruitment

1 Prepare a job description _____

2 Make sure legal and ethical requirements are met _____

3 Look at the general personal qualities of the individual _____

4 Look at the functional skills of the individual _____

Appraisal

5 Develop the appraisal tools _____

6 Make sure that the process is identifying future leaders _____

7 Rate functional performance _____

8 Monitor that appraisals are carried out _____

2 🎧 Now listen to an interview with Jurgen, an HR director, and check your answers.

3 🎧 Listen again. What does Jurgen say about the following topics? Complete his sentences.

1 *Internal candidates* '… opportunities for promotion are an important _____ inside the company and it's important to _____ within the organization.'

2 *The interview* 'In the HR interview we are looking for a positive personality, a flexible attitude, good team-working skills, and other qualities like _____ and the ability to _____ .'

3 *Performance-related pay* 'HR is here to help the business _____ . Bonuses are acceptable if they're seen to be _____ .'

4 *Motivation* 'Apart from the tangible _____ there are what I would call _____ motivators.'

4 Read the listening script (page 118) and make notes on what Jurgen says about the following topics (maximum ten words each). When you finish, discuss the general issues with some colleagues.

● assessing personal qualities in an interview

● performance-related pay

● the appraisal process

Glossary

appraisal formally assessing an employee's job performance
demoralizing making you feel less confident and hopeful
fast-tracking accelerating the progress of a person's career
fit in integrate successfully
job rotation movement through a variety of roles in the organization
matrix organization where people work in a variety of cross-functional teams rather than under one line manager
mindset attitude and way of thinking
rounds similar stages
track record things you have done in your career
underperforming less successful than expected

10 Interview with an IT consultant

Exercises

1 What do these acronyms stand for? How much do you know about them? Make notes.

1 ERP

2 CRM

3 VPN

2 🎧 Now listen to an interview with Jana, an IT consultant, and check your answers.

3 🎧 Listen again. What does Jana say about the following topics? Complete her sentences.

1 *IT consultancy* 'We offer IT solutions – software, hardware, system _____ , maintenance and _____ , consulting – everything.'

2 *The paperless office* 'A document – like an email or a letter or a legal contract or a report – is purely in _____ form and with document management you can _____ and store it.'

3 *Industry trends* '… everything is moving to the network – all kinds of data and all kinds of software. At the end of the day all _____ are the same – just a screen, a _____ of input like a keyboard, and a connection to the network.'

4 Read the listening script (page 119) and make notes on what Jana says about the following topics (maximum ten words each). When you finish, discuss the general issues with some colleagues.

● the benefits and risks of CRM

● using a document management system

● the difference between information and knowledge

● 'The Matrix'

Glossary

applications software computer programmes designed for a specific task, eg word processing, accounting
cold call a telephone call to a potential customer that they were not expecting
downside disadvantage
encryption protecting information by putting it into a special code that only some people can read
flagged up highlighted
IP (address) the IP (Internet Protocol) address is the address of every machine connected to the Internet – it takes the form of numbers separated by dots
log make a record of something
operating system programme that controls all the components of a computer system
print-outs printed information from a computer
stand-alone (package) package that works well on its own
template pre-defined model
track follow the progress of something

Listening Scripts

1 Interview with a venture capitalist

KARL I'd like to explain a little about venture capital, and why I think the lack of a strong VC sector in Europe is holding back our economy, at least as far as the technology sector is concerned.

INTERVIEWER *Very interesting. But before you begin, can you just explain how venture capital works – how it's different to other forms of financing like bank loans.*

KARL Let's think about the objectives of VC. The aim is to take a stake in a small start-up company, and then to sell this stake at a profit in the future, perhaps three or four years down the line. We need a clear exit strategy. We have absolutely no interest in keeping our stake for the long-term.

INTERVIEWER *So how exactly do you sell your stake? When does it happen?*

KARL There are two options, either at IPO when the company goes public, in which case we will sell to institutional and other investors who buy the shares, or in a trade sale, when a large company in the same sector buys the start-up, and the start-up just becomes a part of the other company. Its name disappears.

INTERVIEWER *Is venture capital interested in all start-ups?*

KARL Definitely not. Perhaps 95% of newly founded companies serve a small local market and will either stay small or grow slowly to become medium-sized companies. As venture capitalists we're not interested in that kind of company. These companies will turn to banks for their financing.

INTERVIEWER *So what kind of start-up is a venture capital firm looking for?*

KARL We're looking for companies with enormous growth potential – with a break-through innovation that will allow them to become major players in some specific sector in the global economy. Typically, these small firms will have their origins in some sort of collaboration between university and the industrial world, and they are usually found in the IT and biotech sectors. This type of firm will have little or no income stream – they are developing a product or a process and it's not on the market yet. Or maybe they have just a few pilot customers who are working with them to develop the product. So they need a source of financing, and that's where venture capital comes in. We're prepared to take a very big risk and fund the company.

INTERVIEWER *And in exchange for this risk?*

KARL In exchange for the risk we take a large stake in the company – perhaps 80% of the shares – and in the future we hope to sell these at a large profit. As I said earlier, we need to have an exit strategy.

INTERVIEWER *OK, so when you get involved you take something like 80% of the shares, leaving 20% for the founders of the company.*

KARL That's right. To motivate a team of bright guys you need to leave them with something like 20% of the company. But they are usually very happy with that. Remember that there is no money coming into the company – nothing to pay the bills, nothing to buy equipment. Without VC they have no company.

INTERVIEWER *OK. So venture capital gets involved at an early stage. What role does a venture capitalist have in the management of a start-up?*

KARL We don't get involved in the day-to-day running of the company. As I said, that's not our business. But we're a majority on the Board, and we want to monitor the growth of the company. Initially the most important thing is to get the human resources right – to make sure that the key people in the company are the very best. Then the next thing is to define the road map for the company, with the important milestones – perhaps first a working prototype, then the first customers, things like that. In fact the venture capital will be released in two or three rounds of financing, as different key milestones are reached.

INTERVIEWER *Then after some years the company grows and you get to the point where you want to sell your stake, either as a trade sale or an IPO.*

KARL That's right. A trade sale is by far the most common. It's easier to look for a trade sale. Large, international companies are very interested in buying successful start-ups who have already done all the hard work in developing a new product. It's like outsourcing their own R&D, with no risk. They are buying a technology which would have taken them several years and a lot of money to develop themselves. In addition, they are also buying all those early customers.

INTERVIEWER *That makes a lot of sense.*

KARL It's a trend that is unstoppable. Large companies will buy in more and more innovation. That's how Intel and Microsoft grew, but it's also true for biotech. Right now a lot of pharmaceutical firms are looking for drugs in phase two of development just because their own internal line of new products is not enough to fulfil their future needs. In the pharmaceutical sector all start-ups are looking to be bought, because it makes absolutely no sense to become a stand-alone company.

INTERVIEWER *So the situation is this. You have a small team of smart people working in a start-up. They all know each other and it's a very exciting environment. The focus is all on R&D. Then suddenly they are bought by a larger company and find themselves dealing with bureaucracy, sitting in long meetings and with reports to write. How do they react? Are they happy?*

KARL Well, of course they are very happy. Remember that they will have sold some of their shares as well, and they'll get a lot of money for that. It's their reward for all the years of hard work. They'll buy a new house and generally take their living standard to a new level. But, to be honest, in the case of a trade sale I can say that most of the original founders of the company will leave within a few years. You're right – it's a big culture shock. They get used to being their own boss and working in a company where every minute is dedicated to what is really important. They have a lot of difficulty in adapting to a large corporate environment.

INTERVIEWER *What happens to them?*

KARL They often start another new company.

INTERVIEWER *So they're serial entrepreneurs?*

KARL Yes, that's exactly what they are.

INTERVIEWER *So, just to be clear, very few small companies with a high growth potential will go on to be a success in their own right, through an IPO and a stock market listing. Instead, they'll all be bought, and disappear as stand-alone companies. At least in the technology area.*

KARL Yes, that's the point I was making at the beginning. With a service company it might be different. If it has a business model that is easy to understand, if it has a good revenue stream and the company is already profitable, then it will be able to have a successful IPO and go public. They will find investors to buy the shares. But in the technology sector investors are not ready to take a risk. They see a break-through innovation and a bunch of R&D-oriented managers, and that's not enough – they think the only way forward is a trade sale. It's very difficult in Europe to do a technology IPO. In the US it's different – the financial markets are quite happy to take the risk, and many start-ups go on to become world champions. That's the reason why they have so many successful companies in the technology area.

2 Interview with a CEO

INTERVIEWER *So, Lara, you've had a very interesting career. Now you're the CEO of a medium-sized utility company, but before that you were involved in local government, and in fact you were the mayor of your town! What have you learned about managing people? Let's begin with communication.*

LARA There are really three different channels of communication. There is top-down, there is bottom-up, and then there is also horizontal communication between people at the same level – that's more or less the same as teamwork.

INTERVIEWER *Let's begin with communication from the top to the bottom.*

LARA OK, well things like reports and meetings are obvious. But we do something else. Every quarter we produce an in-house magazine, written by our communications officer, and everyone who works in the company receives it. It describes the most important developments in the company, it has interviews and so on. It's expensive to produce – 80 pages, full colour – but we also send it to important customers, the CEOs of other local companies, local politicians and so on. The staff of the company get it through the mail at their homes.

INTERVIEWER *OK. What about the other way – communication from the bottom to the top?*

LARA You have to encourage an atmosphere where people feel able to speak freely. You don't want low-level employees to think 'the boss is the boss, and I'm going to keep my mouth shut'. You have to build an atmosphere of trust. When I became CEO do you know what I did? I made sure that I got out of my office and spent at least an hour a day just walking around the factory and talking to people on the shop floor. I saw how people worked, asked questions, asked how we could improve things. I think Tom Peters called it 'management by wandering around'. It's a bit like having a 'Suggestions Box', but face-to-face.

INTERVIEWER *A Suggestions Box is anonymous! This isn't!*

LARA But you know people don't really use a Suggestions Box, even if it is anonymous. You have to have human contact to find out what people think. What other examples can I give you? Yes, at the end of the year we have a big meeting with everyone in the company which is like an annual review. We present the progress of the company over the year, but people can also ask us questions. Then a few days later we have an event with food and drink, and again the managers mingle with the other staff and it creates a good atmosphere.

INTERVIEWER *Let's go on to the third type of communication you mentioned – horizontal communication.*

LARA As I said at the beginning, this is really the same as teamwork. This is very important in an organization. If someone is absent from work because of holidays, or illness, then someone else has to cover for them. And nowadays more and more work is organized according to individual projects – people come together as a team for one thing, work on it, and then the project ends. The next day they are in a new team for a new project. So interpersonal skills are really important in the workplace – even for technical guys. If you want to work alone, that's fine, but then you need to be an entrepreneur or a freelance professional, not part of an organization.

INTERVIEWER *Is there anything else about communication that you want to say?*

LARA Yes, there is. It's about email. I hate email. It takes much more time to resolve the smallest problem. In the past people used to sort things out quickly by getting together and talking. Now you have to cc everybody about your issues and read their replies, and then you have to read all the ccs that you receive about their issues. It's crazy. Many people spend two hours a day just answering emails. And people now have to be much more careful because there is a permanent record. It's very bad for communication.

INTERVIEWER *OK. Now let's change the topic completely and talk about motivation.*

LARA I have two things to say about motivation. The first is the importance of positive feedback. It has to be given constantly: face-to-face, through reports, and of course through the results in the figures. But just having the results is not enough – there has to be public acknowledgement and thanks so that people feel valued. The second thing is about the importance of listening. One of the most motivating things for an employee is to have a boss that listens. I love to speak in meetings and show how important I am, but that's a big mistake. I am important and I will take the decisions. But I have to take into account other people's opinions, otherwise they won't support me. So in many meetings I just explain the background to the situation in two minutes and then leave time for other people to speak.

INTERVIEWER *You have worked both in the public sector – in local government – and in the private sector. Public sector employees sometimes have a bad reputation – people say they are less motivated because they have their jobs for life and have no incentives to perform well. Do you think that's true?*

LARA You have to change the system in the public sector so that people are paid more in relation to results and performance. It's not easy and it takes a long time. But remember something else very important – not everyone has drive and energy and wants to get to the top. Some people are happy to stay near the bottom, or in the middle. Perhaps they have other priorities like their families or their outside interests. Some people just want to do their job and go home and forget about work. That doesn't always mean they are lazy. I think that very, very few people are deliberately lazy – everyone can be motivated somehow.

INTERVIEWER *Thanks. The final topic I'd like to talk about is leadership. In a way it's the other side of the coin. Communication and motivation are all about listening and empowerment, whereas leadership is about strength at the top. If you are a leader then I, by definition, am a humble follower.*

LARA No, no, you can't see it that way. The leader has vision, and sees the big picture. Employees like to see that and respect it – it gives them a sense of security, like having a parent figure. The sailors on the ship need to feel that the captain of the ship knows where he or she is going. No-one wants to sail around in circles. But that is not a contradiction with motivation – it's part of the same process. It's motivating for employees to know that the boss is prepared to take important decisions, and be responsible for them.

INTERVIEWER *There's one thing that I've never understood. What is the relationship between the Chairman of the Board – or the President as some people say – and the CEO? You can't have two captains of the ship.*

LARA The CEO – not the Chairman of the Board – is the captain of the ship. The role of the Board is different – it's to monitor and challenge the actions of the senior management. The CEO is there on the Board to represent the management team and explain their actions. So the Board just checks that everything is going well for the share price and the dividends, and it doesn't take many initiatives. But that's most of the time, not all the time. For very big things, like mergers, acquisitions, strategic alliances, entering new markets and so on – for those things the initiative can come from the Board. In those cases the Chairman of the Board is the top person. If I use your analogy of the navy, the CEO is like the captain but the Chairman is like the Admiral. The Admiral lives on land and just visits the ship occasionally to make sure things are going OK. The Admiral lets the captain get on and do his job. But when the Admiral gives an order, even the captain jumps. The Admiral can send the captain to war, and the captain's job depends on the Admiral.

3 Interview with a project manager

INTERVIEWER *Anton, you work in the construction industry as a project manager. I'd like to get an idea of some of the issues that you deal with.*

ANTON Yes. First let me give you some context. We build factories, warehouses and office buildings, but not residential buildings.

INTERVIEWER *And you take part in the whole process – from a greenfield site to the finished buildings.*

ANTON Yes. We can do all the process or just one part. Sometimes we have to rebuild an old factory, or build a new warehouse next to an existing factory. But generally we build in an area that has been designated for urbanization – so there is just the land, no buildings, but the local authority has already put in all the services. There is a water supply, an electricity supply and drains already in the ground.

INTERVIEWER *OK, what is the first step?*

ANTON First you discuss with your client the number of buildings and the layout of the factory. You look at all the initial preparation that will be necessary. So, starting with the movement of earth and the laying of the foundations, and then looking at the different types of engineering that will be involved – the mechanical and the electrical engineering. We call all this the 'master plan'.

INTERVIEWER *What exactly do you mean by 'mechanical' engineering and 'electrical' engineering?*

ANTON Let's take mechanical engineering first. You have the basic structure that sits on the foundations. You need to look at the load on the structure – for example one beam may have a crane attached to it that will carry machinery, and that beam has to be very strong. Then you have the enclosure – that means the roof and walls and doors. We have to consider water exclusion, the position of windows for natural daylight, noise, access doors, security and so on. Then we have climate services. That means heating, ventilation and air conditioning. The next thing is utility services. That includes the water supply, drainage, refuse handling – including handling any pollutants that might be produced – and also mechanical transportation inside the factory, so things like lifts and escalators. Oh yes, another very important thing is safety, and in particular fire safety. We need a sprinkler system, fire-resistant materials, we might even have to compartmentalize sections of the building if there is a high risk. All that affects the insurance costs.

INTERVIEWER *Wow – that's quite a list.*

ANTON Yes, and that's just the mechanical engineering. I still haven't mentioned the electrical engineering!

INTERVIEWER *OK, go on.*

ANTON The electrical side of things includes first the basic supply to the factory. So we need transformers to reduce the high voltage from the grid to the low voltage inside the factory, and also an electrical distribution system inside the building. Then we have lighting – here we look at the level of light, the mix of artificial and daylight, the position of the windows and so on. And then we have all the telecommunications inside the building – the cabling that we are going to need for that.

INTERVIEWER *Have you missed anything out?*

ANTON Let me see. Oh yes, acoustics. That means the properties of the ceiling, walls and floor that absorb or reflect noise. Noise levels inside the factory have to be kept within health and safety limits.

INTERVIEWER *Well, I've driven past many factories in my life but I've never really stopped to think about the work that goes into building them.*

ANTON It's a very complex operation. All the things I've mentioned so far are defined by us working together with the client at the beginning of the project. We have a team of people working with the client on each of those areas – they are like sub-projects that go together to make the master plan.

INTERVIEWER *So what happens next?*

ANTON For each of the sub-projects – we call them 'packages' – we go to the market and ask different suppliers to give us a price. We put out a tender. We tell them the specifications that we need, and they bid.

INTERVIEWER *Can I stop you for one moment. You're saying that each of the areas that you listed earlier has a separate tender that will lead to a separate contractor?*

ANTON Yes. Exactly. And we are the project manager. We define the project at the beginning and then manage it all the way through.

INTERVIEWER *And is it a completely open, public tender?*

ANTON First of all we make a shortlist of suppliers, because not all contractors can do all projects. There's usually around six or seven companies on the list. Most of them will put in a proposal once they've seen the details of the project and had a chance to ask us questions. We need at least three proposals before we can confirm that the prices are reasonable. If not, we look for more suppliers. After that we select just two, and we start negotiating with just one of these. If this fails, we negotiate with the second one. When the negotiations are over, they start work.

INTERVIEWER   *It sounds very competitive.*

ANTON   It is. In the construction sector things are very competitive.

INTERVIEWER   *There must be a lot of planning involved in terms of which contractor starts work when. Some packages need others to be finished before they can begin, some can work in parallel.*

ANTON   You've got it. We do most packages in parallel, and we have to coordinate all the different contractors very carefully. If we get it wrong, they can claim money from you.

INTERVIEWER   *What do you mean?*

ANTON   If one job is late, it has a knock-on effect. Another contractor is halfway through their work and they can't continue. They have their machinery on-site, which they have hired, and they have their people, who are expecting to work. But they can't get on and finish their job because another package is behind schedule. So if it's not their fault, they charge you. Sometimes it's just a simple question of two teams being unable to physically work in the same space – one of them has to stop.

INTERVIEWER   *So in the small print of the contract there's a penalty clause that allows a supplier to claim compensation from you for their lost time.*

ANTON   Yes, when it's not their fault, that's right. We have to pay that. But of course we first go to the other supplier that caused the problem and try to charge them for being late. We negotiate with both companies about how much to pay and whose fault it is.

INTERVIEWER   *You don't make many friends as a project manager.*

ANTON   It's very tough, because at the same time we want to keep them happy so that they do a good job.

INTERVIEWER   *Is there anything else you negotiate about?*

ANTON   Yes, right at the end, at the point when they hand over to us – we call that the 'reception'. At the reception we make a retention until we have checked all their work. They want to be paid the full amount as soon as they finish, but we have to check that all the work is OK in case we want them to redo something. So we retain some money as a way to control the situation, and they don't like that.

INTERVIEWER   *OK, thanks. I found that very interesting.*

4 Interview with a design engineer

INTERVIEWER   *Could you start off by telling me what you do in your job?*

ALEX   I'm a design engineer, working currently in the rail industry.

INTERVIEWER   *Can you give me an example of the kind of work you're doing at the moment?*

ALEX   At the moment I'm working on a mechanism for providing power to a train when it's in the maintenance depot. It's a special piece that is fitted to the train that allows an auxiliary power supply to be attached. The piece has to fit into a specified space – we call that the 'work envelope'. Apart from being the right size, the piece will also have slots and holes, moving parts that have to work together, and so on. I do all the design for that in a CAD package.

INTERVIEWER   *OK, and this process is presumably the same for other industries such as the automobile industry and the consumer goods industry.*

ALEX   It's basically the same, but our engineering process is batch production – we might be producing hundreds of pieces, whereas in the car industry, say, it's mass production – they might be producing tens of thousands of pieces. But of course every piece of every physical object in the world was designed and manufactured by someone somewhere.

INTERVIEWER   *Right. So the whole thing starts with you and a CAD package on your computer.*

ALEX   The whole thing starts with me receiving a specification from the customer regarding the requirements for the particular project. I do an initial design and then there is a degree of refining within the given parameters of dimension, functionality, cost and so on.

INTERVIEWER   *OK, so how does CAD work?*

ALEX   I usually begin with some initial concept sketches on paper – just outline drawings. Then I construct a virtual piece in CAD. I begin with a major part first of all, so for this particular example, that would be the mounting panel – all the other parts are attached to this panel, which itself is attached to the train. I create this first part and then start to think about how the other parts of the mechanism are going to fit and work together. In this particular case there are about fifty or sixty different bits, including all the screws and nuts and so on.

INTERVIEWER   *And you're making modifications all the way.*

ALEX   Yes, the design is iterative. That means repetitive and cyclical. It means you keep going, making slight adjustments, until you reach the result you want.

INTERVIEWER   *There's an important point here. As a design engineer, are you just looking for the most elegant and functional design, or are other factors like cost of materials also important?*

ALEX   Good question. Let me first give you an example where design was the only factor, and cost not important. Steve Jobs famously told the designers at Apple that with the iPod he wanted no visible screws. That was a design constraint that forced tremendous innovation. But the consumer goods sector and the B2B sector are two very different sectors. In consumer goods, design is there to appeal to the end-user. It's about fashion. Whereas in my sector, or any B2B sector, we're looking very much at design for manufacture, DFM, and design for assembly, DFA. These are two well-known methodologies for design.

INTERVIEWER *Can you explain them?*

ALEX Design for manufacture means that the piece can be made easily and cost-effectively. Design for assembly is very similar, but it refers to how to put all the individual pieces together. Making sure that assembly time is minimized, and that the people who fit the pieces can only do it in a certain way and won't make any mistakes. Both ideas reinforce the fact that design is not just about quality and functionality, but also about cost and ease of manufacture.

INTERVIEWER *So there is a trade-off between quality and costs.*

ALEX Very much so. There's no point designing something with the best possible quality that can last for fifty years when the piece itself will only have a working life of ten years. That's called 'over-designing', and it's one of the biggest mistakes that you can make. You end up with a piece that's much too expensive in every respect – materials, manufacturing costs, design time, everything. No, your design must be fit-for-purpose, not the best possible quality.

INTERVIEWER *OK, so you're doing all this design work at your desk using the computer. What kinds of testing are you able to do while it's still in a virtual form?*

ALEX You can simulate movement – for example when one part turns, will it clash with another part? But testing at the CAD stage is fairly limited. We have to wait for the physical prototype to do the majority of the tests.

INTERVIEWER *OK, so let's move on to the next stage of the process, manufacturing. Do you do that in-house or do you outsource?*

ALEX We outsource. We have a supplier network. Different manufacturers are specialized in different things. So for example you might use one company for the welding and sheet metal work, another for the non-metallic materials, and so on.

INTERVIEWER *And do they work off drawings or using your CAD file?*

ALEX With some processes they have to work off drawings because they are done manually – for example welding. But many parts are machined, and in this case we provide the supplier with the CAD file containing the designs. They transfer this to a CNC machine that machines the parts automatically. CNC stands for Computer Numerical Control, and it means that the machine tool is driven by a computer program as it is making the components.

INTERVIEWER *OK, tell me about what happens next.*

ALEX Everything comes back to us, and we do the assembly on our own premises. We are a design and assembly company. So, the parts come in batches. The very first batch is the most important – we do an inspection on a couple of items to make sure that they are within the tolerances specified.

INTERVIEWER *The 'tolerances'?*

ALEX The tolerance means the amount of permitted variation. A part can be half a mil off, but not one mil off. It's a plus or minus figure.

INTERVIEWER *OK, so you have your first batch of parts, and you've checked them. The next stage is to build a physical prototype.*

ALEX Yes. You build your first unit. You work off the drawings – just like making an IKEA wardrobe. And as you go you find that things are not as straightforward as you hoped. Some mechanisms won't fit together or work together as well as they did in your virtual CAD world.

INTERVIEWER *And you may have to go back to the manufacturer to ask them to make small adjustments.*

ALEX Yes. Then finally we have a working assembly, and the next stage is to test it. The customer will normally give their requirements for testing and this can be quite comprehensive. It can include testing against fire, or to check the seals against entry of water, or to check the effects of vibration, and so on.

INTERVIEWER *And would this prototype be fitted to a real train?*

ALEX Yes. That's the idea. And when the customer has seen one working item, and they're happy with it, then we can accept delivery of further parts and go into full production.

5 Interview with a marketing director

INTERVIEWER *So, can you tell me what field of marketing you work in?*

LOUIS Yes, my company manufactures and sells domestic appliances – white goods. That means fridges and freezers, ovens and hobs, dishwashers, washing machines and so on. I have worked in the same company for fifteen years, starting as a salesman and then working my way up to marketing director for the whole company. Now we are part of a very large international group.

INTERVIEWER *OK, can you tell me something about your product range?*

LOUIS An interesting point I'd like to make straight away is that there are some important differences here between the US and Europe. Americans tend to like functionality and are less status-conscious, whereas Europeans want sophistication and design. And then there's also a difference in habits. Americans move house often and take everything with them, so they like free-standing units. Whereas Europeans move house less often and want built-in units, fitted units. A well-designed fitted kitchen is an expression of their personality.

INTERVIEWER *OK, but sticking to Europe for now, tell me about your product range and your distribution channels. For example, I imagine that, as well as selling directly to the end-user, you also have B2B distribution channels to the construction sector?*

LOUIS That's right. For the end-user we have both free-standing and built-in lines. For the construction sector – where everything is built-in – we have cheaper lines for holiday flats and more expensive lines for residential developments.

INTERVIEWER *Is there a big difference in the profit margins between the various lines?*

LOUIS Enormous. In fact for the kitchens in holiday flats our profit is zero. Nothing at all. But we need those items to provide builders with a full range – so that they come to us for everything. Because the units they install in their residential developments are very profitable for us.

INTERVIEWER *How many different models do you have in total?*

LOUIS It's crazy. Across all our different product categories and all our different brands we have about 1,400 models.

INTERVIEWER *Why do you have so many?*

LOUIS Because we have to. First, if we cut our product line, it would look bad in the market. People might think 'They only have twenty dishwashers whereas the competitor has twenty-four so it must be a worse company, or a smaller company, or something.' And second, in the construction sector they build a variety of houses and apartments at different price levels and they want different qualities of kitchen to reflect that.

INTERVIEWER   *And how often do you replace old models with new ones?*

LOUIS   That's a good question. Take washing machines as an example. Every two years we do a facelift – just minor cosmetic changes. Then every three or four years we do a restyling – the line and volume of the product changes, and perhaps the position of the handle or something. And finally every six or seven years we actually have a new generation of products with different technology and so on. So at what stage do you say it's a new product? It's an interesting question.

INTERVIEWER   *Are the new generations of product marketing-led or engineering-led?*

LOUIS   In the case of washing machines, marketing-led. Consumers told us that they wanted a drum big enough for eight kilos of clothes, not five, and we asked engineering to find a way to do that. They had to redesign and reposition the internal components, the motor and so on. It wasn't them who told us they could do it.

INTERVIEWER   *OK. A moment ago you were talking about different price levels and different qualities of kitchen. In what sense does quality vary according to price?*

LOUIS   It doesn't vary in terms of build quality. The build quality has to be excellent for all our products. This is very, very strict. No, the difference is in the number of features, the performance and the design. And in terms of pricing, it's design that adds the most value. A top-of-the-range brand will have its own personality that we have spent a lot of advertising dollars creating. When the customer buys the brand, they buy the image and the lifestyle that goes with it.

INTERVIEWER   *So image adds more value than features.*

LOUIS   Absolutely.

INTERVIEWER   *OK, but it's strange to think about 'brand personality' with something very practical and functional like a domestic appliance.*

LOUIS   As I mentioned earlier, in Europe a kitchen is a status symbol. When someone new comes to your house, to visit you, there is a ritual of showing them round the different rooms. And our research shows that the kitchen is the main area where the homeowner is judged. The brands you have there give other people an idea of which level of society you move in – what you can afford.

INTERVIEWER   *Now I see!*

LOUIS   Maybe you didn't understand because you are a man. With kitchens, women make the purchasing decision, and they know about these things.

INTERVIEWER   *OK, let's change the subject completely now. Can you tell me a little about your market research.*

LOUIS   Yes. We realized early on that the people who come into closest contact with our end-users are actually the service engineers who repair the products. So we give them some training in how to ask questions while they are chatting to people in their homes – after the repair is finished. I suppose you could say it's like a customer satisfaction survey, but qualitative not quantitative. People often come up with good ideas for improvements.

INTERVIEWER   *So that's an interesting way to use existing customers. What are your main ways to get new customers?*

LOUIS   Advertising is of course very important. We use an outside agency for that, and we monitor the success of their campaigns. It's not at all straightforward. For example, immediately following a campaign we often find that the brand awareness of our competitors has increased by as much as our own. One time we found that only 15% of end-users associated our slogan with our brand.

INTERVIEWER   *What does the agency say about that?*

LOUIS   They are very skilled at not taking the blame. Usually the solution involves spending even more money! But anyway, we change our advertising agency every few years – after a time their ideas get stale.

INTERVIEWER   *What other marketing tools do you use?*

LOUIS   Direct marketing is very important for us. I'll give you an example of one thing that we do. Inside many magazines you get a questionnaire with boxes to tick about different aspects of your lifestyle. If you fill it in and return it, you might win a prize. Anyway, we can ask to have one of the questions about kitchens, and in particular to tick a box if you are thinking about having a new fitted kitchen in the next twelve months. Then we buy all those names and addresses, and we contact the people directly and send them our brochure.

INTERVIEWER   *So you increase the amount of junk mail in circulation.*

LOUIS   No, it's not junk – it's targeted and useful. By law the consumer has to actively opt in – they have to tick a box saying they are interested in receiving third-party promotions.

INTERVIEWER   *OK, thanks.*

6 Interview with a communications consultant

INTERVIEWER   *So, Angelika, you work for a communication company.*

ANGELIKA   That's right.

INTERVIEWER   *And why do you use the word 'communication', rather than 'advertising'.*

ANGELIKA   'Communication' refers to a whole range of different tools that we use, and advertising is just one of those, along with PR, the Internet, events, publishing, etc.

INTERVIEWER   *I think most people are clear about what advertising is, but what about public relations – PR? What exactly is PR?*

ANGELIKA   Well, we've got two kinds of PR. We've got relationships with the press, and we've also got relationships with people who perhaps I can describe as 'opinion formers' – leaders of public opinion.

INTERVIEWER   *Do you mean lobbying?*

ANGELIKA   Yes, 'lobbying' in its broadest sense.

INTERVIEWER   *OK, the second thing you mentioned was the Internet.*

ANGELIKA   Yes, we advise clients on their use of Internet websites, so that they have maximum impact, and we also use a whole range of tools like banner ads and so on. A more unusual thing that we do is 'buzz communication' – that's when you create a video clip on a website and then hope that people send the clip, or the link, to their friends and that they send it on to their friends and it spreads.

INTERVIEWER   *Is that called 'viral marketing'?*

ANGELIKA   Yes. Viral marketing.

INTERVIEWER   *OK, what about events?*

ANGELIKA   We've got a big events department, because more and more companies want to create personal links with their end-users. Of course advertising is important, but with events you reach the people who use your products in a very direct way. And you offer them something very important: a good moment in their lives that they will remember. So it could be a party, a conference, a private visit to a museum, or something in the street.

INTERVIEWER   *And the last thing you mentioned was publishing.*

ANGELIKA   Yes, we've got a big publishing department. We produce leaflets and brochures, in-store displays, the annual report, and sometimes even magazines to give away free to consumers.

INTERVIEWER   *Right. Can you put it all together and give me an example of how a communication company works with a specific client?*

ANGELIKA   OK, I'm going to talk about one client in particular – a tour operator that I worked with a few years ago. Their products were holidays, travel in Europe. The first thing you have to understand is who their customers were. Obviously, the end-user was the person who went on the holiday. But there was also a trade customer, the travel agent, who was the intermediary.

INTERVIEWER   *So you had two different communication channels to think about?*

ANGELIKA   Exactly. For the trade customers we decided to invest a lot of money in one specific event. In fact it was a weekend ski holiday.

INTERVIEWER   *Let me get this right. This weekend was for people who worked at travel agencies, not for members of the public.*

ANGELIKA   That's right. Only for staff who work in the agencies. We wrote to them all and invited them to enter a competition. The prize was a weekend in the mountains for a hundred people. This is how it worked. On the first evening we would do some short presentations about our new products, talk them through our new brochure, things like that. During the rest of the weekend we would mix with people and talk to them. That way you start a personal relationship with the agents. It's much easier to contact them again in the future. You also get a lot of useful market information just by talking to people informally over the weekend. It's a good investment because it's not very expensive – if you compare it with an advertising campaign in a major newspaper aimed at end-users, it was peanuts.

INTERVIEWER   *OK. That's a nice example of using an event. Now what about promotion to the end-users – the people who actually go on the holidays.*

ANGELIKA   Yes. Here we're talking about brand recognition. And we decided that the best way to get this was by attending fairs at exhibition centres. We worked with our client to make the maximum impact on the stand. We created the display area around the stand, and we had to think carefully about how to differentiate our products visually from all the others. Then there's the printed material to design and prepare. We also trained the people working on the stand how to interact with the visitors. You talk to a lot of visitors over seven days and it's easy to forget to ask them for their contact details, holiday preferences and so on. You need this information for your customer database – it's one of the most important outcomes of the fair.

INTERVIEWER   *If they just walk away, it's a missed opportunity.*

ANGELIKA   Yes.

INTERVIEWER   *OK, thanks a lot. I want to ask you something different now. In the field of communication there's a lot of small agencies, and the client companies seem to switch agencies a lot. Can you tell me something about how that works?*

ANGELIKA   Of course. For a large company it would be normal to have several agencies working for them – perhaps different ones for different brands. A big company will never, never give all its communications and advertising work to just one agency.

INTERVIEWER   *Because one agency would have too much power?*

ANGELIKA   Yes, too much power. They want competition between them. And they also want different ideas. What is very striking now is the fragmentation of media channels and the fragmentation of the market. In the past you knew where the consumers were. When you ran an advertisement at 8 o'clock in the evening, you knew that 40% of the country were looking at your ads. Now it's more and more difficult. First because of all the communication channels – the Internet, satellite TV, specialized magazines – and second because people's attention span is much less – they only stay on a website or watch TV for a short time, then they lose interest. We have to use a lot of channels and a lot of tools. Now it's a mix, a real mix.

INTERVIEWER   *OK. There's something you haven't spoken about yet. Do you use endorsements and sponsorship deals?*

ANGELIKA   Sometimes, although I've never done that personally. But it is useful. Why? Because products are so similar these days and branding is everything. One way to build a brand is to associate it with famous people that consumers believe in and trust. You pay for an endorsement and you buy the credibility and fame of that celebrity – it transfers to your product. The process is very easy to understand – you can buy anything, even people. You just have to pay enough money. But you have to be very careful. For example if your company sponsors a sports team, the team must win, because if they lose, then your brand is also a loser.

INTERVIEWER   *I'd like to finish with a completely different question. What advice would you give to someone at university who was thinking about a career in communications?*

ANGELIKA   I would say that communication is not to do with market research and collecting data.

INTERVIEWER   *What do you mean?*

ANGELIKA   Research will just tell you that the consumer wants the product they already know but at a cheaper price and with a different colour. It's meaningless. When companies contact a communication agency they want creativity – they want original campaigns to make their brand more powerful. You need inspiration more than market research. You need to understand how to speak to the emotional and intuitive side of people's brain.

7 Interview with an auditor

INTERVIEWER   *Can you begin by telling me a little bit about the company you work for?*

CLAUDIA   I work for an auditing company in Austria – we're a middle-sized company, not one of the big international names like KPMG or PricewaterhouseCoopers. The companies we audit are not listed on the Austrian stock exchange.

INTERVIEWER   *OK. So how would you describe the main responsibilities of an auditor?*

CLAUDIA   Actually, an auditor's job is getting more and more complex. After each scandal which involves some fraud or other – like Enron – there are new regulations. In the old days we just examined the financial statements and we had to state officially that they gave a fair and true picture of the accounts of the business. Now we have to do more than that. We have to check the company's internal control mechanisms, and we have to make an official statement that no fraud is taking place. So now we don't just look at the figures, but at the internal processes as well – we have to audit the way the figures are collected. In fact we used to do this before as well, you can't avoid it, but now there is a legal duty to make a statement about this.

INTERVIEWER   *Can you give me an example of the kinds of things that you do now that you didn't do before?*

CLAUDIA   Now we have to interview the executives of the company. We have to ask detailed questions about any areas where they themselves think we should investigate further. So the senior management has some responsibility to warn us if there are any strange things going on. If there are, and they haven't told us, then they get into big trouble. It puts more of the responsibility on them. Another example would be the company's sourcing policy – who they buy from. We have to examine that very closely now. For example we look for any case where one particular supplier has provided a large amount of raw materials for a suspiciously high price. It might be the case that they are being favoured in exchange for an under-the-table kickback. The whole question of cash management is important to look at here: who wrote the invoice, who accounts for the cash in, and are these people the same or different. We're always looking to make sure that there are checks in the system – more than just one pair of eyes seeing and authorizing all the documents.

INTERVIEWER   *OK, so now you don't just check the consistency of the figures, you check what lies behind the figures.*

CLAUDIA   Yes, but everything is related. Every sum of money has an entry in the financial statements somewhere, and a discrepancy in cash will eventually show up as a discrepancy in the income statement. A good example is how you divide sales income between two years: if you make a sale and deliver the goods in one financial year, but only receive the money in the next financial year, then how do you account for that in the books? You might have a top-line sales figure in the income statement for one year that doesn't correspond to the cash flow.

INTERVIEWER   *OK, your examples so far have been quite specific. What are the really big issues on the income statement?*

CLAUDIA   Well, the first thing is just to make a comparison with the previous years. If there is a big fluctuation, then obviously we look closer and ask why. But I suppose the biggest thing on the income statement is definitely tax.

INTERVIEWER   *And what is the one most useful piece of advice that you can give to a company on how they can reduce their tax?*

CLAUDIA   The most useful advice is often to change the structure of the company so that you change its legal entity. You set up a holding company so that you offset your profits from one subsidiary with the losses from another. There is a consolidated financial statement for the whole group. You pay less tax. We get a lot of work by advising our clients on how to do this.

INTERVIEWER   *Isn't that a potential conflict of interest? Can an auditing company both check that the taxes are correct and also advise on how to reduce taxes?*

CLAUDIA   Yes, why not? There's no conflict of interest. We are in the best position to give tax advice because we are the ones who really know the accounts.

INTERVIEWER   *OK, so far we've been talking about the income statement. Let's turn to the balance sheet. What kind of internal processes do you check?*

CLAUDIA   One big thing for the balance sheet is how to value inventory. When the time comes to do this at the end of the year – it's called 'stock taking' – we have to see how the company values its unsold stock, its work-in-progress, its raw materials. We have to check that they do it properly and have counted every single part, and that they do it at the right time. The question of valuing unsold stock is complex: is it valued at cost price or at sale price? If it is old stock that is not worth as much, then have they made a proper depreciation?

INTERVIEWER   *Anything else on the asset side?*

CLAUDIA   Receivables. Receivables get a lot of focus during an audit because if the trade receivables are not accounted for properly, then the sales are also not correct. In fact we check by sending out letters to the customers to ask them independently how much money they owe the company.

INTERVIEWER   *And on the liabilities side, what's a typical issue that the auditor would focus on?*

CLAUDIA   A typical issue is their provisions for risks. There may be an item for provisions for a particular risk – maybe a lawsuit – but in fact the cost is already partially paid and accounted for. A big thing with provisions is that it's a way to minimize tax. Imagine that you have a big profit one year – you push some of that into provisions and you reduce the profit for that year and you pay less tax. And then imagine that next year you make a loss. No problem – surprise, surprise, you didn't need the provisions after all and the money comes back into the accounts and it looks like the loss isn't so bad.

INTERVIEWER   *Is that legal?*

CLAUDIA   No. You have to check that the amount for provisions is reasonable.

INTERVIEWER   *OK, thanks. I'd like to finish with a big picture question. In the auditing world people talk about 'the big four' – that's Deloitte, Ernst & Young, KPMG and PwC. It used to be 'the big five', but of course Andersen collapsed in 2002 along with Enron.*

CLAUDIA   That's right.

INTERVIEWER   *Four is not much choice for such an important area, and there always seems to be some scandal or other happening. The American arm of Ernst was banned in 2004 for reckless and negligent conduct; in 2005 KPMG in the States was involved in a case of alleged tax fraud, although it never went to court; and in 2006 the Japanese financial regulator suspended PwC's audit licence for two* *months. The suspicion is that the regulators are going easy on these companies in case there's another collapse, and then there would be even less choice.*

CLAUDIA   You're right, and because I work for a medium-sized company I am very critical of all that. I would like to see more use of second-tier companies like us in auditing the big four. But another solution is compulsory rotation – clients should be required by law to appoint a new firm every few years. That would stop the relationship from getting too close, and the incoming firm would have an incentive to look at the work of its outgoing predecessor.

8 Interview with a portfolio manager

INTERVIEWER   *You work as a portfolio manager in an investment bank based in London. Can you begin by briefly describing your job?*

JO   OK. Investment banks advise companies on financing, and on mergers and acquisitions. They help to tackle the legal issues surrounding those things – so they are like financial consultants for companies. I personally work for the asset management arm of the bank – that means looking after a client's money. Our clients are mostly pension funds.

INTERVIEWER   *Just explain what a 'pension fund' is.*

JO   Our clients are US corporates with a global business. Any large company – or any US state authority or public authority for that matter – has a pension fund for its employees. It needs to pay out large sums of money over many years. We manage a part of the capital in the fund. We offer them the ability to earn high investment returns and to diversify their risk.

INTERVIEWER   *You manage just a part of the capital in their fund?*

JO   Yes. There are several asset managers involved. A US pension fund will obviously include a lot of US investments, and these are managed by one or more investment banks based over there. But the fund will also hold equity positions in markets all over the world. It diversifies their risk. And usually we are the sole overseas provider – we offer a high level of expertise in managing these non-US equities. In my own job, I manage just the investments in Japanese companies.

INTERVIEWER   *And what about non-equity holdings such as bonds?*

JO   The manager of their bond funds will be completely different again.

INTERVIEWER   *OK. So the client, the pension fund, gives you a pot of money to invest. Do you have to get back to them with your ideas – how much liaison is there between you and them?*

JO   The normal relationship is that we'll draw up what we call an investment mandate. That puts down on paper some legal restrictions on where we can invest. There will also be guidelines like the percentage of the fund that can be in emerging markets, or in smaller companies. Sometimes there will also be an ethical component in the mandate – types of companies that we cannot invest in. And then we report back to the client on a regular basis – monthly or quarterly – both in written reports and in face-to-face meetings.

INTERVIEWER   *Right. So your job is to look at all of the stocks listed on the Japanese stock market, and then pick the ones that you're going to buy. How do you do that?*

JO   We do a mixture of top-down and bottom-up analysis. In my particular bank the house style is to be more bottom-up.

INTERVIEWER   *Can you explain 'top-down' and 'bottom-up'?*

JO   Sure. Top-down means looking at the economy. Looking at macro themes that will support the business going forward. So for instance if we believe in strong personal consumption trends over the next three or four years, then we will obviously be drawn towards the retail sector, or if we think Japanese auto purchasing is going to be weak, we are unlikely to take big positions in some of the auto stocks.

INTERVIEWER   *And bottom-up analysis?*

JO   Bottom-up means looking at the micro dynamics within a company. It's very company specific. We spend a lot of time talking to company managers, looking at their balance sheet, looking at their product pipeline, and really getting to know our companies very well. If you want me to be more technical, I can say that we look for companies with a very high return on equity, or return on invested capital, and we focus very heavily on the ability to sustain those returns going forward. P/e is also very heavily used, as well as things like price-to-book ratio. Basically these are all metrics that we use to find stocks where the valuation is appealing.

INTERVIEWER   *OK. But other asset management companies are doing exactly the same thing for their clients; they're looking at exactly the same information. How do you get an edge on your competitors?*

JO   Good question. What we're all trying to do is look at inefficiencies in the market. We're trying to find some information somewhere that is not being discounted in the share price. The only way to do that is by the quality of your analysis, and that boils down to the quality of the analysts – the people you have doing the work. We have a global network of analysts and we're very good at picking up trends before they reach others in the market. Let me give you an example. What's happening to sales of PCs in the US is crucially important for a lot of Japanese technology-related stocks, and so our US analysts talk to our Japanese analysts and we get a very clear picture of what's likely to happen. It's the combination of excellent analysts working in a global team that gives us a very powerful competitive advantage.

INTERVIEWER   *OK – and what about you? Are you one of the analysts?*

JO   No, I'm a portfolio manager. The analysts work for me. They are the experts at the company level and the sector level. I listen to all the analysts and then decide on how to make up the overall portfolio for the whole Japanese market. Also, I am a little more aware of some of the macro factors, and I can decide between sectors. I take a broader view of the market. But the interaction between us is very close and very informal – it's very much an ongoing debate.

INTERVIEWER   *Where do you stand on the argument between fundamental and technical analysis? I know that technical people look at charts, look at support and resistance levels, look at momentum and volume, and all of those things can be done without knowing anything at all about the company or the market. It's a very different approach.*

JO   Generally we don't use technical analysis here. We think it has very little to offer, at least for equities. But you have to be careful – for example in Japan local investors do look at key price points for stocks, and so automatically it does have some relevance. You find that technicals are used a lot more in areas like commodities and currencies where people move in and out of the market very quickly. And also with currencies there's very few drivers of the price movement – very few fundamentals to analyse like we do with stocks – and so it's helpful to use the charts.

INTERVIEWER *Great. I'd like to finish with a very different question.*

JO OK.

INTERVIEWER *What is a typical crisis in your job? What's your worst nightmare when you walk in at nine o'clock in the morning?*

JO There are two big things that can go wrong. One is that you walk in and you find that a company that you have invested in has a profit warning. So basically it's not going to make as much money as you or the market think. Obviously the first reaction is a big drop in the share price. How do you cope with that? Well, you have to adjust to the new reality very quickly. Normally the biggest question is: is it a structural problem with the company, or is it a temporary decline in earnings? If you think it's a structural deterioration, then you need to sell your holding, and to decide when – maybe very fast. If it's temporary, then normally you'll be looking at a good price to add to your position – in effect looking to challenge the market which you think has an incorrect assessment of events. Another problem would be if you came in and you heard that a company was issuing a lot more shares. That means that the equity is diluted – with the shares you hold, you own less of the company than you did yesterday. That is generally destructive of share prices. But you have to look at why they are issuing more shares – what they'll be using the money for. For instance, if they were to use that money to buy a competitor and you thought it was a very good deal, then it could be very supportive of the share price.

INTERVIEWER *OK, thanks.*

9 Interview with an HR director

INTERVIEWER *Jurgen, you've worked in human resources for more than 30 years, including as part of the senior management team. I'd like to go through some key HR issues with you. We'll begin with recruitment. Can you talk me through a typical recruitment process?*

JURGEN Yes. It's a shared responsibility between the line manager who has the vacancy and the HR department. The four steps in the process are: first of all, to define the requirements of the job and prepare a job description, and usually it's the line manager who'll do that because they know the job better than anyone in HR does. But HR has a role in making sure that all the legal and ethical requirements are met, so as not to discriminate – even unintentionally – on grounds of race, gender, religion and increasingly age. The second step is to attract the candidates. You can go inside or outside the company, or both. The third step is to select the candidates. You compile a longlist when you've got the applications in, and then a shortlist. First consideration is normally given to internal candidates, because opportunities for promotion are an important motivating factor inside the company and it's important to grow talent within the organization. You'd soon lose your best people if they can't progress and develop their careers within their own organization. But sometimes you're looking for new skills that your organization needs, or perhaps new mindsets, or it might be a new location where your

company hasn't previously operated and it makes more business sense to hire locally.

INTERVIEWER *And then you do the interviews.*

JURGEN That's right, that's the final step. In many companies the interviews will be in two rounds. First someone from HR will do an interview where they'll look at the general personal qualities of the individual, and then the line manager will do a separate interview where they look at the functional skills. In the HR interview we are looking for a positive personality, a flexible attitude, good team-working skills, and other qualities like honesty and the ability to handle pressure. We want to know whether this person can fit in around here in terms of company culture, and whether they can grow with the business. We want to employ and promote somebody who can be doing bigger jobs in five years' time.

INTERVIEWER *How do you assess these personal qualities? You can't quantify them.*

JURGEN Well it's an art, not a science, you're right, but the answer is that you look at the track record. Let's go through some questions one might ask to get that kind of information out. 'What have been the most notable achievements in your career?' 'What sort of problems have you successfully solved recently?' 'What have you learnt from your present job?'

INTERVIEWER *Of course we're assuming here that the person has a track record. What about an interview with someone straight out of university?*

JURGEN Well I suppose that basically we're looking for energy, determination and drive, and an interest in learning new things. There are many ways to see that, even if the candidate doesn't have a career history to refer to. For example, sport, travel, involvement in voluntary associations – all those kinds of things. Then interest in current affairs and what's going on in the world, interest in other cultures. Language skills is another obvious point. And it's usually a good sign if they take the initiative in the interview and ask us questions. It shows they've got self-confidence, they are interested, they want to find out more.

INTERVIEWER *OK. Can we talk a little about pay and compensation? In the modern business world performance-related pay is a well-established idea. But it has its critics.*

JURGEN HR is not a charity department. We're not here to be nice to people. HR is here to help the business meet its objectives. Bonuses are acceptable if they're seen to be fair. Some sales people, for example, will have as much as 50, 60 or 70 per cent of their earnings based on what they sell. Other people will have a percentage of their pay based on their annual appraisal, or the general success of the business over the year. The system is designed to create a high performance culture. You reward good performance and you do not give money to people who are not delivering. People don't complain – in fact they complain about the opposite, when a colleague is demotivated and underperforming and yet they receive the same salary.

INTERVIEWER *You mentioned appraisal just now, and of course appraisal is important for many things apart from salary – promotion, identifying training needs, and so on. What are the key issues in the appraisal process?*

JURGEN Appraisals, or performance reviews as they're often called, are absolutely fundamental to good management practice. They are usually annual, and involve looking at criteria that are agreed between the line manager and the employee beforehand. The aim is to take an overall view of the progress that the individual has made, and then use that to plan that person's job for the following year. But the process of appraisal is becoming more complex – people work in a global environment in different countries and work in a matrix organization with different managers. We have to collect data from a number of sources in order to discuss with the employee how things have been this year, what's gone well, what hasn't gone well, where do you think you need to improve, what skills or training you might need for the future and so on. That joint discussion will then result in some kind of performance rating, and this will often be directly linked to pay increases or opportunities for promotion.

INTERVIEWER *What is the division of responsibility between HR and the line manager in the appraisal process?*

JURGEN The line manager knows how to rate functional performance. We don't do that. Our role is to develop the appraisal tools and train the managers in how to use them, to make sure that a wide range of skills are being assessed, to make sure that the process is identifying and fast-tracking future leaders, and quite simply just to monitor that it's being done. But I want to emphasize that the employees are fully involved and they themselves are often the best people to judge their own job performance.

INTERVIEWER *Right. Finally I'd like to turn to the question of motivation. We talked earlier about salary and about opportunities for promotion, but we know that these are not the only way to motivate people.*

JURGEN Absolutely. Apart from the tangible rewards there are what I would call intrinsic motivators. The first is autonomy. This is the amount of control that you have over your work. The responsibility that you have. The second is variety – a lot of evidence suggests that different types of work, even job rotation, can help improve motivation. The third is the extent to which the job uses your abilities. An individual will enjoy doing a job that requires them to use abilities that they have and that they value. The fourth aspect, I think, is consistent meaningful feedback. People want to know how they are doing – they want to be advised from time to time about their own performance and they want also to be involved in evaluating their own performance. The fifth thing I think is the belief that the task is significant. Nothing is more demoralizing than to feel that your company doesn't really care about the project you're working on. And notice that all these five things are exactly the kind of things that can be discussed in an appraisal interview.

INTERVIEWER *Right. That's a very complete answer. Thank you very much.*

10 Interview with an IT consultant

INTERVIEWER *You work for an IT consultancy. Is that right?*

JANA That's right. We offer IT solutions – software, hardware, system integration, maintenance and support, consulting – everything. We don't represent any one hardware or software company – we can recommend to our clients whatever solution is best for them. So we talk to our clients, we analyse their needs, and we suggest how their IT budget can be spent most effectively. It's a business approach – we see IT very much as a way for a company to add value. We don't see it as toys for the boys – we're business people, not techies.

INTERVIEWER *OK. So what kind of solutions are we talking about?*

JANA I'll tell you about applications software because it's the most interesting. But I do want to emphasize that applications software cannot be seen in isolation – it sits on top of systems software like the operating system, and also the hardware.

INTERVIEWER *Is that called the platform?*

JANA Yes, and it's important to know which applications can run on your platform. OK, let's begin with ERP, because ERP is the umbrella. ERP stands for Enterprise Resource Planning. It integrates and automates the business practices of the organization. It's modular. It can include modules for the supply chain, manufacturing, operations, sales, distribution, finance, e-commerce, everything. It has functionality right across the organization.

INTERVIEWER *Can you give me an example of one specific module?*

JANA A good example is CRM, Customer Relationship Management. In the past, information about one individual customer could have been anywhere on the system – financial information in one database, sales information in another database, and maybe customer support interactions not recorded anywhere – someone on a helpdesk just dealt with a phone call and then forgot about it. With CRM you can bring all that together and have a single view of your customer. It means that whoever comes into contact with them – pre-sales, post-sales, accounts, whoever – they all see the same information, and they all log the results of their interaction for others to see. You can also analyse information from all the customers together, and that helps you to see trends in buying behaviour, make forecasts and so on. From the customer's point of view they get a more unified and intimate experience – it feels like they are dealing with the same company, regardless of the point of contact.

INTERVIEWER *Is there any downside for the customer? I'm thinking about privacy issues, or aggressive direct marketing from a sales person who knows everything about you.*

JANA You have to be careful. It's true that it's very easy to see someone's buying habits. You can easily see a history of what a customer has bought, and when, and also why – because sales staff will have made notes about the sales conversation and entered them on the system. And you're right, the next step from that is to anticipate what the customer might want to buy and make a cold call to them about a new product or something. But customers don't like that, and if you overdo it, they resist and you lose their trust.

INTERVIEWER *You said that ERP was modular, and you've given us an example of one module. Can you buy just one module and nothing else?*

JANA You can, but it wouldn't make sense. If you were a small company and you just wanted CRM, you would buy a stand-alone CRM package. ERP is for large organizations – we use the big vendors like SAP and we recommend a whole series of their modules across the different business departments.

INTERVIEWER *Can you give me one more example of an ERP module, besides customer relationship management?*

JANA Yes, a good example that shows the importance of

integration across the organization is document management. In the early days of computing people talked about the paperless office, but in fact the amount of paper increased because of all the print-outs and photocopies. Now we really can have a paperless office. A document – like an email or a letter or a legal contract or a report – is purely in electronic form and with document management you can track and store it. For example, you can specify exactly who should see it, and what they should do with it, and where it should go next. Take a sales contract: the sales person creates the contract based on an existing template, then it is sent to a financial person for checking, maybe a legal person also has to see it, and the sales director will also want to see it. Each person might want to modify it, in which case the changes have to be flagged up and the document sent back to everyone else for checking again. Finally all the key decision-makers have to sign it electronically to say that it's OK. It's a complex process, and document management software makes it all very easy.

INTERVIEWER   *OK, so a big company has all these different modules. But not everyone in the company needs the same information. There's a huge amount of information on the system – but that's not the same as useful knowledge.*

JANA   You're right. And so we have another kind of software, called a portal, that can access every application but that is set up individually for different people so that they only see the information that is useful for them. There's also something new called 'meaning-based computing' that includes advanced search of a company's databases, knowledge management and so on. It allows managers to analyse unstructured information.

INTERVIEWER   *Right. That's very interesting. To finish, I'd like to ask you about the future. What do you think are going to be the trends in your industry over the coming years?*

JANA   The big trend is the way that everything is moving to the network – all kinds of data and all kinds of software. At the end of the day all devices are the same – just a screen, a means of input like a keyboard, and a connection to the network. It doesn't matter whether we're talking about a PC, a mobile phone, a fixed-line phone, a games console, a television, a security camera in your home, or something built in to your fridge door in the kitchen. You don't need much computing power in the device itself – just a connection to the network. Any data or software that you need is right there on the network ready to access and use. It makes working from home easy, or working from a hotel room, or working off-site with a client. All you need is a device and, for security, a VPN – a Virtual Private Network.

INTERVIEWER   *A VPN?*

JANA   When you connect to a private company network using the public telecommunications infrastructure it's called a virtual private network. The VPN gives you security with a firewall, encryption and so on.

INTERVIEWER   *It's clear that things like laptops and mobile phones can talk to the network and to each other. But what about other everyday household objects – like your fridge?*

JANA   You need wireless connectivity and an IP address. That's all. With an IP address you have a unique identification on the network.

INTERVIEWER   *It sounds like that film 'The Matrix'. In the future every object will be on the network and we will be able to experience everything from everywhere. Whoever controls the network controls reality.*

JANA   It's going to come sooner than you think.

Answer Key

1 Industries and companies

Exercise 1.1
1 freight   2 household   3 appliances   4 apparel / beverages
5 facilities   6 real estate   7 brokerage   8 utilities

Exercise 1.2
1 equipment   2 machinery   3 device   4 appliance

Exercise 1.3
1 consumer staples   2 consumer discretionary

Exercise 1.4
1 ExxonMobil / Oil and gas
2 PwC / Auditing
3 Citigroup / Diversified financial services
4 Intel / Semiconductors and semiconductor equipment
5 Proctor & Gamble / Household and personal products
6 GE / Industrial conglomerates
7 Pfizer / Pharmaceuticals, biotechnology and life sciences
8 Wal-Mart / Food and drug retailing
9 UPS / Air freight and logistics
10 Cisco / Communications equipment

Exercise 1.5
1 raw materials / finished goods / fabrication
2 Consumer durables / household appliances
3 Non-durable goods / food and beverages
4 business solutions

Exercise 1.6
1 Board / senior management team   2 venture / enterprise
3 debt / liability   4 self-employed / freelancer
5 firm / partnership   6 merger / acquisition

Exercise 1.7
1 issue   2 run   3 appoint   4 guarantee   5 underwriting
6 reinvested   7 held   8 constraints

Exercise 1.8
1 d   2 h   3 g   4 e   5 a   6 b   7 f   8 c

2 Globalization and economic policy

Exercise 2.1
1 merge / joint ventures   2 subsidiary / subsidy   3 red tape
4 tariffs / quotas   5 exchange rates   6 assets

Exercise 2.2
1 recovery / upswing   2 growth / boom / expansion
3 recession / contraction / downturn / slowdown
4 depression / slump

Exercise 2.3
1 inward investment   2 competitive advantage
3 deeper involvement   4 contractual agreement
5 mobile communications   6 trading partners / trade surplus

Exercise 2.4
1 licensing   2 franchising   3 import / export   4 joint venture
5 strategic alliance   6 outsourcing   7 foreign subsidiary

Exercise 2.5
1 T   2 F   3 T   4 F
5 increasing / provide a stimulus to / inflation
6 increasing   7 increasing   8 increasing   9 increasing

3 Corporate strategy and structure

Exercise 3.1
1 key accounts   2 Chief Operating Officer
3 cross-functional teams   4 grassroots   5 subordinates
6 development / consolidation / withdrawal

Exercise 3.2
1 f   2 e   3 h   4 d   5 a   6 g   7 b   8 c   9 i   10 j

Exercise 3.3
1 human resources   9 production
2 customer services   10 legal
3 quality control   11 shipping
4 research and development 12 finance
5 public relations   13 marketing
6 project management   14 accounts
7 administration   15 purchasing
8 billing   16 procurement

Exercise 3.4
market research / cost centre / earnings growth / management hierarchy / customer needs / product portfolio / core business / distribution channel / mission statement / market share / shareholder value / brand loyalty

Exercise 3.5
1 market research   6 cost centre
2 core business   7 earnings growth
3 shareholder value   8 management hierarchy
4 product portfolio   9 mission statement
5 brand loyalty   10 distribution channel

Exercise 3.6
1 check   2 coordinate   3 assign   4 implement   5 control
6 ensure   7 adapt   8 monitor   9 evaluate   10 determine

Exercise 3.7
1 state-of-the-art   2 tailor-made   3 one-stop   4 depth
5 outdated   6 debt   7 workflow   8 range
9 overhead (BrE overheads)   10 climate   11 alliance
12 transfer   13 start-up   14 barriers   15 shortage

Exercise 3.8
1 lack (*or* shortage)   2 over-reliance   3 reps (representatives)
4 facility   5 saturation

Exercise 3.9
2

Exercise 3.10
Specific, Measurable, Agreed, Realistic, and Time-specific

4 Managing people

Exercise 4.1
1 morale   2 esteem   3 acknowledgement   4 self-fulfilment
5 achievement   6 empowerment   7 enabling   8 assertive
9 commitment

Exercise 4.2
1 L   2 M   3 M   4 L   5 L   6 M   7 M   8 L

Exercise 4.3
1 enrichment   2 outcome   3 autonomy   4 meaningfulness
5 enlargement   6 assignment

Exercise 4.4
a) 2   b) 3   c) 4–7   d) 8–9   e) 10–11

Exercise 4.5
achieve, meet, fulfil, reach an objective / define, establish, identify, set an objective / fail in, fall short of an objective

address, deal with, handle, tackle a problem / cause, create, give rise to a problem / clear up, overcome, resolve, solve a problem

accept, agree to, agree with, take up a suggestion / come up with, make, offer, put forward a suggestion / reject, rule out, turn down a suggestion

arrive at, come to, make, reach, take a decision / defer, postpone, put off a decision / overrule, overturn, reverse a decision

collective, joint, unanimous decision / critical, crucial, important, key, major decision / difficult, hard, tough decision

anticipated, expected, likely outcome / desirable, favourable, satisfactory, successful outcome / eventual, final, outcome

Exercise 4.6

1 Innovator   2 Evaluator   3 Specialist   4 Implementer
5 Shaper   6 Finisher   7 Coordinator   8 Team worker
9 Promoter

Exercise 4.7

1 inaccurate / imprecise   2 careless   3 innovative / radical
4 indecisive / hesitant   5 inefficient / wasteful
6 unenthusiastic / bored   7 inflexible / rigid   8 laissez-faire
9 hard-working   10 impatient   11 impolite / rude   12 unreliable

Exercise 4.8

1 sensitive   2 sensible

5 Operations management

Exercise 5.1

1 lead 2 concept brief   3 feasibility   4 vulnerability
5 first-tier / upstream   6 Procurement / sourcing   7 vendor
8 core competencies

Exercise 5.2

1 technical expertise   2 a high level of productivity
3 fast throughput   4 a frequently updated product range
5 downside risk   6 vertical integration   7 economies of scale
8 an error-free process

Exercise 5.3

1 draw up a bill of materials   2 reduce design complexity
3 migrate an operation to the web   4 put upward pressure on prices
5 have a competitive advantage   6 roll out a new product
7 carry out a feasibility study
8 turn an initial idea into a concept brief

Exercise 5.4

1 c   2 f   3 d   4 i   5 a   6 j   7 g   8 k   9 b
10 h   11 l   12 e

Exercise 5.5

1 specifies   2 builds   3 tested   4 compile   5 hooked up
6 drilling   7 welding

Exercise 5.6

1 parameters   2 specifications   3 criteria

Exercise 5.7

1a define = specify = establish = set   1b meet = fulfil = satisfy   2 a

Exercise 5.8

1 sophisticated   2 foreseeable   3 penalties   4 straightforward
5 show up   6 quotation   7 surcharge   8 forecast
9 driving down   10 run

Exercise 5.9

1 setbacks   2 stakeholders   3 Gantt chart   4 small print
5 milestones   6 constraints   7 scope   8 track

6 Production

Exercise 6.1

1 bottleneck   2 throughput   3 capacity utilization
4 fit-for-purpose   5 value-for-money   6 reliability
7 durability   8 defect

Exercise 6.2

planning 3, sequencing 6, scheduling 5, dispatching 2, loading 1, monitoring 4

Exercise 6.3

1 steel making   2 an automobile plant   3 clothing manufacture
4 aircraft manufacture   5 construction of a building

Exercise 6.4

1 downtime   2 changeover time   3 lead time   4 cycle time
5 overtime   6 set-up time   7 time-to-market   8 lag time

Exercise 6.5

1 improvement   2 culture   3 process   4 marketplace
5 competitors   6 metrics   7 cycle   8 resistance

Exercise 6.6

first-rate, high, top, outstanding quality / low, poor, inferior quality / uneven, variable quality

assess, evaluate, measure, test quality / demand, insist on quality / keep up, maintain, preserve quality

begin, go into, start up production / boost, increase, ramp up, speed up production / cut back (on), reduce, scale down production

be in charge of, supervise the process / keep track of, monitor the process / rationalize, simplify, streamline the process

excess, spare capacity / full, maximum, peak, total capacity / limited, reduced capacity

carry, have, hold, keep inventory / dispose of, get rid of, reduce inventory / reorder, replace inventory

Exercise 6.7

1 cover a wide range of activities   2 determine customer needs
3 deal with complaints   4 be adopted worldwide   5 keep records
6 carry out internal audits   7 be expensive to implement
8 be dedicated to improving processes
9 measure performance against a standard
10 match the best practice of your competitors

7 Marketing strategy and Product development

Exercise 7.1

1 quantitative / qualitative   2 end-user   3 value-for-money
4 benefits / features   5 trademark   6 mark-up / breakeven

Exercise 7.2

1 product lines   2 product mix   3 brand names
4 brand loyalty   5 brand awareness   6 market leader
7 market share   8 profitability

Exercise 7.3

1 making a loss   2 early adopters   3 similar offerings
4 advertising budgets   5 differentiate products
6 reaches saturation   7 consumer tastes
8 withdrawn from the market

Exercise 7.4

1 consumer needs   2 gaps in the market   3 published sources
4 the activity of competitors   5 a representative sample of people
6 statistically reliable   7 carrying out a survey

Exercise 7.5

1 requirement   2 USP   3 specification   4 benefit   5 feature
6 characteristic   7 estimate   8 quotation   9 budget

Exercise 7.6

1 d, i, k   2 b, f, h   3 a, e, j   4 c, g, l

Exercise 7.7

sales campaign, drive, promotion / sales figures, volume / sales force, personnel, staff, team

disappointing, poor, weak sales / export, foreign, overseas sales / global, international, worldwide sales

bring out, introduce, launch a product / discontinue, take … off the market, withdraw a product / improve, modify, upgrade a product

attractive, fair, reasonable price / exorbitant, high, inflated price / retail, selling price

agree on, agree to, arrive at, establish, set, work out a price / bring down, cut, lower, reduce a price / increase, push up, put up, raise a price

booming, expanding, growing, healthy, strong market / depressed, flat, sluggish, weak market / niche, specialist market

be forced out of, withdraw from the market / break into, enter the market / corner, dominate, monopolize, take over the market

8 Distribution and Promotion

Exercise 8.1
1 fulfilment　2 outlet　3 prospect　4 billboard
5 repeat purchases / cross-selling　6 middleman　7 warehouse
8 merchandising

Exercise 8.2
1 customer / client　2 catalogue / brochure
3 promotion / advertising　4 commercial / spot
5 endorsement / sponsorship　6 agent / broker

Exercise 8.3
1 brand identity　2 convenience store　3 direct mail
4 distribution channel　5 in-store display　6 press release
7 product placement　8 public relations

Exercise 8.4
1 Prospecting　2 Approach　3 Presentation　4 Demonstration
5 Closing　6 Answering objections　7 Follow-up

Exercise 8.5
change 5 and 6 so that 'Answering objections' comes before 'Closing'

Exercise 8.6
1 newspapers　2 magazines　3 television　4 radio
5 outdoor　6 direct mail　7 internet

Exercise 8.7
1 coverage　2 placed　3 target　4 junk　5 eyeballs

Exercise 8.8
1 inbound logistics　2 materials handling　3 outbound logistics
4 customer returns　5 end user　6 warehouses　7 retail outlets
8 ex-works　9 fob　10 cif

9 Accounting and financial statements

Exercise 9.1
1 own / owe　2 depreciation / written off / amortization
3 receivable / payable　4 inventory　5 accrued　6 leverage

Exercise 9.2
1 variable costs　2 direct costs　3 fixed costs　4 indirect costs
5 operating costs　6 capital expenditure　7 marginal costs

Exercise 9.3
1st group: costs, expenditure, expenses, spending
2nd group: earnings, profit
3rd group: income, revenue, sales, turnover

Exercise 9.4
Preparation of accounts: ledger, trial balance, invoices
Profit and Loss Account: cost of goods sold, EBITDA, operating expenses
Balance Sheet: accounts payable, shareholders' equity, current assets

Exercise 9.5
Credit control: 2, 4　　Stock control: 1, 5　　Expenditure control: 3, 6

Exercise 9.6
Debt financing: 2, 3, 6　　Equity financing: 1, 4, 5

Exercise 9.7
1 d　2 c　3 b　4 e　5 a

Exercise 9.8
bring down, cut, lower, reduce costs / calculate, figure out, work out costs / meet, pay costs

bring in, earn, generate, make profits / jeopardize, put at risk profits / plough back, reinvest profits

accurate, exact, precise figure / approximate, ballpark, rough, round figure / deceptive, dubious, misleading figure

announce, issue, publish, release the figures / check, examine, go over, go through, study the figures / cook, doctor, falsify, manipulate, massage the figures

Exercise 9.9
1 c　2 b, d, f　3 a　4 e

10 Financial markets

Exercise 10.1
1 securities　2 equities / shares / stocks　3 bonds
4 money market instruments

Exercise 10.2
1 mutual　2 dividends　3 principal / term　4 treasury

Exercise 10.3
1 tracker fund　2 capital growth　3 fixed rate　4 junk bond
5 risk management

Exercise 10.4
1 first group: booming / bull / rising / strong
　　second group: bear / depressed / falling / weak
2 first group: acquire / buy / purchase
　　second group: have / hold / own

Exercise 10.5
1 S&P　2 Nasdaq　3 Dow　4 DAX　5 CAC　6 FTSE

Exercise 10.6
a) 2　　b) 1　　c) 4　　d) 3

Exercise 10.7
1 growth　2 income　3 income + growth

Exercise 10.8
1 investment bank　2 pension fund　3 mutual fund
4 insurance company　5 endowment

Exercise 10.9
1 price elasticity　2 capital requirements　3 ease of substitution
4 market penetration　5 barriers to entry

Exercise 10.10
1 market capitalization　2 earnings growth　3 return on equity
4 p/e ratio　5 dividend yield

Exercise 10.11
1 market capitalization　2 p/e ratio　3 earnings growth
4 dividend yield　5 return on equity

Exercise 10.12
1 resistance　2 support　3 volume　4 breadth
5 momentum　6 trading channel　7 leadership　8 liquidity

Exercise 10.13
1 buyer　2 seller　3 exports　4 imports　5 raises　6 rises
7 Reserve　8 Bank

11 Human resources

Exercise 11.1
1 payroll　2 discrimination / disability　3 in-house
4 headhunting　5 shortlist　6 track record　7 appraisal

Exercise 11.2
Appraisal process: 3, 6
Training and development: 1, 5
Worker-management relations: 2, 4

Exercise 11.3
1 salary / wage　2 candidate / applicant　3 mentoring / coaching
4 employees / staff　5 commission / bonus
6 retirement / pension

Exercise 11.4
1 ability　2 competence　3 skill　4 experience
5 qualification　6 background　7 knowledge　8 aptitude

Exercise 11.5
Group A: be employed / be appointed / be headhunted / be hired / be recruited / be taken on
Group B: be dismissed / be fired / be sacked
Group C: be laid off / be let go / be made redundant

Exercise 11.6

1 qualification   2 experience   3 knowledge   4 skills
5 ability   6 competence   7 background   8 experience
9 knowledge   10 aptitude

Exercise 11.7

1 collective bargaining   2 individual grievance   3 layoffs
4 length of service   5 official dispute   6 strikes   7 picketing
8 boycotts   9 court injunction   10 mediation   11 arbitration
12 legally binding

12 Information and communication technology

Exercise 12.1

1 legacy   2 documentation   3 device   4 bandwidth
5 platform   6 embedded   7 browser   8 warehouse

Exercise 12.2

1 stability / downtime   2 ensure / secure   3 translate / solution
4 measure / efficiency   5 retrieve / trends
6 accessibility / intranet   7 enable / devices   8 aggregate / portal

Exercise 12.3

1 ensure   2 backed-up   3 requirements   4 retrieve
5 enable   6 charge   7 downloading   8 aggregate   9 portal

Exercise 12.4

1 stand-alone PC   2 workstations   3 LAN   4 servers
5 WAN   6 intranet   7 firewall   8 encryption

Exercise 12.5

1 off-the-shelf package   2 wireless connectivity
3 processing power   4 storage capacity   5 back-office functions
6 intellectual property   7 click-through rate
8 web page (often written as one word: webpage)

Exercise 12.6

1 design / develop   2 provide / supply   3 run / use
4 application / package   5 environment / platform
6 supplier / vendor   7 old-fashioned / out-of-date
8 customized / tailor-made   9 defective / faulty
10 the latest / up-to-date

Exercise 12.7

1 running   2 running on   3 software   4 some   5 upgraded
6 updated   7 updates

Exercise 12.8

1 off-the-shelf   2 customization   3 forecast   4 project
5 procurement   6 stand-alone   7 quote   8 fulfilment
9 alerts

13 Trends, graphs and figures

Exercise 13.1

1 g   2 c   3 h   4 a   5 b   6 e   7 d   8 f

Exercise 13.2

1 d   2 e   3 a   4 f   5 b   6 c

Exercise 13.3

1 bring / down   2 put / up   3 bottom out   4 bounce back
5 pick up   6 take off   7 level off   8 slip back

Exercise 13.4

1 grow   2 cannot   3 cannot   4 first two examples

Exercise 13.5

1 ✓   2 ✗   3 ✗   4 ✓   5 ✓   6 ✗   7 ✗   8 ✓
9 ✓   10 ✓   11 ✗   12 ✓

Exercise 13.6

1 shrinking   2 expanding   3 growing   4 rising   5 soaring

Exercise 13.7

1 rapidly   2 gradually   3 steadily   4 slightly   5 marginally
6 significantly   7 sharply   8 dramatically

Exercise 13.8

1 ✓   2 ✗   3 ✗   4 ✓   5 ✗

Exercise 13.9

1 cut   2 deterioration   3 fall   4 growth   5 half
6 improvement   7 increase   8 recovery   9 reduction
10 rise

Exercise 13.10

1 slight fall   2 steady rise   3 gradual improvement
4 sharp reduction

Exercise 13.11

1 pie chart   2 heading   3 title   4 labeled with   5 steep

Exercise 13.12

1 i, k, p   2 c, e, f   3 a, l   4 m   5 j   6 b, d, g, h, n, o

Exercise 13.13

1 from / to / of   2 in / of   3 at   4 in
5 no preposition   6 between   7 in   8 in / with
9 to (YTD is a common abbreviation in graphs and charts)
10 on (YOY is a common abbreviation in graphs and charts)
11 down   12 into

14 Presentations – structure and key phrases

Exercise 14.1

a Could I have your attention, please?
b I'm responsible for new product development here at InfoCom. (or Here at InfoCom I'm responsible for new product development.)
c For those of you who don't know me already, my name is Nancy Holmes.
d It's always a pleasure to speak to an audience of experienced professionals like yourselves. I know that many of you have travelled a long way to be here.
e On behalf of the company, may I welcome you to this presentation.
f The aim of my talk is to give you some information about our new product line.
g Please feel free to interrupt me if you have any questions during the talk. (or Please feel free to interrupt me during the talk if you have any questions.)
h Okay, I'd like to begin by looking at this first slide. Can the people at the back see okay?
i My presentation will take around forty minutes.
j I've divided my talk into three main parts. First, I'll give you an overview of the different models in the range. Then I'll move on to describe the key benefits of each model. And finally I'll say a little about prices.

Exercise 14.2

1 a   2 c   3 b   4 e   5 d   6 f   7 j   8 i   9 g   10 h

Exercise 14.4

1 a   2 c   3 b   4 e   5 d   6 f   7 j   8 i   9 g   10 h

Exercise 14.7

1 start / looking   2 come / later   3 Right / far   4 moving / talk
5 Going / moment   6 digress / little   7 getting / to
8 turn / question   9 As / see   10 finish / summarize
11 let / attention   12 pleased / answer

Exercise 14.8

Answers given in 14.7

Exercise 14.9

1 I'm glad you asked that.
2 Leave me your contact details and I'll send it to you.
3 Could you be a little more specific?
4 Well, it's a very complex issue.
5 We have time for one last question.
6 Let me check that I understand.
7 What are your own views?
8 I don't know that off the top of my head.

Exercise 14.10

a 1   b 3, 6   c 4, 7   d 2, 8   e 5

15 Presentations – being lively and persuasive

'A persuasive presentation' (page 64). How many techniques can you spot?

Answers: fiftieth-fifty (repetition of words); life-life (repetition of words); we've seen / we've seen (repetition of words + structure); anger / joy (contrast); bad / good (contrast); change / constant (contrast); innovation, quality and value (rule of three); customers / customers (repetition of words); want / want (stop-and-start repetition); for now, and for the generations who follow (contrast); changing / solid (contrast); they want / they want (repetition of words + structure); What about you? (rhetorical question); Perhaps you want (repetition of words + structure / rule of three); We have a plan that's right for you (repetition of words + structure / rule of three); an accident – or worse? (emotional language); golden years (emotional language); families / families (stop-and-start repetition); pension plans, health plans and life insurance (rule of three); those are the things (repetition of words + structure); happy worker / productive worker (repetition of words + structure); individuals, families and business owners (rule of three); take time today (repetition of sounds); to … today to … tomorrow (repetition of structure / contrast).

Exercise 15.1

1 What / waiting   2 Where / go   3 How / do
4 When / expect   5 Why / keep on   6 How much / is

Exercise 15.2

1 improvement / progress   2 helpful / effective   3 grow / boom
4 choice / variety   5 wonderful / glorious   6 important / major

Exercise 15.3

1 knowledge / information   2 line / range   3 explanation / reason
4 topic / issue   5 international / global

Exercise 15.4

1 one / two   2 light / strong   3 classical / modern
4 not cheap / cheap (or cheap / special)   5 today / tomorrow

Exercise 15.5

1 clean / maintain / running costs   2 commitment / drive / vision
3 highly profitable / well-run / future
4 customer needs / distribution channels / time-to-market

Exercise 15.6

a) make a killing   b) corner the market   c) get off the ground
d) cook the books   e) come under fire   f) keep an eye on things
g) get a piece of the action   h) put my foot in it
i) spend money like water   j) be in the red   k) sell like hotcakes
l) be a real high-flyer   m) see it in black and white
n) get more bang for your buck   o) be a big fish in a small pond

Exercise 15.7

1 h   2 o   3 e   4 l   5 g   6 j   7 b   8 d   9 n
10 m   11 f   12 a   13 k   14 i   15 c

Exercise 15.8

1 a   2 j   3 h   4 f   5 c   6 e   7 g   8 d   9 k
10 i   11 o   12 l   13 b   14 m   15 n

16 Discussions

Exercise 16.1

a way / looking   b business   c Going (or Coming or Getting)
d sight / point (or issue)   e just / moment   f specific   g by
h just   i get / on   j kind (or sort) / mind   k sense   l put

Exercise 16.2

1 a   2 d   3 e   4 h   5 b   6 c   7 i   8 f   9 g
10 l   11 j   12 k

Exercise 16.3

1 down / to   2 on / to   3 of / at   4 back / to   5 of
6 back / to / on   7 about   8 of / of   9 in   10 over

Exercise 16.4

1 get down to   2 move on to   3 go back to   4 get back to
5 go over

Exercise 16.5

a) You're absolutely right.
b) Yes, I'm in favour of that.
c) That might be worth trying.
d) I agree with you up to a point, but …
e) I can see one or two problems with that.
f) I'm sorry, I can't agree to that.
g) Really? Do you think so?
h) That's not how I see it.

Exercise 16.6

1 a   2 d   3 g   4 h   5 b   6 c   7 e   8 f

Exercise 16.7

1 Shall we move on?   2 I think we're losing sight of the main point.
3 Can I get back to you on that?   4 Yes, exactly.
5 Let me put it another way.

Exercise 16.8

1 suggestion   2 proposal   3 offer

Exercise 16.9

1 put forward / make   2 accept / take up   3 reject / dismiss
4 come up with / think of   5 take part in / be involved in
6 come to / reach   7 raise / bring up   8 deal with / tackle
9 reconsider / reassess   10 throw it open for / open it up for
11 a sensible / reasonable   12 a sensitive / difficult
13 a realistic / feasible   14 a minor / side
15 an absurd / ridiculous   16 a constructive / fruitful
17 a hard / tough   18 a detailed / in-depth
19 an easy / straightforward   20 an exploratory / initial

Exercise 16.10

1 come up with / feasible   2 take up / reasonable
3 put forward / ridiculous   4 bring up / sensitive   5 tackle
6 involved in / exploratory   7 took part in / fruitful
8 open it up for / in-depth   9 reached / tough
10 straightforward

Exercise 16.11

1 ✓   2 ✗   3 ✓   4 ✓   5 ✗   6 ✓   7 ✗

Exercise 16.12

1 a proposal   2 an effort to do sth   3 a demand
4 a difficult challenge   5 an issue

17 Social English and cultural awareness

Exercise 17.1

1 this   2 too   3 Pleased   4 doing   5 going   6 life
7 introduce   8 must   9 Fine   10 good   11 appreciate it
12 take   13 us   14 Still or sparkling?

Exercise 17.2

1 a ✓
  b ✗ (only used for people we know)
  c ✓ (formal and a little old-fashioned, but appropriate after the formal opening)
2 a ✗ (only used for first meetings)
  b ✓
  c ✗ (it is true that the opening phrase is a real question, but it is inappropriate to mention personal problems in a business context)
3 a ✗ (used to respond to a request, not a factual question)
  b ✓
  c ✗ (see a)
4 a ✓   b ✗   c ✓
5 a ✗ (questions with 'mind' mean 'is it a problem for you?', so a 'yes' answer means it is a problem)
  b ✗ (see a)
  c ✓

6 a ✓ b ✗ ('I do mind' means 'it is a problem for me') c ✓
7 a ✗ (too dry and unenthusiastic)
   b ✗ (used to respond to a request)
   c ✓

Exercise 17.3

1 a   2 d   3 b   4 h   5 e   6 c   7 f   8 i   9 g

Exercise 17.4

1 Wow, that's fantastic.   2 You're kidding, right?
3 How awful. I'm so sorry.   4 Poor you.
5 You must be delighted!   6 Yes, of course. Sure.
7 What a nightmare!   8 That makes a change.   9 Well done!
10 That's great news! Congratulations!

Exercise 17.5

1 Are you? Lucky you, I wish I was going! Whereabouts?
2 Did you? Congratulations – you must be delighted! What are your responsibilities going to be?
3 Were they? How awful for them. Which areas were affected?
4 Is it? Three days – what a nightmare! Can I give you a lift anywhere?
5 Did he? That's not like him. What did the boss say?

Exercise 17.6

1 have you got a moment?   2 bear with me
3 was wondering if you could help me   4 do my best to sort it out
5 have an apology to make   6 didn't do it on purpose
7 happens all the time

Exercise 17.7

1 Excuse me   2 Sorry

Exercise 17.8

1 make a move   2 so soon   3 rush off   4 How about
5 must be going   6 really nice meeting   7 thank you so much
8 really appreciate it   9 Don't mention it   10 my pleasure
11 safe trip   12 say hello to Isabel for me   13 best of luck
14 Keep in touch

18 Style – clarity and emphasis

Exercise 18.1

1 We will need to ask for more help.
2 You can choose your own colour.
3 These days the unions have less influence on government.
4 My boss fired Claudia because of her poor performance.
5 We expect commodity prices to rise.
6 Because their needs are so specific, let's check the details very carefully.

Exercise 18.2

1 I know how we can use better credit control to improve our cash flow.
2 The new rules say we must not use the company PCs for personal emails.
3 While we were talking she asked a lot of questions about the recent changes in our product range.
4 Your line manager will decide your bonus, even though the HR department is officially responsible.

Exercise 18.3

We have not definitely determined the causes for the decline in sales for March. We know, however, that during this period construction work on the street limited the number of customers who entered the store. In addition, we know that promotion efforts were reduced as a result of staff changes in the advertising department.

Exercise 18.4

Thank you for your email regarding invoice D970. We will give you until May 15 to pay the outstanding amount.
If you have any further problems please contact us immediately.
(or Please contact us immediately if you have any further problems.)

Exercise 18.6

1 We really can't afford to ignore such a good opportunity.
2 I'm absolutely certain that we're in a far better position now.
3 Actually, it's (It's actually) much cheaper to use an outside firm for all the graphic design work.
4 There is absolutely no truth at all in what they are saying – their whole story is complete lies.
5 It's a highly risky project – I strongly recommend that we take the greatest care.
6 It's just so difficult to know whether the advertising campaign is actually going to work.
7 I fully support the entire Board – they are doing an extremely important job.
8 I really hope we see a significant rise in sales at Christmas – even more than last year.
9 We really can't decide so quickly – the issue is far too important.
10 I completely agree – upgrading our entire computer network will take us way over budget.

19 Style – politeness and softening

Exercise 19.1

1 It seems we have a slight problem.
2 Could I just interrupt for a moment? (or Could I interrupt just for a moment.)
3 There might be just a small delay.
4 I understood that you could deliver by the end of March.
5 I'm afraid our competitors are not very cheap.
6 Wouldn't it be better to ship to Rotterdam?
7 There are one or two things I wanted to discuss.
8 I am assuming that the paperwork is okay.
9 I'm sorry but we're not very happy with the quality of this repair.
10 We were hoping for a slightly more flexible response.
11 I would be grateful for the chance to have a look round your factory.
12 I was wondering if I could have (take) a quick look at your designs for next season.
13 With respect, you don't seem to understand how important this is.
14 We would appreciate it if you could give us a little more time.
15 I suppose I could speak to my boss about it, but I'm not promising anything.
16 Apparently, their business is not going very well.
17 As far as I know there are (or there's) just a couple of technical problems to sort out.

Exercise 19.2

1 I mean   2 At least   3 Or rather   4 That's to say

Exercise 19.3

1: I was given this list just last month.
2: Unfortunately, we had to raise all our prices by 4% from the beginning of this month.
3: Well, you could switch to another product with a slightly lower performance.
4: If you did that, you'd save money.
5: But that's not going to be easy.
6: How many more units were you thinking of?
7: I'm sorry, but an increase of that size would not be enough to give you a bigger discount.

Exercise 19.4

1 we are willing to do   2 suitable for resale
3 this is clearly stated   4 terms and conditions
5 with the relevant section highlighted   6 in the circumstances
7 consider the sale final   8 within ten working days

Exercise 19.5

Paragraph 1: b, e
Paragraph 2: c, a, h, g
Paragraph 3: d, f, i

Exercise 19.6

1 ✓
2 ✓
3 no ('unfortunately' is a negative word, but is polite in this context)
4 ✓
5 no (and a formal ending as a sign of respect is an old-fashioned idea)

20 Developing an argument – linking words 1

Exercise 20.1

1 and / furthermore / moreover   2 but / however / nevertheless
3 so / therefore / consequently   4 because / since / as

Exercise 20.2

1 Since   2 Due to   3 so as to   4 so that
5 In spite of the fact that   6 In spite of   7 while   8 though

Exercise 20.3

1 Because, because of   2 In order that, in order to
3 Although, despite   4 Although, whereas

Exercise 20.4

1 as / since   2 due to / as a result of / owing to   3 to / so as to
4 so / so that   5 though / even though / in spite of the fact that
6 in spite of   7 while

Exercise 20.5

1 But   2 Also   3 because of   4 So

Exercise 20.6

1 However   2 Furthermore   3 due to   4 Consequently

Exercise 20.7

1 Broadly speaking / Therefore   2 On the whole / However
3 As a matter of fact / For instance   4 In fact / To a great extent

Exercise 20.8

1 As a matter of fact / In fact   2 Broadly speaking / On the whole

Exercise 20.9

1 Due to   2 In fact   3 As a result   4 as   5 Even if
6 finally   7 on the other hand   8 in spite of

21 Developing an argument – linking words 2

Exercise 21.1

1 c   2 b   3 e   4 d   5 a

Exercise 21.2

1 Actually   2 Ironically   3 Presumably   4 Amazingly
5 Unfortunately   6 Frankly   7 Clearly   8 Predictably

Exercise 21.3

1 It is true that / however   2 Firstly / Secondly
3 In most cases / but   4 As far as / is concerned
5 Unless / it will

Exercise 21.4

1 Unless   2 Provided that   3 otherwise   4 whether
5 in case

Exercise 21.5

1 provided that   2 whether

Exercise 21.6

1 recruited / would be   2 had recruited / would have been
3 hadn't recruited / wouldn't have been

Exercise 21.7

1 On the one hand … but on the other …
2 On the surface … but deep down …
3 On paper … but in reality …
4 At first … but in the end …
5 In the short term … but in the long term …
6 Under normal circumstances … but in the current situation …
7 At the time … but in retrospect …

22 Developing an argument – linking words 3

Exercise 22.1

a 3   b 4   c 1   d 2   e 2   f 1   g 4   h 3

Exercise 22.2

1 b   2 a   3 b   4 a   5 b   6 a

Exercise 22.3

1 Up to   2 In   3 To / extent   4 To / degree   5 To / best
6 As / as / know

Exercise 22.4

1 What companies need is a set of standards.
2 What I'm talking about is a completely new approach.
3 What we want is good quality at competitive prices.
4 What I would like (is) to have (is) a chance to speak to him.
5 What I will do first is give you the history of the project.
6 What we mustn't do is go over budget.
7 What we should do is employ more local staff.

Exercise 22.5

1 Never before has business ethics been such a hot topic.
2 Under no circumstances can we accept this deal.
3 On no account should this information be shown to the press.
4 Only in some respects do I agree with you.
5 Only on rare occasions do we do business without a bank guarantee.

Exercise 22.6

1 a technical point of view   2 a commercial point of view
3 a political point of view   4 an ethical point of view
5 a legal point of view

Exercise 22.7

1 c   2 b   3 a

Exercise 22.8

In particular

Exercise 22.9

1 especially / specifically   2 principally / predominantly

Exercise 22.10

1 apart from = except for
2 in comparison with = compared to
3 in short = to put it briefly
4 on balance = taking everything into consideration
5 similarly = likewise

Exercise 22.11

1 Apart from   2 Similarly   3 In comparison with   4 In short
5 On balance

Exercise 22.12

1 eg   2 ie   3 ie   4 eg

23 Writing paragraphs

Exercise 23.1

a 1   b 4   c 2, 3   d 5, 7   e 6, 8

Exercise 23.2

1 ✓ (substitution to avoid monotony)   2 no
3 ✓ (repetition for stylistic impact)

Exercise 23.3

1 c   2 a   3 b

Exercise 23.4

1 → 3 → 2 → 5 → 4

Exercise 23.5

1 → 5 → 3 → 4 → 2

24 CV (resume) / Job interview

Exercise 24.4

a 2   b 1   c 9   d 10

Answer Key: Listening practice

1 Interview with a venture capitalist

Exercise 2

1 Companies with enormous growth potential (with a break-through innovation); with their origins in some sort of collaboration between university and the industrial world; in the IT and biotech sectors; with little or no income stream
2 Monitor the growth of the company; get the human resources right; define the road map
3 Yes, they are very happy. (They'll get a lot of money from selling their shares.) They'll buy a new house and generally take their living standard to a new level. Most of the original founders of the company will leave within a few years (big culture shock).

Exercise 3

1 F   2 T   3 T   4 F   5 F

2 Interview with a CEO

Exercise 1

Lara's opinion: 1 No (people don't really use it)   2 No (takes much more time to resolve the smallest problem)   3 Yes (so that people feel valued)   4 No (people who just want to do their job and go home and forget about work are not necessarily lazy)

Exercise 3

1 top-down, bottom-up, horizontal   2 interpersonal   3 listening
4 pay people more in relation to results and performance
5 the leader   6 Chairman

3 Interview with a project manager

Exercise 1

a 7   b 2   c 4   d 1   e 6   f 5   g 3

Exercise 3

1 air conditioning   2 handling   3 escalators   4 fire-resistant
5 voltage   6 artificial   7 cabling   8 acoustics

4 Interview with a design engineer

Exercise 1

a 6   b 1   c 4   d 5   e 7   f 2   g 3

Exercise 3

1 window envelope   2 iterative   3 Design for manufacturing
4 Over-designed   5 Computer Numerical Control   6 Tolerance

5 Interview with a marketing director

Exercise 1

1 End-user and construction sector
2 Train the service engineer in how to ask the end-user questions after they've repaired their appliance
3 Include a question about kitchens in questionnaires in magazines

Exercise 3

1 F   2 F   3 T   4 T   5 F

6 Interview with a communications consultant

Exercise 1

1 e   2 h   3 g   4 f   5 b   6 a   7 c   8 d

Exercise 2

She mentions: lobbying, Internet advertising, viral marketing, event, publishing, endorsement
a) lobbying   b) viral marketing   c) endorsement

Exercise 3

1 personal links   2 the credibility and fame
3 emotional and intuitive

7 Interview with an auditor

Exercise 1

1 d   2 e   3 a   4 f   5 b   6 c

Exercise 2

Make sure that internal accounting processes comply with government regulations.

Exercise 3

1 The executives of the company
2 The company might favour the supplier in exchange for an under-the-table kickback.
3 Valuing inventory
4 To check the trade receivables
5 To minimize tax

8 Interview with a portfolio manager

Exercise 1

Bottom-up analysis: a company's balance sheet, a company's product pipeline
Top-down analysis: macro trends, the economy
Technical analysis: key price points, support and resistance levels

Exercise 3

1 F   2 T   3 T   4 F   5 F

9 Interview with an HR director

Exercise 1

1 LM   2 HR   3 HR   4 LM   5 HR   6 HR   7 LM   8 HR

Exercise 3

1 motivating factor / grow talent   2 honesty / handle pressure
3 meet its objectives / fair   4 rewards / intrinsic

10 Interview with an IT consultant

Exercise 2

1 ERP 'Enterprise Resource Planning': an application that integrates and automates the business practices of the organization
2 CRM 'Customer Relationship Management': a module of ERP that allows you to bring together information such as financial information, sales information, customer support interactions to give you a single view of your customer
3 VPN 'Virtual Private Network': a secure connection to a private company network using the public telecommunications infrastructure

Exercise 3

1 integration / support   2 electronic / track   3 devices / means